Sara Dehkordi
Segregation, Inequality, and Urban Development

Political Science | Volume 99

This open access publication has been enabled by the support of POLLUX (Fachinformationsdienst Politikwissenschaft)

and a collaborative network of academic libraries for the promotion of the Open Access transformation in the Social Sciences and Humanities (transcript Open Library Politikwissenschaft 2020)

This publication is compliant with the "Recommendations on quality standards for the open access provision of books", Nationaler Open Access Kontaktpunkt 2018 (https://pub.uni-bielefeld.de/record/2932189)

Karl-Franzens-Universität **Graz** | Universität **Wien** Bibliotheks- und Archivwesen | Bergische Universität **Wuppertal** | Carl von Ossietzky-Universität (University of **Oldenburg**) | Freie Universität **Berlin** (FU) (Free University of Berlin) | Georg-August-Universität **Göttingen** | Goethe-Universität-**Frankfurt/M** (University of Frankfurt am Main) | Gottfried Wilhelm Leibniz Bibliothek – Niedersächsische Landesbibliothek | Gottfried Wilhelm Leibniz Universität **Hannover** | Humboldt-Universität zu **Berlin** | Justus-Liebig-Universität **Gießen** (University of Giessen) | Ludwig-Maximilians-Universität **München** (LMU) | Martin-Luther-Universität **Halle-Wittenberg** | Max Planck Digital Library | Ruhr-Universität **Bochum** (RUB) | Sächsische Landesbibliothek Staats- und Universitätsbibliothek **Dresden** (SLUB) | Staatsbibliothek zu **Berlin** (Berlin State Library) | ULB **Darmstadt** | Universität **Bayreuth** | Universität **Duisburg-Essen** | Universität **Hamburg** (UHH) | Universität **Potsdam** (University of Potsdam) | Universität **Vechta** | Universität zu **Köln** | Universitäts- und Landesbibliothek **Düsseldorf** (University and State Library Düsseldorf) | Universitäts- und Landesbibliothek **Münster** (University of Munster) | Universitätsbibliothek **Bielefeld** (University of Bielefeld) | Universitätsbibliothek der Bauhaus-Universität **Weimar** (University of Weimar) | Universitätsbibliothek **Erlangen-Nürnberg** (FAU University Erlangen-Nürnberg) | Universitätsbibliothek **Hagen** (Fernuni Hagen) (University of Hagen) | Universitätsbibliothek **Kassel** | Universitätsbibliothek **Koblenz-Landau** | Universitätsbibliothek **Konstanz** (University of Konstanz) | Universitätsbibliothek **Leipzig** (University of Leipzig) | Universitätsbibliothek **Mainz** (University of Mainz) | Universitätsbibliothek **Marburg** | Universitätsbibliothek **Osnabrück** (University of Osnabrück) | Universitätsbibliothek **Passau** | Universitätsbibliothek **Siegen** | Universitätsbibliothek **Würzburg** | Zentral- und Hochschulbibliothek **Luzern** (ZHB) (Central and University Library of Lucerne) | Zentralbibliothek **Zürich** (Central Library of Zurich) | Bundesministerium der Verteidigung | Landesbibliothek **Oldenburg** (State Library of Oldenburg) | Leibniz-Institut für Europäische Geschichte | Stiftung Wissenschaft und Politik

Sara Dehkordi is a lecturer at the Department of Political and Social Sciences at the Freie Universität Berlin. She teaches postcolonial and decolonial theories, on colonial genocide, the Negritude and Black Consciousness Movement, neoliberal urbanism, and critical peace and conflict studies. She has received the German Tiburtius Prize for outstanding research for her work leading to the book »Segregation, Inequality, and Urban Development«.

Sara Dehkordi
Segregation, Inequality, and Urban Development
Forced Evictions and Criminalisation Practices in Present-Day South Africa

D188

Bibliographic information published by the Deutsche Nationalbibliothek
The Deutsche Nationalbibliothek lists this publication in the Deutsche Nationalbibliografie; detailed bibliographic data are available in the Internet at http://dnb.d-nb.de

This work is licensed under the Creative Commons Attribution 4.0 (BY) license, which means that the text may be be remixed, transformed and built upon and be copied and redistributed in any medium or format even commercially, provided credit is given to the author. For details go to http://creativecommons.org/licenses/by/4.0/
Creative Commons license terms for re-use do not apply to any content (such as graphs, figures, photos, excerpts, etc.) not original to the Open Access publication and further permission may be required from the rights holder. The obligation to research and clear permission lies solely with the party re-using the material.

First published in 2020 by transcript Verlag, Bielefeld
© Sara Dehkordi

All rights reserved. No part of this book may be reprinted or reproduced or utilized in any form or by any electronic, mechanical, or other means, now known or hereafter invented, including photocopying and recording, or in any information storage or retrieval system, without permission in writing from the publisher.

Cover layout: Maria Arndt, Bielefeld
Cover illustration: Sara Dehkordi: The ruins of the evicted pensioners' houses in Pontac, Nelson and Aspeling Street - District Sx, Cape Town

Print-ISBN 978-3-8376-5310-6
PDF-ISBN 978-3-8394-5310-0
EPUB-ISBN 978-3-7328-5310-6
https://doi.org/10.14361/9783839453100

Contents

Acknowledgements 9

Introduction 13
Beginnings 13
Impressions 16
The book 21

Chapter one

The colonial archives repertoire 31
Introduction 31
Thinking archive with Derrida 34
Coloniality and the archive 38
The archive, institutionalisation, and the making of memory ... 40
Archive and method 43
Thinking the forbidden archive 46
Coloniality and the Urban Development Discourse 51
Imagining a third space 62
Conclusion 64

Chapter two

Policies of Displacement – Forced Evictions and their Discursive Framing 69
Introduction 69
The District Six evictions 75
The evictions of the Joe Slovo Residents 79
The evictions in Symphony Way 84

The Tafelsig evictions 87
Blikkiesdorp 91
Conclusion 94

Chapter three

"Cleaning" the streets – Urban Development Discourse and criminalisation practices 99
Introduction 100
Politico-economic violence and the coloniality of the present 103
The category of "the poor" and the disciplining effects of space 107
Superfluous informal traders 117
The security sector and the production of fear 126
The business elite 136
Urban Development Discourse and media 148
Conclusion 156

Chapter four

Architectures of Division 163
Introduction 163
First coordinate: Table Mountain 166
Second coordinate: Vredehoek Quarry 178
Third coordinate: Victoria Road 189
Fourth coordinate: Imizamo Yethu 194
Fifth coordinate: Main Library, University of Stellenbosch 198
Conclusion 205

Chapter five

Intervention through art – Performing is making visible 211
Introduction 211
Steven Cohen – The Chandelier 215
The Xcollektiv – *Non-Poor Only* 220
Ayesha Price – Save the Princess 226
Donovan Ward – Living on the Edge 231

Conclusion 237

ConclusionS 241

Epilogue 247

Bibliography 251
Books, journal articles, reports and court judgments 251

To the memory of Siyamthanda Betana and Nuri Dehkordi who were murdered, and Thabiso Betana and Maziar Dehkordi who died whereas they could have lived.

Acknowledgements

This book is indebted to the inputs, analyses, theoretical discussions and attentive criticism of many. I would like to start with Mrs. Magdalene George, Jerome Daniels and Faeza Meyer Fouri. Their openness and analyses of their struggles, the ways in which they relate to their communities and their recalling of their memories allowed me to develop the analysis of this study. Their words lived with me throughout the years. Their resoluteness and above all, their power of endurance, will remain a life-time reminder of fight and hope. Their critical stance towards the role of research and researchers have essentially shaped the book's entire approach. This study would have been impossible without our conversations and the amount of what I have learned from them.

Heidi Grunebaum has shaped and challenged this work over almost six years. The time she invested in our conversations and the ways in which she supervised the work throughout all its critical stages, cannot be compensated. Especially the methodology this book undertook has been thoroughly influenced by her painstakingly deconstructing imprecise assumptions, use of sources and theoretical framings. Ulrike Schultz's extensive and committed supervision is irreplaceable for the direction this book undertook. Her straightforwardness and and at the same time, humanness, became the most productive sources.Oddveig Nicole Sarmiento accompanied this work from its very beginning. Conversations with her contributed to various frameworks and concepts. I remain indebted to her guidance and intellectual generosity she invested down through the years. Sara Abbas's patience and analytical interventions made me rethink the book's structure and use of method and has influenced my whole understanding of the themes I was working on. I am deeply grateful for her sincere friendship. Countless conversations with Ilham Rawoot have enabled a whole set of subjects related to exclusion and criminalisation to impact this work. I do not want to miss one single of them.

Ala Hourani has enriched this work in many different ways. To list all of them is impossible, although it would make the reader sincerely laugh, because his humour is a gift to anyone who wants to learn how making fun of ourselves releases the uptightness that our everyday imposes on us. His scholarly input and ways of articulation has made me rethink many of my own fixed notions and paradigms. Donovan Ward's contributions in conversations and discussions and his commitment to the themes this book focuses on, tremendously helped the idea of this book to emerge. My deepest gratitude to his analysis and humbleness in all these years. From Xolile Masoqoza I learned the anti-apartheid struggle songs. His tireless commitment has, I think without him knowing, helped me through the different stages of this work. Sabelo Mcinziba's political analysis has strongly influenced the angle from which the book's themes were chosen. I cannot thank him enough for our theoretical debates. I also would like to express my profound respect and gratitude to Andreas Feldtkeller. His motivating words have enabled me to continue at times when I became doubtful.

I am deeply indebted to Manjanigh Collective and our comradeship over the years. Would we not have approached countless discussions and working methods together, I would have lacked the theoretical and practical means that were essential to conduct this study the way it was done.

Different contents of this book have been strongly nurtured by the scholarly generosity of the Centre for Humanities Research – University of the Western Cape, during my time at the Centre as a visiting fellow. Discussions at the Centre on theory and method have been substantial to the whole path this book undertook. The study leading to this book was conducted through the Otto Suhr Institute of Political Science of the Free University Berlin. It owes much to the institute's manner in which doctoral fellows are encouraged to continue their studies despite all kinds of social and economic hardships. I would like to thank Bettina Engels and Daphne Stelter for exceptional mentoring and administrative guidance.

Hardly can I find words for expressing my gratitude to my husband, best friend, and comrade, Behzad Yaghoobpour, who has taught me to remain calm and never surrender. His ability to conceptualise thought, to allow emotions to flow the way they have to, and to hold theoretical discussions until the early morning, enabled me to constantly reflect on content and approach. Asal Akhavan, Greer Valley, Chrisoula Lionis, Dror Dayan and Renate and Kiana Klysch have been great companions who supported this work particularly in the moments when I lost my ability to think clear.

This book owes much to Schohreh Baddii, my mother, and to Masoumeh Fooladpour and Maryam Zia, my late grandmothers, whose strength and truthfulness have determined the whole path through.

Introduction

> In my language
> every time we suddenly fall silent
> a policeman is born.
> In my language
> on the back of each frightened bicycle
> sit three thousand dead words.
> In my language
> people murmur confessions,
> dress in black whispers,
> are buried
> in silence.
> My language is silence.
> Who will translate my silence?
> How am I to cross this border?
> *Mohsen Emadi, from the poem - In Memory of Khavaran —*

Beginnings

In the country where my history was made, countless people are classified as kaffir, the term that South African media services refer to as the "k-word". It comes from the Arabic word for "infidel" or "unbeliever". The original meaning is "the one who hides the truth" and serves as a mark of identification used by the Iranian regime to humiliate, stigmatise and denounce its opponents. Thousands of people marked as kaffir were tortured and killed during the mass executions of communists, and religious and ethnic minorities between 1981 and 1989. The number of dead is still unclear today. In South Africa, the term implies a different complexity of memories of humiliation and pain. With the beginning of colonialism, it was taken from the Arabic language for officials of the Dutch East India Company to verbally categorise those enslaved, who they promised to "uplift" from slave to servant, if they would serve as warders and guardsmen to keep the slaves in their determined order and daily rhythm that was defined by forced labour and physical punishment in its most violent forms.[1] In such a way, officials of the Company distinguished between slave and kaffir. During segregation and apartheid, it would not only brand a person's beliefs or potential resistance against colonial rule and later against the apartheid regime, but it particularly targeted the flesh, so as to underline and celebrate the constructed hierarchy and classification of human bodies, always reminding the black majority of the population, that the power to humiliate was handed over to every single person that was referred to by the government as white.

In February 2012, in Woodstock, Cape Town, a man whose name I unfortunately do not know, around the age of 45, was shivering and walking down Nerina Street. At first glance, I felt that he was frightened. Hesitantly, I asked him if everything was ok. He looked at me, still distressed or perhaps somehow shocked and said: "I am not a *kaffir*. You understand? I am not a *kaffir*." I asked him what had happened. He explained: "I had a job as a gardener in Woodstock. The landlady just fired me today and let me know that I have to leave. Without *any* reason....without aaaaany reason. But I am not a *kaffir*. Do you understand? I am not a *kaffir*." He was not asking me for any help. While shedding tears, he walked away, towards Woodstock Main road.

In April 2008, I was standing in front of a university seminar class in Berlin, giving a presentation on Walter Benjamin and the relation of his essay, *Critique of Violence*[2] with the South African negotiated revolution, when my lecturer became more and more nervous about the content of my presentation. In fact, I had put together fragments of a narrative and discourse that celebrates the Truth and Reconciliation Commission (TRC), the element of forgiveness during the negotiations, and of course, the beginning of multiculturalism. After my presentation, the lecturer made a very clear statement about how she could see a serious lack of understanding and a deep ignorance from my side, which in her view, emerges from a specific dominant discourse.

---

1 Cf. for example: Shell, Robert; Shell, Sandra and Kamedien, Mogamat (eds.): *Bibliographies of Bondage*. Cape Town 2007: p.viii; Crais, Clifton: *White Supremacy and Black Resistance in Pre-Industrial South Africa – The Making of the Colonial Order in the Eastern Cape, 1770-1865*. Cambridge 1992: p.32.

2 Benjamin, Walter: *Critique of Violence / Zur Kritik der Gewalt*. In: *Walter Benjamin – Gesammelte Schriften*. Frankfurt a.M. (first published in 1921).

Even though these were not literally her words, I realised that I might have read Walter Benjamin, Michel Foucault and Giorgio Agamben in order to pass the course, but that it was a superficial reading paired with ignorance. When I saw her passion and commitment to question what it means to, in her words, "read history against the grain", I went home, thinking about my arrogance of planning an exchange semester in a South African University, without even considering to get in touch with academic texts, novels, poetry or art work that speak outside of narratives, which do not fit into the specific dominant discourse that the lecturer was criticising.

I began to think about silences. What is it that gets silenced in the narrative that markets the new *Rainbow-Nation*, the concept provided by governmental institutions and different media in South Africa and abroad? What did I silence in my short presentation? What "facts" about South Africa's transition had I read and seen before that day in the seminar? The answer to the last question fails briefly. I had read Nelson Mandela's *Long Walk to Freedom*[3]; *Country of my Skull*, Antje Krog's book about her witnessing the TRC in its actual time period[4], and had seen Frances Reid's documentary film about the TRC[5]. What I would like to call the "Rainbow-Nation discourse", as Zimitri Erasmus and Edgar Pieterse already did in 1999[6], reproduced itself through my presentation in the implied seminar. Articles about and interviews with liberal-democratic Iranian political analysts like Akbar Ganji and Masoud Behnoud, added to the narrative of a successful negotiated revolution in South Africa that would have ended with bloody revenges and civil war, were it not for the selflessness of Archbishop Desmond Tutu, Nelson Mandela and other members of the African National Congress (ANC) in particular, who intervened and asked the population to forgive the apartheid government and move forward.[7] Since 1998, when a serious reformist approach developed in between Iranian opposition forces inside Iran and in exile, influenced by the election campaign of Mohammad Reza Khatami and his ministry candidates, the negotiated revolution of the South African context became utilised by Ganji,

---

3   Mandela, Nelson: *Long Walk to Freedom*. Boston 1994.
4   Krog, Antje: *Country of my Skull*. New York 1999.
5   Reid, Frances: *Long Night's Journey into Day*. Australia 2000.
6   Erasmus, Zimitri and Pieterse, Edgar: *Conceptualising Coloured Identities in the Western Cape Province of South Africa*. In: Palmerg, Mai (eds.): *National Identity and Democracy in Africa*. Uppsala 1999: pp.171-172.
7   Cf. Ganji, Akbar: Interview title: *Liberty and Democracy*. Voice of America – Persian section. June 18, 2006.

Behnoud, and other opposition members to rationalise and implement a discourse of forgiveness, negotiations, free elections, and a liberal parliamentarian democratic system.[8] This specific narrative does not only repeat the official one of the ANC after the negotiations, but it also celebrates the transition from apartheid to liberal-democracy as a cornerstone in human history.

I am pointing to this discourse and its production and reproduction, as it envisions the main starting point for me to think about silences.

The reaction of the lecturer in that seminar was the first wind that shook my reading of the South African transition in that time. The second long-lasting wind started blowing, when I finally arrived in South Africa, to study in the small university town of Stellenbosch. Starting from the *Coca-Cola* signs all over Khayelitsha township that I encountered on the way from the airport to Stellenbosch, I began trying to put together a perpetual puzzle. Walking on the one-and-a-half-kilometre long road that leads from Stellenbosch to Kayamandi township, intensified my thinking about the architecture of space and constructions of land and city scape that create division. Encountering the narratives produced in museums and memorial sites that I was able to visit - some in the Western Cape, and some in other provinces such as the Eastern Cape, KwaZulu Natal, and Gauteng - questions of silence and power reappeared and started their journey through my mind that eventually led to this work. Whereas Western mediatic framings of my country, Iran, but also of most other Middle Eastern countries, would predominantly highlight state violence and oppression, South Africa's path from apartheid state violence to democracy had become a permanent mediatic event that celebrates the country's transition as an example for liberal-democracy as the one and only political concept in which people could live "freely".

Impressions

Part of the journey that led to this book were the works of South African scholars, writers and political activists that continue unremittingly to point to different silences and to a specific relation of violence that entails concepts of superiority versus inferiority based on the hierarchisation of human bodies

---

8   Cf. Ganji, Akbar: *Cooperation with an Oppressive Regime?* Article in Gooya News (first published in Radio Zamaneh Website): http://news.gooya.com/politics/archives/2013/03/156947.php. June 17, 2013.

and with it, a classification of social groups into more or less valuable. In this part of the introduction I would like to honour these works and draw a mindmap of the way they became relevant to this book.

While staying away from a comparison of levels of violence or from a determination of any artificial hierarchy of catastrophe and trauma, I draw from Premesh Lalu when he asks the question of the continuation of the modes of evidence of the colonial archive and the ways in which "the nagging resilience of racial formation, not as mere ideological formations but as deeply entrenched cultural effects and formations in South Africa"[9] has been addressed by scholars and writers. He points to apartheid as the incarnation of colonialism and the functions of the colonial archive that remain unquestioned in many spheres of knowledge production up until now in present-day South Africa.[10] Ashwin Desai's book on the Abahlali baseMjondolo shack dwellers movement in the province of KwaZulu Natal, titled *We are the poors*, deals with the marginalisation, attempted isolation, and systematic criminalisation of the active shack dwellers and their families. It delves into how the shack dwellers see themselves, how they express what they struggle for, and how they see their struggle related to the past, present and future.[11] The book helped me to formulate questions, but also to understand urban development and planning as part of a project that is as much economic as it is political. Anna Selmeczi's work that focuses on that same movement, made the relations between shack dwellers and neoliberal urban planning clearer.[12] Related to Desai's analysis of segregated city spaces and their links to forced eviction and criminalisation is Heidi Grunebaum's and Yazir Henry's work. They, to put it in Henry's own words, choose to "objectify" themselves rather than to look at others as subjects of research and analysis,[13] when they write about the ways in which everyday life in Cape Town is corroded by the duality of unquestioned privileged life and a huge lower class that is obliged to live in

---

9   Lalu, Premesh: *The Deaths of Hintsa. Postapartheid South Africa and the Shape of Recurring Pasts.* Cape Town 2009: p.191.
10   Ibid.
11   Desai, Ashwin: *We are the Poors – Community Struggles in Post-apartheid Soutrh Africa.* New York 2002.
12   Selmeczi, Anna: *Abahlali's vocal politics of proximity: speaking, suffering and political subjectivization.* in: Journal of Asian and African Studies. October 2012, Vol. 47, Issue 5.
13   Henry, Yazir: *The Ethics and Morality of Witnessing – On the Politics of Antje Krog's Country of My Skull.* Conference: *Ethnographic Approaches to Transitional Scenarios: Perspectives from the Global South.* Organised by Rechtskulturen.

the apartheid-created and postapartheid-perpetuated townships of the Cape Flats. The mountain that separates the middle and upper classes from the majority of the city's inhabitants in the townships, they use as a metaphor that emphasises how physical segregation and exclusion are actually constituted. Going beyond a mere personal reading, in *Where the Mountain Meets Its Shadows*, Gruenbaum's and Henry's conversation reflects on the relationship of *race*-concepts with social and political exclusion. Further to this, they zoom in on the role constructed city spaces play in the locating of "the Other" in determined possibilities of interaction and movement.[14] Not unrelated to this understanding and to the structural analysis of city spaces, is Grunebaum's critique of the *Truth and Reconciliation Commission* that evolved out of her long-term research and engagement with dominant narratives on the one hand, and the narratives silenced, on the other hand. Here, she focuses on how knowledge was produced through a specific conceptualisation of "truth" and "reconciliation" and how these concepts were distributed through the Commission.[15] Sarah Nuttall, Carli Cotzee, Njabulo Ndebele and others add to the analytical critique of the commission and of the creation of dominant narratives.[16] Reading these critiques was important for the whole discussion on the relation between those dominant narratives and the silences they construct. Whatever politicians in South Africa, national and international media, and the so-called "International Community" portrayed as a righteous step towards the desired Rainbow Nation and what I therefore could not properly locate in the discussion on political transition in South Africa, was turned upside down through my own observation but also through the engagement with these texts. This brought the possibility to set discursive silence as the starting point of my own work, while deliberating its functions throughout the whole process.

Amongst others, Nick Shepherd, Noeleen Murray, Martin Hall, Steven Robins and Matthew Barac write about the space and architecture of the township and how the "landscape of apartheid" still characterises South

---

14 Grunebaum, Heidi and Henri, Yazir: *Where the Mountain Meets Its Shadows: A Conversation on Memory, Identity, and Fragmented Belonging in Present-Day South Africa*. in: Strath, Bo and Robins, Ron: *Homelands: The Politics of Space and the Poetics of Power*. Brussels 2003.

15 Grunebaum, Heidi: *Memorializing the Past: Everyday Life in South Africa after the Truth and Reconciliation Commission*. New Jersey 2012.

16 Nuttall, Sarah and Coetzee, Carli: *Negotiating the Past – The Making of Memory in South Africa*. Cape Town 1998.

African cities[17]. Writing about the power of *race* concepts in the city of Johannesburg, Achille Mbembe draws a line between the history of their emergence, and the conceptualisation of the city today.[18] Zimtri Erasmus speaks of the constructed category of the *coloured*, its imposition on the categorised subjects, and the restrictions that are forced on *coloured* identity.[19] Harry Garuba delves into the historical articulation of the construct of race and its survival through the continuation of racial othering, respectively the construction of "otherness", as he puts it. He disapproves of the notion that racism is a phenomenon of the past, just because it is currently generally seen as a construct and emphasises the "intense racialization of the social space of daily life in South Africa".[20] Rafael Marks and Marco Bezzoli write about the privileges of minorities and the exclusions of majorities through specific business constructions such as private cities. In their structural analysis, they focus on the private city project of Century City, that was built between the N1 and Milnerton, a 10 minute drive from Cape Town's city bowl, so as to demonstrate how the free market has led to new segregation and divided spaces embedded in sharp contrasts between the concentration of poverty on the one hand, and of privileged life on the other.[21] J.M. Coetzee has presented an extensive study of the ways in which the Khoi and the San were constructed in anthropological writings and letters during the first decades of the colonisers' arrival in 1652. With his detailed work, Coetzee clarifies with which language and concepts the "inferior native" was created discursively,[22] a discourse that I zoom in onto in the first chapter of this book, because it will help to understand the rhetoric and metaphors used to discredit the majority of the South African population as "lazy" and "not motivated enough to change their lives".

Several studies reveal the high level of inequality in the South African educational system. Three of them, conducted by Jeremy Seekings, Justine Burns

---

17 Shepherd, Nick; Murray, Noeleen and Hall, Martin (eds): Desire Lines: *Space, Memory and Identity in the Post-apartheid City*. New York 2007.
18 Nuttal, Sarah and Mbembe, Achille (eds): *Johannesburg – The Elusive Metropolis*. Johannesburg 2008.
19 Erasmus, Zimtri: *Coloured by History, Shaped by Space – New Perspectives on Coloured Identities in Cape Town*. Roggebaai 2001.
20 Garuba, Harry: *Race in Africa: Four Epigraphs and a Commentary*. New York 2008.
21 Marks, Rafael and Marco Bezzoli: *Palaces of Desire – Century City and the Ambiguities of Development*. Dordrecht 2001.
22 Coetzee, J.M.: *White Writings – On the Culture of Letters in South Africa*. New Haven 1988.

and Michael Cosser, specifically deal with *racial* and class discrimination in the school- and higher educational system.[23]

A recent study by Lindsay Blair Howe, *City-making from the Fringe: Control and Insurgency in the South African Housing Landscape*, has substantially helped to understand national, provincial, and city governments housing policies and discourse, the further conceptualising of displacement and criminalisation and its anchoring in the bigger debate on housing.[24]

After *A History of Inequality in South Africa*, Sampie Terreblanche's last work before his death focuses on the politico-economic reasons for the rapid intensification of poverty, unemployment and inequality between 1986 and 2012 in South Africa. After interviewing Terreblanche in January 2012, his later published new book allows for comparison with his statements in that time.[25]

The killings of the mine workers by the South African police that followed the platinum miners' wage strikes in Marikana in the North West province, created a deep shock that probably shook any romanticising narrative of the achievements of liberal-democracy after the transformation in South Africa. Peter Alexander, Thapelo Lekgowa, Botsang Mmope, Luke Sinwell and Bongani Xezwi, were the first to record the workers' testimonies and to interview the workers in order to analyse the institutional mechanisms that led to the massacre.[26]

To summarise, the above-listed works deal with related topics without which the perspectives this book undertook would have been impossible. They range from the discursive power of the colonial archive in the postapartheid; the relation of *race*-concepts with social and political exclusion; the producing of dominant narratives of the past through the *Truth and Reconciliation Commission*; the socio-political engineering of the township and of segregative architecture; the power of *race* concepts in South African city spaces; the making of *coloured* identity and the restrictions that are up until now forced upon it; the connections between racialised social spaces and their pasts; the

---

[23] Centeno, Miguel Angel and Newman, Katherine S. (eds.): *Discrimination in an Unequal World*. New York 2010.
[24] Blair Howe, Lindsay: *City-making from the Fringe: Control and Insurgency in the South African Housing Landscape*. Zurich 2016.
[25] Terreblanche, Sampie: *A History of Inequality in South Africa*. Sandton 2002; Terreblanch, Sampie: *Lost in Transformation*. Sandton 2012.
[26] Alexander, Peter; Lekgowa, Thapelo; Mmope, Botsang; Sinwell, Luke and Xezwi, Bongani: *Marikana – A View from the Mountain and a Case to Answer*. Johannesburg 2012.

role of the free market; the creation of the "inferior native" through anthropological texts, letters, pictures and film material and its inextricable links to the present; *racial* and class discrimination in the educational system; and state violence against mine workers and its meaning in the context of the postapartheid.

The book

This is not a book that 'discovers' or 'unveils'. Thousands of texts have been written by South African and other African scholars and writers, thousands of artworks and poems have been produced on the matter of postapartheid social inequality and segregation, and most importantly, people affected by forced evictions and criminalisation practices do not need researchers to make themselves heard. In all four cases of forced eviction that this book delves into, residents took their demands and formats of resistance into the public sphere. Let us be reminded of Jacques Depelchin, when he points out that, "In the realm of social sciences, so-called discoveries attributed to social scientists are usually made long after they have been discovered by the people who have lived through what the researchers study".[27] Thus, this book is rather an analysis from an internationalist perspective that asks the question of how silences in politico-economic discourses become produced and what it is that can be learned from the people who shared their testimonies, and in a broader sense, from the South African political experience of the past 25 years.

In order to be able to respond to these questions, this book will specifically focus on urban space. Its process of evolution emerged as a challenge to my own understanding of how urban space can be studied. I had to negotiate a way of accepting my position as a member of the middle class in the socio-economic structure of Cape Town and Stellenbosch and the privileges this brings with. I did not live through apartheid nor through the brutal manifestations of colonial and apartheid modes of production still inherent in the postapartheid. The spaces I inhabited were spaces of tension, contradiction, pain, struggle and political self-organisation. But the inevitable outsider-position was a permanent companion that at times I neglected, at times misunderstood and at times embraced. The fact is, that I would most probably

---

27   Depelchin, Jacques: *Silences in African History*. Dar Es Salaam 2005: p.7.

not have had the opportunity to speak with heads of governments, business sector figures, and key officials in governmental and semi-governmental institutions, if I had not made use of this same position that at times irritated me so much.

The book zooms in on the practice of forced evictions of residents in the broader Cape Town Metropolitan Area[28] and the criminalisation of residents with low income who live in townships, other working-class areas and informal settlements. It especially tries to disentangle and deconstruct the discursive and politico-economic practices that make the normalisation of forced evictions possible. The policies of provincial and city governments and the interests and exercises of business and security sectors, as well as the representation of Urban Development Discourse in local media, form the central fields of the work.

Urban Development Discourse I define as an umbrella term for dominant government and business sector discourses on urban planning, on the role of the market, on the relation of the cities' inhabitants with the market, on housing, evictions, and socio-economic exclusion and inclusion.

My questions are, how are postapartheid dominant discourses that rationalise and justify forced evictions and the rendering as undesirable, criminalisation and marginalisation of lower-income groups of society constructed? I also want to know how the relationships between government (national/provincial/city) and the business sector are structured and to which extent forced evictions are systematic. As I understand that forced evictions are coupled with criminalisation and marginalisation practices that target people with lower or very low income, I also analyse how the Urban Development Discourse frames the rationalisation of ongoing segregated city spaces. What role do private and public-private security companies play? How are middle and upper-class suburbs guarded and what are they guarded against? How are city spaces being narrated and conceptualised? How are laws and by-laws being used and what connections exist between colonial and apartheid law, and present-day law?

---

28   The metropolitan municipality of Cape Town governs over the greater Cape Town area, which covers an expanse of 2.445 square kilometres. It reaches from Mamre in its north, to Somerset West in its south-east, to Robben Islands in its west, down to Cape Point in its most southern point. The City of Cape Town is the official name given to its governing institution.

"Low-Income Residents", **"Working Class"**, **"Lower Class"** and **"The People"**, are the terms that are used to define the people affected by forced eviction and criminalisation. Depending on which term is more explicit for the specific content I am looking at, each one has its own particular connotations. "Low-income residents" is a more precise term, when it relates to the structural analysis of an area/city space, or to a case of forced eviction. "Working class" or "lower class", I mostly use when pointing out a criminalisation process related to individual subjects on the streets, or their systematic exclusion from certain city spaces. "The people" is a term that I learned from the people affected by forced eviction, when they would explain their relation to politicians, business sector representatives, and security companies. "They don't care about *people*", or, "We are the *people* of this country", reoccurred as a self-description in various conversations. This self-description made me think of using the term as in the representation of a political subject that is "the people". Sometimes, I use the three terms more interchangeably, favouring the one over the other depending on which one I deem as closer to the meaning of the specific content.

My focus on the Western Cape province speaks to its high concentration of class inequalities and divided urban and rural spaces that are still underpinned by *race* concepts. Although inequality is highly visible all-over South Africa, the Western Cape comprises a very extreme formation of unequal access to a decent life that manifests in its architecture, city spaces, infrastructure, social life, and socio-economic conditions of people. Visibility and invisibility of different categories of violence alternate in highly raced, gendered, and classed urban and rural landscapes.

My approach might be genealogical in the Foucauldian sense or following different methods of Historical Materialism/Marxist Historiography, as it traces lineages of discourses and studies the ways in which they were constructed historically and how political powers influenced epistemes and modes of production whose rationalisation models survived until today. It confronts conditions of the social and looks at why and in which ways they have been dehistoricised and depoliticised. At the same time, giving the approach a title just to be able to categorise it will not necessary help to introduce it. Most important for this work was understanding what Depelchin conceptualises as paradigmatic silences:

"Whereas it is fairly easy to figure out the contours of paradigms because of their visibility, it is much more difficult to decide what paradigmatic silences are...The genealogy of paradigms is easy to map out, but the same cannot be said of paradigmatic silences."[29] Earlier in his book he explains: "Among those who have suffered enslavement, colonisation, steady and relentless economic exploitation, cultural asphyxiation, religious persecution, gender, race and class discrimination and political repression, silences should be seen as facts...Silences are facts which have not been accorded the status of facts."[30]

The **first chapter** concentrates on questions of epistemology, knowledge production, archive and method. While rethinking methodology is a key challenge to this work and will be discussed in this chapter, I will also look at the extent to which the Urban Development Discourse draws from justification and rationalisation models of the colonial project. What metaphors and rhetoric are being repeated to denounce people affected by forced eviction and poverty and how does the colonial archive relate to these questions? To which extent do ideological and conceptual relations exist here between the criminalisation and marginalisation practices of today and those of the *black* subject in the colonial and apartheid past? I also want to know how the archive itself can be theorised so as to understand its function in discursive practices of the past and the present.

The **second chapter** zooms in on four cases of forced evictions in the broader Cape Town metropolitan area. This journey starts in District Six, where in 2012, pensioners have been forcibly evicted from a block of houses in a small part of the district that, during apartheid, had remained untouched by the Group Areas Act. As all families affected by eviction from formal houses and structures in the Western Cape, they were offered to move to a so-called Temporary Relocation Camp (TRC) by the city government, an offer which they were able to refuse. Their struggle against the evictions lasted eight years.

The journey continues in Joe Slovo, a section of the Langa township, where, in 2009, approximately 20,000 people were forcibly evicted to give way for the so-called N2 Gateway Project, a housing project of the City in which none of the residents living in that space were considered or included. The N2 is also the very highway that leads from Cape Town International Airport to the city centre, whereas Joe Slovo comprised that part of Langa shacks that bordered on the highway. In light of the Soccer World Cup that was hosted by South

---

29   Depelchin, Jacques: *Silences in African History*. Dar Es Salaam 2005: p.10.
30   Ibid.: pp. 3,4.

Africa in the year after the evictions, court decisions, and the business sector and government's aims and strategies have been carefully put into context.

The next eviction case I looked at is Symphony Way, a street in the City of Delft, where backyarder families[31] had occupied social housing units built by the State, after a mayoral committee member had written open letters, in which he suggested and guaranteed that he will back the occupation of houses. The families were evicted from the houses, but before they were forcibly removed to a TRC in the end of 2009/beginning of 2010, they held a struggle for two years, in which they lived in tents and semi-structures, demanding dignified housing for themselves and their children.

The last stop in this journey is two open fields in Mitchell's Plain, to which backyarder families had come in May 2011 in order to build structures and start a community life from scratch. An 18 months-long struggle against their eviction left them living in tents without any access to water or electricity, a space that they could not defend. After being evicted over 15 times, the remaining families had no choice but to accept their relocation to Blikkiesdorp by the end of 2012.

In short, here I look at how people being criminalised and marginalised, and how residents being forcibly evicted from their homes without being offered a dignified alternative to live, define and construct their own subjectivity and take initiative, but also at how their criminalisation and eviction is being justified discursively.

The **third chapter** delves into the discursive practices of the Urban Development Discourse itself. Politicians speak about their aims and investors unveil their motivations and how they see inclusion and exclusion and the people that have no access to their businesses. The *People's Post*, a free community newspaper with different editions for different areas in Cape Town, as the most accessible weekly local newspaper will be analysed. I want to understand the arguments that governments, business sector and mainstream media use and the role they play in the construction of the Urban Development Discourse. In this regard, I also zoom in on the security sector, on its role in guarding specific neighbourhoods against 'others', and on its function as a facilitator of social and spatial division. Hence, I move from the more specific angle of the criminalisation of residents affected by forced evictions, to the broader perspective on the criminalisation of people with low income

---

31   "Backyarders" is the self-description of people who live in backyards of other people's houses, mostly within townships, informal settlements and other working-class areas.

in general and expand the study in that sense. This I do with regards to their exclusion from certain city spaces and the discursive framings that enable this exclusion, but also through the lens of the informal trade sector and the criminalisation of traders. I also examine the politico-economic meanings of the concept of the by-law itself and their influence on the practice of forced evictions and criminalisation today. Furthermore, I ask the question: do ideological and/or conceptual relations exist between forced evictions as politico-economic practice of the present and forced removals during colonialism and apartheid? The latter involves removals as part of the implementation of the *Group Areas Act*, approved by the apartheid state in 1950.[32] The former points to the very first practice of forced removals that was supported by the *Dutch East India Company*, when in a systematic process, European settlers expelled the Khoikhoi and the San from their areas of living and systematically pushed them into the Cape interior. Khoikhoi and San people were either indentured as forced labourers and worked "alongside slaves on the Cape farms",[33] or were forced to leave, together with their herds and flocks, for the settlers to be able to build the first farming and cattle frontiers in which settler's life could be initiated.[34]

In the **fourth chapter**, I will walk, hike, and drive the city of Cape Town and neighbouring Stellenbosch - two central points of interest in the Western Cape. The first one, a relatively huge city with various economic interests of the business sector as well as a reference example of neoliberal policies run by the political sector; the other, a small university town, - the very place where apartheid was theorised and its architecture designed[35] -surrounded by wine farms and constantly romanticised by the new narrative of a diverse South Africa. Movement is the central theme of this chapter. Cape Town and Stellenbosch will be approached from five different physical coordinates. Each

---

32 Cf. Mare, Gerhard: *African Population Relocation in South Africa*. Johannesburg 1980; Platzky, Laurine and Walker, Cherryl: *The Surplus People: Forced removals in South Africa*. Johannesburg 1985; Desmond, Cosmas: *The Discarded People - An Account of African Resettlement in South Africa*. Harmondsworth 1971.
33 Worden, Nigel and Crais, Clifton: *Breaking the Chains: Slavery and its Legacy in the Nineteens-Century Cape Colony*. Johannesburg 1994: p.122.
34 Elphick; Richard: *Kraal and Castle – Khoikhoi and the Founding of White South Africa*. New Haven and London 1977: p.217.
35 Cf. Roth, Mia: *The Rhetorical Origins of Apartheid – How the Debates of the Natives Representative Council, 1937-1950, Shaped South African Racial Policy*. Jefferson 2016: p.48; Coetzer, Nicolas: *Building Apartheid: On Architecture and Order in Imperial Cape Town*. New York 2016: 61,67-68.

coordinate opens a new angle and perspective on inclusion and exclusion, on the historical meanings of the sites themselves, and on segregated city spaces that seem so insurmountable in the present-day setting of city, its suburbs, townships and informal settlements.

The **fifth chapter** will look at artworks that respond to the practices of forced eviction, exclusion and criminalisation. I read the works as the building of counter-archives that are created to prevent the dominant discourse from swallowing all memories and narratives that explain what is happening to the people affected. This might mean that critical art is set as in rebellion and not as an independent entity that can be read outside the formation of discourse and anti-discourse. My argument is that the creation of a third discursive place clear of the effects of social, political, and economic violence is impossible in the world's current social and politico-economic condition. Following this logic, I will concentrate on one of Xcollektiv's[36] public art works; on one of Donovan Ward's artistic productions; Ayesha Price's work against the building of a shopping mall in historical Princess Vlei; and Steven Cohen's art intervention in the middle of a forced eviction in Johannesburg.

To find answers to my questions, I have held conversations with people affected by forced evictions, conducted interviews and held conversations with functionaries in provincial and city governments, in related institutions, as well as in the business sector; held conversations with artists whose art works speak about forced eviction and criminalisation and have analysed their art works; conversations with informal traders; conversations with security guards that are employed in the public-private security sector; have analysed urban planning schemes, access and non-access to city spaces, law, infrastructure, government and business plans, and processes of forced evictions; discourse analysis that looks at statements of governments and business sector - made in our conversations or press statements-, and articles in local media; and a discussion on the role of archive, epistemology, and method.

Since the massacre of the workers in Marikana in August 2012, many of us are haunted every day by the images of the dead. I hope that the on the 22nd of September 2017 people who were shot and beaten to death by the Red Ant Security Relocation & Eviction Services in the Lenasia-South land occupation in

---

36   The Xcollektiv is a group of artists and writers that challenge the urban development plans of the City of Cape Town and actively oppose spatial segregation through interventionist art on the streets. (read further in chapter five).

Johannesburg,[37] the murdered members of the Abahlali baseMjondolo shack dwellers movement in KwaZulu Natal province,[38] and all the other people shot dead in protests, or assassinated elsewhere, will infiltrate our everyday lives not only as reminders of present-day political violence, but also as an appeal to the future. My friend Mohammad Shabangu who recently handed in his doctoral thesis at the English department of the University of Stellenbosch[39] once said, "Maybe we have to kill the idea of hope to be able to start from anew. Maybe we have to say, 'people, let us stop hoping', as hope has made us passive beings within the violence of the everyday."[40] Being haunted by the dead also means that many have not become used to living with catastrophes, against which writing has remained a tool to disrupt the normalisation of political murder, death under custody, people shot in protests, and massacre. I will leave it to the readers to judge how much this book was able to contribute to this task.

---

37 Khubeka, Thando: *Paul Mashatile 'Shocked' by Deadly Land Clashes in Lenasia*. Eyewitness article. September 23, 2017.
38 See chapter five.
39 Shabangu, Mohammad: *Globality: The Double Mind of African Migrant Writing*. Stellenbosch University. September 2017.
40 Conversation with Mohammad Shabangu, July 14, 2017.

Chapter one

The colonial archives repertoire
Discursive power of archive in the face
of forced evictions

"They could evict us, take the houses and demolish them. But they can never take away our memories. Our memories will always stay with us [...]. This suitcase will go with me, wherever I go."
Magdalene George, February 2015

"... the postapartheid is unimaginable without effecting a strategic invalidation of the modes of evidence of the colonial archive which enabled the violence of apartheid...apartheid was inconceivable without the apparatus of the colonial archive. The colonial archive provided apartheid with its multiple metaphors and strategies of demarcation and segregation...The modes of evidence specific to the colonial archive were not only the foundation on which apartheid was built but its very discursive condition. Apartheid was, we might say, entangled in colonial modes of evidence and born in the shadow of the colonial archive."[1]
Premesh Lalu

Introduction

A suitcase full of memories. A story untold. Documented evidence of a struggle against the forced eviction from houses in which the pensioners where born. Mrs. George, Jerome Daniels, and Faeza Meyer, each of whom were

---

1   Lalu, Premesh: *The Deaths of Hintsa. Postapartheid South Africa and the Shape of Recurring Pasts.* Cape Town 2009: p.194-195.

evicted from different places in the greater Cape Town Area, insist on narrating what has happened in the eviction process themselves. The ways they organised themselves, formed committees, how they were framed and presented their court cases, and the ways in which police and Anti-Land Invasion Unit treated them – all these issues they are determined to raise awareness around by providing access to their narratives and the related material they have collected over the years. The arrangements of that material have formed archives that tell a different story to the official narrative of the particular eviction process. In this chapter I want to know, how can these archives be understood? What does the dominant discourse on forced evictions try to erase, what archives nurture the discourse and how can that what remains untold be read?

This chapter wants to find answers to this question and will discuss **memory**, **method**, **historiography**, and **epistemology** in relation to this question. The discussion and use of theory evolved out of the necessity to formulate what the people affected by forced eviction and criminalisation were expressing and narrating, their living conditions and the ways in which they accessed their memories on the one hand, and the mechanisms used by governments, business sector and media to undermine histories of eviction, removal, relocation, criminalisation and unequal access to the city, on the other hand. In this vein, this chapter starts from **Thinking archive with Derrida**, and continues with the discussion on **Coloniality and the Archive**. It then discusses and formulates answers to the relation between **The archive, institutionalisation and the making of memory**, and subsequently, between **Archive and method**. As its next step, the chapter thinks of the people evicted as archivists and will discuss their archives in the section **Thinking the *Forbidden Archives***. The aim here is to formulate an understanding of how their archives relate to the dominant discourse on forced eviction, while the concept of *forbidden archives* will become clearer as well. Through accessing and analysing the colonial archive, its ways to name and frame the *black* subject, the reciprocal relationship between **Coloniality and the Urban Development Discourse** will be illustrated and analysed. As the chapters last endeavour, **Imagining a third space**, in which epistemology can be critically reviewed, will point a way forward for building and formulating the approach this book will undertake.

As in many other works that evolve from an open decolonial perspective, questions of archive, methodology, language and the power to knowledge production are not only central to the study this book emanates from, but they function as a permanent critical voice that challenges, seeks reflection and re-reflection, and that shatters normalised and dominant epistemologies that were/are complicit in the construction and reproduction of colonial/neo-colonial discourse. This perspective evolved out of the necessity to rethink orders of knowledge that were manufactured by the colonial regimes in order to maintain political, economic and cultural hegemony. Coloniality, then, is a power structure that accumulated and settled in the different layers and institutions of society, beginning with its most influential domain in relation to knowledge production, the academy. Considered further, not a single discipline could have been spared, on the contrary, some branches of the humanities and the natural sciences assumed an essential role as actual artisans of colonial discourse. Ann Laura Stoler alludes to "anthropology's longstanding complicity in colonial politics".[2] Indigenous peoples[3] as subjects - those whose study was so desirable-, were at the same time subjects of colonial rule, a condition without which the anthropological encounter would have been impossible. Wendy James points to this dependency when she asserts that, "there was little possibility of a European traveller knowing the people intimately in the pre-colonial period [...] the situation of a lone European living for months or years in an ordinary village without a retinue was only possible when benevolent colonial administration was well-established".[4] Accordingly, the interconnectedness of colonialism and anthropology was thus implicated as a logical consequence. This remained the case even if in some instances anthropologists directly contravened colonial administrations and were accused by colonial officials of defending their informants against the colonial regime and acting as their spokesperson.[5] As certain as colonial administra-

---

2 Stoler, Ann Laura: *Colonial Archives and the Arts of Governance*. in: Hamilton, Carolyn, amongst others (eds.): *Refiguring the Archive*. Dordrecht 2002: p.83.
3 Linda Tuhiwai Smith argues for using the term "indigenous peoples", underlining the "s" at the end: "Indigenous peoples" is a relatively recent term which emerged in the 1970s out of the struggles primarily of the American Indian Movement (AIM), and the Canadian Indian Brotherhood. It is a term that internationalizes the experiences, the issues and the struggles of some of the world's colonized peoples. The final "s" in "indigenous peoples" has been argued for quite vigorously by indigenous activists because of the right of peoples to self-determination." Tuhiwai Smith, Linda: *Decolonizing Methodologies - Research and Indigenous Peoples*. London and New York 2008: p.7.
4 James, Wendy: *The Anthropologist as Reluctant Imperialist*. in: Asad, Talal (ed.): *Anthropology and the Colonial Encounter*. London 1975: p.50.
5 Cf. Ibid.: pp.47-49, 69; and Asad, Talal (ed.): *Anthropology and the Colonial Encounter*. London 1975: p.15

tions employed anthropologists as advisors on the "Native Problem"[6], such as the *Union of South Africa* did officially after 1925[7], the formation and implementation of colonial discourse was co-supervised by anthropologists whose work benefited from and was informed by the colonial condition. But when we speak about *colonial discourse*, we will have to at the same time admit that the complexity of the colonial project's structures and mechanisms, aims and processes, allowed a certain multiplicity, albeit limited, of discourses to coexist. Nevertheless, we will need to inquire into the commonalities of these discourses, to understand whether a tangible leitmotif, or better to say, recurring themes of the colonial project exist. To that effect, Lalu's concluding statement (that heads this chapter) on the role of the colonial archive was chosen purposefully to indicate the suggestion this chapter makes: to include the question of archive as crucial to all layers of one's approach, and in particular, to the theoretical framing one's work adopts.

Lalu's work forms an important pillar in postapartheid theory that had an extraordinary decisive impact on the analysis of the colonial archive's discursive power in South Africa. Adam Sitze writes in his book review of Lalu's exercise into the operations of the colonial archive: 'But *The Deaths of Hintsa* is no ordinary text. It's a text that asks us to think twice – both more searchingly and more responsively – about what it is exactly that we want to know, insofar as our intellectual curiosity takes the form of a demand for historical knowledge'.[8] What in my view Sitze describes here is a general approach that seeks to not only re-read History and to scrutinise its function as a 'discursive condition', but to see this condition as preparer and organiser of the epistemological realities of the present: *History* here not as merely events of the past, but rather as discipline.

Thinking archive with Derrida

In the discussion about emergence and evolution of the archive, about its substance and structures, Jacques Derrida's exceptional deconstructivist response

---

6   Cf. Cape Times article. Mtimkulu, Abner: *The Native Problem*. May 30, 1924; Feuchtwang, Stephan: *The Colonial Formation of British Social Anthropology*. in: Asad, Talal (ed.): *Anthropology and the Colonial Encounter*. London 1975: p.95.
7   Cf. Ibid.: p.84.
8   Sitze, Adam: *History and Desire*. in: Safundi - The Journal of South African and American Studies. Volume 13, No 1-2. 2012: p.171.

appears as the most concrete, but also as the most essential one. Without claiming to have written a theory of the archive, he provides suggestions for a possible future theory. He argues that the substance/content of the archive are elected documents in a "privileged topology" that are housed in a residence/a "domiciliation". This domiciliation of documents then shifts from the representation of a private space and collection, to the manifestation of a public entity, and therefore, to the establishment of an institution that produces knowledge - its ultimate institutionalisation. The particularity of this institutionalised and released entity is that it is a limited structured corpus. Limit here is understood not as shortage but as active limitation – that unifies, identifies, classifies and brings together an arrangement of signs. This gathering together of signs Derrida articulates as "consignation", since it turns the different documents into a unit that is "a system or a synchrony in which all the elements articulate the unity of an ideal configuration".[9] This configuration does not allow heterogeneity, because, if it would, it would bring with separation and discordance inside the discourse that is constructed or that is aimed to be constructed.[10] This does not mean that not every archive bears inside a certain amount of heterogeneity. But what is unified, identified and classified, is at the same time systematically configured, which also means that it is named and structured. This "topo-nomology"« now becomes protected by the "archontic" principle of guarding the "arkheion"/the archive and, as such, gains authority and legitimacy through the law and right that enable its existence.[11] Further, what guards and limits the archive is neither structurally embedded in mysterious entanglements of society, nor is it coincidental or unintended. In my view, one of Derrida's key statements comes in an extended footnote, where he emphasises, "There is no political power without control of the archive, if not of memory".[12] It is this sentence in the only book that he ever dedicated fully to the question of archive, that I want to underline, and subsequently let breath.

How can we understand what Derrida is suggesting here? I suggest that this conclusion provides the essential answer to the whole inquiry underscoring the question. To control the archive, and therefore memory, means to

---

9   Derrida, Jacques: *Archive Fever*. Chicago 1995: p.3.
10 Ibid.: p.2-3. Derrida explains further: "In an archive, there should not be any absolute dissociation, any heterogeneity or secret which could separate (secernere), or partition, in an absolute manner". (p.3).
11 Ibid.: p. 2-4.
12 Ibid: p. 4.

control the ways in which history is perceived, but also, how it becomes reconstructed and imagined. Implied violences of the present can in this way be cut off from their historical background and reside as isolated conditions of the social, but not of the political. Dehistoricising then means at the same time a depoliticising of the event. We may take the German genocide on the Herero and Nama in Namibia as an example. It is impossible to read the catastrophe of the holocaust as a historical one[13], without taking into account the brutal manifestations of fascism within the German colonial apparatus. Put more clearly, the genocidal practices and technologies in both cases, the manner in which colonialists and leaders of the national socialist party viewed themselves, the racialised regimes in which they ordered, administrated and made law, and the epistemological foundations through which they rationalised their notion of superiority and their relationship to violence, are inextricably linked. Around three years ago, two of my students asked the whole group a carefully considered question after their presentation on the representation of colonialism in German history school books: "Did you, no matter in which country you went to school, had ever any lesson on colonial violence or, on colonialism in general?"[14] The answer of all of us, people who went to school in Germany predominantly, but also in the Netherlands, in Belgium, in France, in Greece and in Georgia, was no. Only one of about 32 in the seminar group explained that she had 3 lessons on colonialism in her High School in France, of which the first was on the British Empire, and two about the so-called French "protectorates". Interesting is also, that one of the students who went to school in Germany, had changed his high school 8 times, from the federal state of Baden-Württemberg to Nordrhein-Westphalen, and still, no lesson on colonialism, not to mention colonial violence. The historical records are simply not generated. The archive on genocide committed by Germans misses the period in which the original act itself began to take place.[15] The question arises as to how we should be able to look at one genocide, if another one that

---

13 Cf. Bogues, Anthony: *Empire of Liberty. Power, Desire & Freedom*. New Hampshire 2010: p.30,40.
14 Leutiger, Lea and Bräu, Miriam: Seminar *Introduction to Postcolonial Theory*. Otto-Suhr Institute of Political Science. Freie University Berlin. Session May 4, 2016.
15 Aimé Césaire's arguments about why the Holocaust is not an anomaly in European history and systems of thought and what he calls Hitlerism, are central to this understanding. Cf. Césaire, Aimé: *Discourse on Colonialism*. Originally published in Présence Africaine. Paris 1955.

took place only 26 years before (1904-1907), became silenced and erased. Amputated from their past, the holocaust and fascism are set free to be narrated as an anomaly in German history, or as the fabrication of a sick mind, that was Hitler, without whom the Jewish genocide is rendered unimaginable.

What remains is to look at the processes and political formations that led to the silencing and erasure and at the discourse that the present archival documents form, or conversely, to pose the question of how that what is absent can be understood. Through a focus on forced evictions in the Western Cape and by explaining the relation between dehistoricisation and depoliticisation, what becomes clear is that which neither government officials or media report speak about regarding eviction cases: forced evictions have a historical predecessor that comes in the forced removals that took place under colonialism, and later were highly systematised during apartheid. As we will see in chapter two, there is a deep political meaning to the fact that the pensioners of the District Six houses were evicted from an area that was built on a tiny island not declared *white* area under apartheid and therefore not subject to forced removals as was the rest of District Six. The evictions of these pensioners 18 years after apartheid has ended, must be read against the historical "technologies of power"[16] applied. Put differently, rehistoricised, forced evictions are not only a social issue, but a political one as well. It is interesting that in all eviction cases I have studied, the people affected were very much aware of the historical weight of the violence they were exposed to. It is not a coincidence that during the struggle against eviction from the District Six houses, one of the main slogans that was also painted on placards was, "Don't let history repeat itself". The connection between the past and the present is made almost automatically, because the residents know that they have to historicise what is happening to them, so as to release the issue of eviction from its intended isolation as a purely social phenomenon and move it into the centre of a political debate, to be able to discuss and dispute it publicly.

With reference to Sonia Combe, Derrida then raises awareness about the "repressed archive", or, with Combe's own words, about the *Forbidden Archive*. He uses the terms "repressed" and "forbidden" interchangeably as part of one concept, because an archive that is forbidden, is at the same time repressed

---

16   The term "technologies of power" in Foucault summarises the complex strategies, tools and methods of implementing and maintaining state power: Foucault, Michel: *Discipline and Punish*. London 1977: p.23.

and vice versa. And, what is repressed and forbidden is controlled by state power, distinctively, by its institutions and apparatus.[17]

Coloniality and the archive

"Coloniality"[18] can be defined as the new shapes that colonial knowledge production took/takes, the new artefacts that it designed/designs, and its new manifestations that are either visible, or remain hidden in the many layers of the institutional, academic, economic, political, juridical, and procedural, everyday. The archivisation of documents in South Africa for example has taken place, long before we could even think of a postcolonial critique of the archive, throughout the colonial and apartheid era. "South Africa's national archival system has its origins in the legislative and administrative mechanisms that regulated colonial rule, which saw extensive official and non-official record generation and keeping: by, among others, British colonial officials, missionaries, travellers, public figures, and scholars".[19] Colonial regimes articulated very well what documents were to be repressed and what circulated. Colonial publishing houses selected eligible documents, duplicated, circulated and catalogued them, and at the same time, destroyed those that were

---

17   Derrida looks at institutions and apparatus more closely. He continues and names "family or state law, the relations between the secret and the nonsecret, [...] between the private and the public, whether they involve property or access rights, publication or reproduction rights, whether they involve classification and putting into order: What comes under theory and under private correspondence, for example? What comes under system? Under biography or autobiography? Under personal or intellectual anamnesis? In works said to be theoretical, what is worthy of this name and what is not?" (p.4-5).

18   See various conceptualisations of the term 'Coloniality' in Anibal Quijano's, Arturo Escobar's, Ramon Grosfoguel's, Walter Mignolo's and Nelson Maldonado-Torres's work. Cf. for example Cultural Studies. Volume 21: 2-3. 2007: Quijano, Anibal: *Coloniality and Modernity/Rationality*. in: Cultural Studies. Volume 21: 2-3. 2007; Escobar, Arturo: *Worlds and Knowledges Otherwise*. in: Cultural Studies. Volume 21: 2-3. 2007; Grosfoguel, Ramon: *The Epistemic Decolonial Turn: Beyond Political Economy Paradigms*. in: Cultural Studies 21: Volume 2-3. 2007; Mignolo, Walter: *Delinking: the rhetoric of modernity, the logic of coloniality, and the grammar of de-coloniality*. in: Cultural Studies. Volume 21: 2-3 2007; Maldonado-Torres, Nelson: *On the Coloniality of Being*. Cultural Studies. Volume 21: 2-3. 2007.

19   Archival Platform: *State of the Archives: An Analysis of South Africa's National Archival System*, 2014. Cape Town 2014: p.20.

declared undesirable.[20] Although political transition does not necessitate an automatic transition of archive, this does not mean that the archives of the postapartheid era did not negotiate a new form of institutionality, or instil change in the face of the new political formation within which they were engaged. Of course, the state of the archive is a different one under a dictatorship as the apartheid regime than under a parliamentarian democracy. But what I adopted from Lalu's argumentation is that the archives of the postapartheid could not set themselves free from the colonial archive, and that the colonial archive is continuing to reproduce itself through the documents archived in the postapartheid. This is clear in *The State of the Archives* report by the Archival Platform of the University of Cape Town which reveals how difficult it is to transform the colonial and apartheid archive, despite the fact that the transformation of the archives was been explicitly set as a political goal at the beginning of political transition in the early 90s.[21]

As an example, the monolinguality of archives in South Africa that Bhekizizwe Peterson writes about, does not only pass parts of itself on; it remains character and founding narrative of archive. To put Peterson's critique in context, "Except for a few cases, archives, and, in particular, public archives in South Africa, have been monolingual: they have embodied and voiced only the experiences and discourses of the successive white oligarchies that have governed throughout the twentieth century. The experiences and insights of Africans, women, workers and other communities were generally either ignored or criminalised, at times even banned and destroyed".[22] Monolinguality applies to language as well. The dominance of language itself with English and Afrikaans as *the* archival languages[23] forms another site of oppression and exclusion. The hierarchical power relationship between the language of the conquerors and the language of the vanquished, as Ngugi wa Thiong'o puts it,[24] remains intact. Keeping this complexity of coloniality and archive in mind, the focus in this book lies on the role coloniality plays in the formation of the present-day archive, on the determining of its limits, on its filters,

---

20   Cf. Stoler, Ann Laura: *Colonial Archives and the Arts of Governance.* in: Hamilton, Carolyn, amongst others (eds.): *Refiguring the Archive.* Dordrecht 2002: p.91
21   Archival Platform: *State of the Archives: An Analysis of South Africa's National Archival System, 2014.* Cape Town 2014.
22   Peterson, Bhekizizwe: *The Archives and the Political Imaginary.* in: Hamilton, Carolyn, amongst others (eds.): *Refiguring the Archive.* Dordrecht 2002: p.31.
23   Ibid.: p.32.
24   Wa Thiong'o Ngugi in several speeches. Cf. speech in Cape Town, March 3, 2017.

in short, on its *arkheions*. Here coloniality, thus, is the articulation of the very colonial condition of the archive, its discursive place and apportionment of function.

The archive, institutionalisation, and the making of memory

In regard to the institutionalisation of the archive, it is not solely written and spoken text that constitutes the archival documents, but the formation and implementation of these texts, inside the different institutions of society. It is for example the content of a university lecture, or the texts that are chosen to be read in a seminar; it is the educational material with which the general teaches his soldiers; the printed or recorded instructions that security services receive; it is what is exhibited in libraries and in book shops; the guidelines on the base of which mass media accepts a documentary proposal; the historic records and written policies that influence the naming of buildings, streets, districts and cities; the academic concepts behind city planning, or the references, engineers, architects and city planners use when presenting their plans and maps; it is study reports and statistics with which politicians justify their policies; the imaginaries that are created through text and audio-visual record for pre-primary school children to see, think, judge, agree or disagree in a certain way; and so on. To archive is therefore to write and print, to audio-visually record, to publish, to hold a speech in a public context, to exhibit in a museum, to write law etc. The archive, then, can be both; it can hold a specific physical address, a *domiciliation* whose archival documents are gathered in one compact and enclosed space; or it can be documents that are accumulated by diverse institutions of society, forming a supra-spatial *domiciliation*. The power of the archive can thus be measured through the frequency to which it is referred institutionally or extra-institutionally. In this regard, institutionalisation holds two dimensions: on the one hand, it is the process from private to public of the archive itself, and on the other it is how documents penetrate, underwrite and configure the governmental, semi-governmental and non-governmental institutions inside the nation-state, and in so doing, force themselves unto general social, political, economic and cultural mindsets and agendas. This I imagine is what Derrida points to when he speaks about "archival violence" and the maturing of archive into law that as such cannot exist without its external playground which is the political system through which it can memorialise, repeat, reproduce, and reimpress.[25] He further explains, "there is no archive without a place of consignation, without a technique of repetition, and without a certain exteriority. No archive without outside".[26]

At the same time, the technologies of archivisation differed in different historical time periods and progressed from handwritten letters and other texts to the products of telecommunication and digitalised print, amongst others.[27] But the creation of a dominant archive has always been about creating memory and about constructing and generating knowledge in a certain way. These processes of memorialisation and generalisation attempt not only an immortality of the archive, but also its omnipresence. In this regard, dominant discourse on forced evictions creates the social perception that evictions are a justified approach in order to enhance urban development. Here the relationship between discourse and archive is reciprocal, where discourse creates archive and archive creates discourse. And it wants this perception to gain omnipresence nationally. Through positioning a document in an archive, the way for it to become part of memory and history is opened. Put differently, it means that next to memorialisation stands its historicisation, respectively, its joining of history. As such, the document becomes primed as a reference, to be pointed to, and therefore, prepared to potentially become part of common knowledge: since its placement as a historical document facilitates its operation within a toolbox used to explain, rationalise, and justify the present. To summarise, a document placed in an archive gains historicity and in this way, evolves to a historical document that in the next step becomes equalised with what is called *historical fact*. The inscribing of *historical* and *fact* on a document positions its content as superior to other readings and narratives.

Simultaneously, in order to achieve omnipresence, the archive works to create absence. Absence as the antonym of memory is one of the key concepts inside the construct of the archive. What is absent stands in dynamic contradiction with what is present. As direct produce of power relations and dominance, archival documents in order to exist, repress their counterparts and their intrinsic paradoxes. Thereby, to disentangle the power relations behind archival documents, this facet of them must be illuminated, because, if looked at from this angle, each of them, in order to gain visibility, must at the

---

25   Derrida, Jacques: *Archive Fever.* Chicago 1995: p.7,11.
26   Ibid.: p.11.
27   Cf. Ibid.: p. 16.

same time silence. It is precisely this absence or the absent document, that evokes gaps in memory and remembrance, which in the worst cases lead to historical blackouts, as indicated in the discussion on the erasure of the German genocide on the Herero and Nama and the dehistoricisation of forced evictions in South Africa above. In summary, what becomes clear is that in order to be able to create dominant discourse, the repressive archive darkens, erases and replaces, and in this way, purposefully organises forgetting.

Referring to the South African *Truth and Reconciliation Commission* in a seminar on archive in Johannesburg, Derrida explains, "...the archive – the good one – produces memory, but produces forgetting at the same time".[28] To darken/to produce forgetting here means to illuminate certain historical events and events of the present everyday to the extent of them placing other events in their own shadows - an erasure "which produces forgetting by remembering".[29] Through this fading in the dark of certain other events, not the events themselves disappear, but their historical or present-day importance. Often certain events will be kept purposefully to function as alibi, testifying to the inclusiveness of the respective archive. But they will hardly be illuminated in the sense of allowing them space to unfold. Remaining in the dark, they are rendered present and absent at the same time. Entire series of events can hereby be rendered as irrelevant. Archival documents can therefore, as much as they function as providers of memory, be at the same time treated as tokens of absence. This does not mean that the absent documents do not exist. They surely do and their trajectories can be found in the households of people whose experiences and knowledge do not conform to the dominant discourse that tries to silence them. But they are not arranged in a way that provides access to them. Even though they constitute a permanent threat to the power that represses them, and although they feature the ability to seriously disrupt the official narrative, without accessibility in practical terms they do not exist. The only material that attests to their existence is the threat that they represent.

As we will see later in this chapter, people who were forcibly evicted keep all the records of their eviction process as a counter-narrative to what the

---

28   Derrida, Jacques: *Transcript of the seminar on Archive Fever at the University of Witwatersrand, August 1998.* in: Hamilton, Carolyn, amongst others (eds.): *Refiguring the Archive.* Dordrecht 2002: p.54.
29   Ibid.: p.68.

dominant archive on evictions propagates. They are ready to prove with documented evidence to anyone who approaches them that what happened was violent and unjust. That said, these records are to be found in their homes, thus they did not gain voice and they are not publicly accessible. To summarise, every archive that is created in order to generate dominant discourse, inhabits a dominant repressive character, even if it appears to be inclusive. Inclusiveness, therefore, stands in direct contradiction to its very nature. This is the quintessence of processes through which the making of memory succeeds, or, if seen optimistically, in which it is attempted. To end this section with Achille Mbembe's inquiry into the question of archive, "...the archive is primarily the product of a judgment, the result of the exercise of a specific power and authority, which involves placing certain documents in an archive at the same time as others are discarded. The archive, therefore, is fundamentally a matter of discrimination and of selection..."[30]

Archive and method

The imposed omnipresence of the archive can be seen as the main reason why it cannot be circumvented. Circumvention is not the aim in this work, too. What is pursued here, is the attempt to develop an awareness that pervasively challenges and scrutinises orders of knowledge and methodologies, which remained untroubled inside academic structures of approval and disapproval, of welcoming and refusal of certain meaning-making material. The question of archive, then, is not only the question of its documents and institutionalisation, of memorialisation and generalisation, but also of its methods. The manners in which data is recorded, classified, framed, and consequently turned into objects of representation are restricted. Scales of credibility and incredibility are inscribed upon them. Certain epistemologies and historiographies are more accessible than others, but also determined as more valuable than others.

The archive prescribes adequacy and inadequacy. It therefore pre-determines what is of scientific nature and what is not. Scientificity, in that sense, is occupied by formalisation mechanisms of the archive that serve adaption,

---

30   Mbembe, Achille: *The Power of the Archive and its Limits*. in: Hamilton, Carolyn, amongst others (eds.): *Refiguring the Archive*. Dordrecht 2002: p.20.

because they generate "schemas of reading, of interpretation and of classification"[31], in short, of method. Derrida mentions in this regard "...the norms of classical scientific discourse".[32] Research outcomes that are not formalised and assimilated in this regard, respectively, do not apply as legitimate forms capable of meaning making of the world, thus they cannot reach the necessary grade of credibility and validity to be read and used. Through these formalisation processes, legitimisation processes are initiated. In other words, what follows formalisation is in fact, legitimisation. The constructed product that evolves out of this legitimisation is the claim of *truth* in its various dimensions: historical truth, biological truth (I am thinking here specifically of the dispersion of scientific racism), psychological truth, sociological truth, political truth, and so on. It is these mechanisms of the archive that build the condition through which an academic discipline evolves into an institution itself.

To sum up, as unfolded in the past pages of this chapter, the archive governs over four columns, in every which it suppresses, aggresses, or, accentuates and values certain contents: memory, method, historiography, and epistemology. The disciplinary regime is born.

The three main disciplines at stake in this process are history, with the archive as its primary instrument and source; and anthropology and sociology, with method as their starting point that instructs not only the pole position of the research, but also the ways in which the researcher sees, frames and discusses. Method displays also the very domain that raises the most questions and debates in anthropological and sociological discussions.

In his critique and analysis of Josef Hayim Yerushalmi's work that attempts to place psychoanalysis as a Jewish science, Derrida points to objectivity as one of the "classical norms of knowledge, of scholarship and of epistemology which dominate in every scientific community". He explains further that in Yerushalmi's work these classical norms are defined as, "the objectivity of the historian, of the archivist, of the sociologist, of the philologist, the reference to stable themes and concepts, the relative exteriority in relation to the object, particularly in relation to an archive determined as already given...".[33] Building on this argument, Derrida asks for a critical engagement with artificial and coerced distance that necessitates in order to be

---

[31] Ibid.: p.36.
[32] Ibid.: p.41.
[33] Ibid.: p.51.

treated as "scientist" or "researcher", must create distance in relation to the subject onto which he or she looks. In emphasising the importance of this distance, I argue, the subject is created as object, which serves a certain research outcome, a certain analysis or discourse. Through this exploitative use, a power relation is indicated that implies a specific situation of violence. Especially when the subjects are already exposed to violent power relations in their personal history or everyday life or both, this exploitation constitutes a reproduction of violence, not as the same violence that is inflicted on the subjects, but as its continuation, and as, what we can recall here, epistemological violence. It can be helpful at this point, to draw on Susan Sontag's discussion of photography as a potential violent tool: "to photograph people is to violate them, by seeing them as they never see themselves, by having knowledge of them they can never have; it turns people into objects that can be symbolically possessed. Just as the camera is a sublimation of the gun, to photograph someone is a sublimated murder..."[34] Here, Sontag opens up an important angle from which we can look at objectivisation differently. What is interesting here for reflecting on method in the context of this work is not so much the analysis of the camera use itself, but the fact that Sontag critiques its objectification of people whose experiences are now available to be "possessed". Drawing on Sontag's notion, the evocation of a vertical and therefore unequal power relation between researcher and researched should be critically rethought. Besides, the preconditioned exteriority in scientific discourse cannot be understood if treated separate from its colonial history. Distance and objectivity in the process of studying Others went hand in hand with governing over them. Anthropologists, missionaries, and travellers, who were either tolerated or supported by the colonial regimes to study the subject that they were colonising, positioned themselves inside this exteriority from which they constructed indigenous populations as exotic and/or inferior. The exterior position was not the only precondition for racist othering processes, but it provided a platform to strike out for one's argumentation. Edward Said points his finger at this exact matter when he says that "...it is anthropology above all that has been historically constituted and constructed in its point of origin during an ethnographic encounter between a sovereign European observer and a non-European native occupying, so to speak, a lesser status and

---

34   Sontag, Susan: *On Photography*. New York 1977: p.14-15.

a distant place...".[35] To recall what Heidi Grunebaum emphasised in one of our conversations,[36] it is to turn the relation of African peoples treated as empirical data and Europeans theorising *them* upside down, through disrupting the epistemology that makes this relation possible.

Thinking the forbidden archive

In its own terms and conditions, the colonial archive holds, as any other dominant archive, several reciprocal relationships to society. One of these relations can be active opposition; another one can be passive disagreement. It is important to consider how this applies to the ways in which people who stand on eviction lists are being framed by the official narrative and the final eviction that is itself not being approved by all members of society that stay silent. Silence is often the result of the feeling of powerlessness that does not let people imagine that their active objection could possibly have an impact. So silence does not necessarily mean approval. On the other hand, through the sometimes conscious, sometimes subconscious positioning of single people or social groups against memorialisation and historicisation processes that dominant discourses generate, certain spaces attempt to be created, for narratives that differ from the dominant ones to gain voice. To this effect, I suggest that in the face of present-day forced evictions of low-income residents in South Africa, small counter-archives are being built by the people affected, allowing for their stories not to be swallowed by systematic processes of criminalisation and marginalisation. With Combe's words and as illustrated above, the erection of "forbidden archives"[37] as an accumulation of the material of repressed histories, represents the manifestation of a visible opposition towards the dominant discourse's claim for totality and total truth. Counter-narratives, respectively, *forbidden* narratives try to hold against, them being described and categorised to the benefit of the dominant discourse's credibility. Furthermore, I would like to illustrate how justification and rationalisation models are directly being drawn from the colonial archive's repertoire.

---

35   Said, Edward W.: *Representing the Colonized: Anthropology's Interlocutors.* in: Critical Inquiry, Volume 15, No. 2. 1989: pp.211-212.
36   Conversation with Heidi Grunebaum. March 2014.
37   Combe, Sonia: *Forbidden Archives.* Paris 1994.

In the context of the bigger research project this chapter is woven into, I delved into present-day forced evictions in the Western Cape province of South Africa and into the joint structures that are erected by government officials and the commercial sector in order to create a specific dominant discourse that justifies and rationalises the everyday reality of forced evictions and what is named "relocation". Here I encountered Mrs. Magdalene George, a 77-year-old woman, who was forcibly evicted from the house in which she lived 33 years, during apartheid and until 2012. I myself met her the first time when I went to knock on her door, after I had found out through a former neighbour of hers, who was similarly evicted, that she was currently living with her grandson in Kensington. I was surprised with how openly and warmly Mrs. George received me, after I had told her the reason for my visit. Without knowing me, she sat down introducing me to what she had experienced and what had happened to her and the other families, who were evicted from the houses in Pontac-, Aspeling-, and Nelson Street in District Six. After these first 10 minutes had passed, she asked me to wait, only to come back with a little suitcase - one of the old leather sort that I had only seen in movies. Before she opened it, she explained that her children and grandchildren always tell her to just throw the suitcase away. She said that they would tell her, "Mama, why do you still keep this? This struggle is over. Just throw it once and for all away". She then continued, "But I don't. I keep all of it, and I don't even know why. And now you are coming here, knocking on my door to ask about what happened". She smiled.

The suitcase was filled with every possible newspaper article on the case; with pictures of the resident's struggle against the evictions; with handwritten letters that the residents wrote to city officials and the South African Heritage Agency; with letters that they received from their lawyers; and with the printed judgment of the Western Cape High Court that granted the permission to evict. Every single time we met, Mrs. George went to get the suitcase, while always telling me that it would not be any problem to photograph or scan the documents, as she would be happy that somebody came after "all this" to dig deeper into the case. My role as a researcher was less important to her. She did not receive me as the academic rescuer that has come to listen to her story, a story that nobody else wanted to listen to. On the contrary, Mrs. George had told her story to many journalists, filmmakers, and activists. In fact, a whole documentary film was made that included this particular case of eviction by filmmakers from overseas.[38] She didn't need my presence to be reminded of the immense time and effort she and her former neighbours had invested in the struggle against the eviction.

I suggest it was more the presentation of her archive to an unknown listener that allowed her to access her memories from a different perspective than during the peak of the struggle. Of course, some of the documents archived in the suitcase I could have found access to differently, especially the newspaper articles and the court judgment. But it was precisely the manner in which Mrs. George presented them, one after another, with full patience and concentration, and with her particular postures and vocal pitch that opened up the possibility for understanding the actual experience of "all this". In one of our meetings in May 2014, she reminded me that she had always told me about some missing pictures that she could not find. She then said victoriously, that she had found them, and added, "You must have them. You don't need to make copies, just have them. Because I know you can use them. What can I do with them?"

The last time we saw each other she said almost victoriously, "They could evict us, take the houses and demolish them. But they can never take away our memories. Our memories will always stay with us". I asked her what she would do with the suitcase, as she told me about her plans of moving from her Grandson's house and live together with her son in a bigger house down the road. She assured me that "Of course I'll take it with! This suitcase will go with me, wherever I go".

Another instance of what I would like to introduce as a manifestation of a *forbidden archive*, I came across through Jerome Daniels. A father of six children, Daniels together with his wife, took part in the occupation of RDP houses (Reconstruction and Development Programme houses built by the state) in Symphony Way/Delft. This occupation took place after a member of the City of Cape Town Mayoral Committee had sent letters to about 300 low-income families mostly living in backyards of other people's houses. In this letter, the Mayoral Committee member granted the permission for the occupation of the RDP houses and promised to take full responsibility for this encouragement. The experience of their eviction, their continued struggle and life on the pavement in Symphony Way, and their relocation to what is called a Temporary Relocation Camp (TRC), I elaborate on in the next chapter.

---

38 Kleider, Alexander and Michel, Daniela: *When the Mountain meets it's Shadow*. Germany 2010.

Mrs. Magdalene George at the stoop of her house in Pontac Street, District Six, from which she and her family were forcibly evicted in 2012 ; and images of the community's protests against their forced eviction

However, what I would like to focus on here, is a DVD that Daniels gave me the last time we met, where he had saved "all the pictures and films of the whole struggle on the pavement". Daniels was cautious with "researchers", as he had seen many times how they run into Blikkiesdorp (the TRC they were relocated to) to observe, to interview, and to take pictures. Knowing that his mistrust was justified in the face of research that instrumentalises the interviewed /observed /photographed subject for career purposes, I was grappling with my responsibility, when he handed over the DVD with a proud undertone in his voice. In that moment I was hoping that he could sense my pride as mirroring his own. This pride for a community with whom I tried to imagine myself; a community that I see as having tried to live differently in light of a social condition that is equal with "bare life"[39]. I also realised that

---

39 Agamben, Giorgio: *Homo Sacer: Souvereign Power and Bare Life*. 1998.

Daniels had just handed over an archive that contained documents which did not represent an adequate repertoire for the dominant discourse on forced evictions and relocations. Inadequacy in relation to a discourse is one thing, the other is to represent the paradox, the antonym of what is attempted to be constructed as total truth.

This book was written, compiled and edited by members of the Symphony Way Shack Dweller's Movement. It contains 25 narrations of the struggles and views of 25 different families who were part of the occupation and following struggle for dignified housing. Cape Town 2011

I suggest that it was this same logic in which Faeza Meyer wrote a diary of their struggle against their eviction from the Tafelsig fields in Mitchell's Plain. Having lived as backyarders for most of their lives, people came together to occupy two empty fields and build structures they could finally call a home of their own. Day to day, all documented with the exact date, Meyer provided her account of the happenings: their encounters with the police, with the Anti-Land Invasion Unit of the City, of their belongings being taken away, of how the children would cope with the rough circumstances, and of their hopes and fears. Not only the diary itself, but also the way she had to hide and protect it to make sure it would not be taken away together with other belongings is a meaningful example of a forbidden archive that has to survive in order to tell the story of the people evicted – a story that will contradict the official narrative of the City. When I met Meyer in February 2014, she explained that she is working with a professional writer to publish the diary, as she wants to tell the truth about what happened in Tafelsig. She then emailed me the diary to be able to use it for this study.

When I first encountered Combe's concept of the "forbidden archive", I realised how much it was applicable for different struggles against authoritative conditions that different social groups experience and define as unjust. These archives are constructed as part of what we might call counter-lives that the people affected by the specific violence are living. Having to outlive a forced eviction causes a restructuring of the whole social and economic conditions one is living under, but also has a deep emotional and psychological impact. One has to create a whole new life and ways of dealing with and withstanding the powers to whose subversion one is exposed. Thus counter-life can be defined as this new life that is fully shaped by standing in opposition to those powers and the dominant discourses they create. Therefore, emphasising these archives does not mean to read them as the revelation of absolute truth, but rather to receive them as a creation of space of the ones marginalised in the story to represent their histories themselves.

Coloniality and the Urban Development Discourse

To now draw a line to the first discussion in this chapter, we will have to look at in which ways dominant discourses that try to schematise low-income residents of an area, are constructed through making use of the colonial archive's ideological repertoire. This repertoire that governmental officials, different journalists, and representatives of the business sector resort to has a lot to offer. In order to be able to define and categorise the everyday life of the labelled residents, their habits, attitudes, worldviews, social network mechanisms, and what is seen as their abilities and inabilities, a specific stigmatising scheme of the past becomes activated. Urban planning is part of a specific politico-economic project that excludes and marginalises the majority of society, not only from specific city spaces, but also from the very imaginaries of a world-class city. The logic of profit and investment, in short of the market, determines whose life is superfluous and whose is not, who must be silenced, displaced and rendered invisible and who is conducive to the desirable city that is placed on rivalry and competition for capital investment. Forced eviction of residents to make space for new development projects, the "cleaning" of city spaces of people who do not hold the acquired social status, and criminalisation practices that business sector, media, and city governments fabricate, become justified against the argument of city improvement. Further to this, city improvement has become an authoritative slogan under which violent urban control policies become implemented and rationalised.

In the following chapters, I look at how low-income residents in different areas of the Greater Cape Town Metropolitan Area are positioned as the opposite of what forms the Urban Development Discourse: that is to say cleanliness, safety, liveability, investment and profit. What concerns me at this point however is that this positioning is particularly possible, because of an archive that defined people - who it categorised as *black* and *coloured* in opposition to *white* – as idle (therefore not profitable), as dirty (therefore not clean), as criminal (therefore a threat to society), and as not willing to integrate in the dominant and authoritative cultural system (therefore an obstacle to liveability). The Urban Development Discourse reproduces concepts of the human that were central to colonial and apartheid discourse. It draws on metaphors about urban cleanliness, public health, hygiene, and valuable life that have a longer history of circulation and an enduring life, reproduced in documents of power and policy making, long after the end of apartheid.

Except for the label "criminal" that supervened later and especially with the beginning of official apartheid in 1948, J.M. Coetzee shows in his analysis of what he titles *White writing: On the culture of letters in South Africa*[40], that this specific argumentation recurs in the letters and other writings of early figures of colonialism at the Cape. Anthropologists, traders, officials, and other European travellers, missionaries and other settlers (outlined by Coetzee as "travel writers"[41]) – wrote accounts in both Afrikaans and English language. Many of these accounts became documents of the colonial archive. They comprise

---

40   Coetzee, J.M.: *White writing: On the Culture of letters in South Africa*. New Haven 1988.
41   Ibid.: p.23 – Coetzee takes account of letters and other texts of Jan van Riebeeck, Ten Rhyne, Peter Kolb, Anders Sparrman, Johan Schreyer, O.F. Mentzel, C.F. Damberger, Francois Valentijn, Francois Leguat, John Ovington, William Dampier, Christopher Fryke, Georg Meister, Volquart Iversen, Johan Nieuhof, amongst others. see p. 16-19.

documents that were produced throughout the years, from the first handwritten letters after Jan van Riebeeck's arrival until the late 19th century, forming what Coetzee determines the "Discourse of the Cape".[42] With the racialised regime in which the colonial archive was produced in mind, Coetzee highlights idleness as a key argument inside the frame of this discourse. The discourse proved efficient for the colonial and later apartheid authorities to systematically inferiorise the created Other and rationalise all sorts of racial and exploitative policies, so that it became reproduced throughout the centuries and especially during the years of official apartheid. The *Van Riebeeck Society* as an important example, which was founded by John X. Merriman among others (a former prime minister of the Cape Colony), reprinted and recirculated many of the travel reports and other writings that formed the discourse.[43]

Since the publication of Edward Said's *Orientalism*, decolonial theories remained focused on how texts produced by dominant narrators play a key role in constructing actual colonial discourse. Generally speaking however, within most texts that are written from a white supremacist point of view the writer insists on, and repeatedly emphasises, the inferiority of the "backward", "lazy", "indolent", "stupid", "uncultured", "savage" etc., Other.[44] The inscription of these labels on *black* subjects implies their construction as living

---

42 Ibid.: p.16, 17, 18, 22.
43 Examples of reprintings of the Van Riebeeck Society: Sparrman, Anders: *A Voyage to the Cape of Good Hope, 1772-1776*. Reprinted in 1975; Schapera, Isaac (ed.): *The Early Cape Hottentots. Writings of Olfert Dapper, Willem Ten Rhyne and Johannes Gulielmus de Grevenbroek*. Reprinted in 1933; Mentzel, O.F.: *A Geographical and Topographical Description of the Cape of Good Hope*. Reprinted in 1944; Valentijn, Francois: *Description of the Cape of Good Hope with the Matters Concerning*. Reprinted in 1975.
44 Cf. Merriman, Archdeacon: *The Kafir, The Hottentot, and the Frontier Farmer – Passages of Missionary Life*. London 1853: p.28; Dart, Raymon A.: *Racial Origins*. in: Schapera, Isaac (ed.): *The Bantu-Speaking Tribes of South Africa*. London 1937: p.23-24; Dapper, Olfert: *Kaffraria or Land of the Kafirs*. originally published: Amsterdam 1668. in: Schapera, Isaac (ed.): *The Early Cape Hottentots. Writings of Olfert Dapper, Willem Ten Rhyne and Johannes Gulielmus de Grevenbroek*. Cape Town 1933: p. 45; Rhyne, Wilhelm Ten: *A Short Account of the Cape of Good Hope*. originally published: Schaffhausen 1686. in: Ibid.: p.123, 125, 127, 139; Marais, J.S.: *The Cape Coloured People 1652-1937*. Johannesburg 1962: p. 6,8, 79, 84, 153; Elphick; Richard: *Kraal and Castle – Khoikhoi and the Founding of White South Africa*. New Haven and London 1977: p.205; Kidd, Dudley: *Savage Childhood – A Study of Kafir Children*. London 1906: Preface, p.6, 116; Comaroff, Jean and Comaroff, John: *Ethnography and the Historical Imagination*. Colorado and Oxford 1992: p.275.

beings without social value, and thus without history. This constructed historylessness of indigenous peoples produced one of the most central arguments of a rationalisation model that denied them the free use of their native land. Okwui Enwezor argues that, "These distinctions, [the ontological and epistemological distinction between the settler population and the indigenous populations – quoted from Edward Said], which lie at the root of the colonial project, worked on the premise of two inventions: one, the ontological description of the native as devoid of history, and two, the epistemological description of the native as devoid of knowledge and subjectivity."[45] Historylessness, then, implied not only the disqualifying from what was imagined as civilisation, but also from humanity.[46] A discourse that was at the same time founding narrative of the Cape Colony, because it composed a framework, setting the European in his *righteous* place of the sovereign over the *inferior black* subject. It dictated this form of engaging as the only possibility of defining oneself in the encounter with that Other. As Stoler stresses, "'Whiteness' was a palpable obsession"[47], based on the "Calvinist ethic of racial purity" as argued by Enwezor.[48] Whiteness is therefore not only a position but also a perception. The self and the demarcated community are *perceived* as superior. A concept that was set free to manifest itself as cultural, epistemological and economic predominance. Later the emergence of lower-class settlers, also termed as "poor whites", was also seen as a threat to the notion of white superiority and supremacy, so much so that they were treated as no longer part of *white* community, bringing forward the racist argument that they could only be poor because they must have "crossed racial boundaries"[49]. As part of othering processes that were so fundamental to the establishment of colonial apparatus and to the creation of the dichotomy that were the superior "us"

---

45 Enwezor, Okwui: *Reframing the Black Subject: Ideology and Fantasy in Contemporary South African Representation*. in: Oguibe, Olu and Enwezor, Okwui (eds): *Reading the Contemporary: African Art from Theory to the Marketplace*. London 1999: p.382.
46 Tuhiwai Smith, Linda: *Decolonizing Methodologies - Research and Indigenous Peoples*. London and New York 2008: p.25.
47 Stoler, Ann Laura: *Carnal Knowledge and Imperial Power – Race and the Intimate in Colonial Rule*. Berkeley and Los Angeles 2002: p.13.
48 Enwezor, Okwui: *Reframing the Black Subject: Ideology and Fantasy in Contemporary South African Representation*. in: Oguibe, Olu and Enwezor, Okwui (eds): *Reading the Contemporary: African Art from Theory to the Marketplace*. London 1999: p.379.
49 Sibanda, Octavia: *Social pain and social death: poor white stigma in post-apartheid South Africa, a case of West Bank in East London*. in: Anthropology Southern Africa, 2012, 35 (3&4): p.81.

and the inferior "them", lower-class settlers were hustled into the camp of the undesirable Other. As superiority was newly acquired, it had to be secured and made incontestable. This entailed the rejection and silencing of what would disprove the discourse/the representation of whiteness. It also presupposed a militarising of the spaces of encounter between the *white* self and the racially distinguished Other.

These positionings administered the relationship between new and old inhabitants of the Cape, legitimising the hierarchical society that was later so well-established. It is almost an ordeal to read through the writings that construct the discourse, as they disclose a very bare and normalised racism that became systematised, for it was propagated in all settler ranks, beginning with the first Commander of the Cape, Van Riebeeck, who insisted that the Khoikhoi were "by no means to be trusted but are a savage set, living without conscience..."[50], as well as a "dull, rude, lazy, stinking nation"[51]. Furthermore, this quote of a missionary and superintendent of the *London Missionary Society in South Africa* introduces us to the specific pejorative tone with which *black* subjects were pictured and racist conceptions were pronounced, multiplying the discourse far beyond mere governmental propaganda:

> "In the year 1800, when Mr. Anderson went among the Griquas they were a herd of wandering and naked savages, subsisting by plunder and the chase. Their bodies were daubed with red paint, their heads loaded with grease and shining powder; with no covering but the filthy Kaross over their shoulders, without knowledge, without morals, or any traces of civilization, they were wholly abandoned to witchcraft, drunkenness, licentiousness, and all the consequences which arise from the unchecked growth of such vices."[52]

Jean and John Comaroff contemplate more specifically how missionaries took ambitious agency in the systematising of racist conceptions.[53] As for racism, its history did not begin only with colonialism. It much more constitutes a system of thought, a discursive formation that was embedded in the canon

---

50   Elphick; Richard: *Kraal and Castle – Khoikhoi and the Founding of White South Africa*. New Haven and London 1977: p.88.
51   Ibid.: p.96.
52   Philip, John: *Researches in South Africa*. Cape Town 1828. cited in: Marais, J.S.: *The Cape Coloured People 1652-1937*. Johannesburg 1962: p.33.
53   Cf. Comaroff, Jean and Comaroff, John: *Ethnography and the Historical Imagination*. Colorado and Oxford 1992: p.216.

of European philosophy, placing settler colonialism only as one station on its itinerary.[54]

My point of departure here is the same as Linda Tuhiwai Smith when she argues that,

> "Views about the Other had already existed for centuries in Europe, but during the Enlightenment these views became more formalised through science, philosophy and imperialism, into explicit systems of classification and 'regimes of truth'. The racialization of the human subject and the social order enabled comparisons to be made between the 'us' of the West and the 'them' of the Other. History was the story of people who were regarded as fully human. Others who were not regarded as human (that is, capable of self-actualization) were prehistoric. This notion is linked also to Hegel's master-slave construct which has been applied as a psychological category (by Freud) and as a system of social ordering".[55]

It is not a coincidence, for example, that Winston Churchill saw himself backed by a secure discursive platform, when he proudly proclaimed that, "I do not admit for instance, that a great wrong has been done to the Red Indians of America, or the black people of Australia. I do not admit by the fact that a stronger race, a higher grade race [...] has come in and taken its place".[56] As Arundhati Roy has pointed to, this is not the statement of an ordinary person; it is racist propaganda uttered by a head of state,[57] the same man that later was handed over the Nobel Peace Prize by the *Norwegian Nobel Committee*.

About 200 years before Churchill's strategic speech that was part of the colonial and imperial propaganda of that time and continues to be repeated

---

54 The discussion about the relation between philosophy that evolved out of a European sociality, racism and the argument that concepts of otherness and racism are intertwined with the development of that philosophy and as a result, with Western policy making, touches on a very complex matter. The elaboration of this perspective is content of many academic writings and discussions within decolonial/postcolonial studies. The chapter's brief introduction into racist notions of enlightenment thinkers was necessary to anchor racist thought in the broader philosophical context it was produced in.

55 Tuhiwai Smith, Linda: *Decolonizing Methodologies - Research and Indigenous Peoples*. London and New York 2008: p.32.

56 Churchill, Winston to Palestine Royal Commission, 1937.

57 Cf. Roy, Arundhati: *Come September*. Speech in San Francisco. September 29, 2002.

as a mode of argumentation, the author of *The History of England* and Enlightenment philosopher David Hume, who clearly influenced Adam Smith's political and economic philosophy[58] and let us not forget was also referred to by Immanuel Kant as having interrupted his "dogmatic slumber",[59] philosophically framed what he articulated as the naturally intrinsic inferiority of "Negroes...to the whites".[60] Emmanuel Chukwudi Eze underlines how Hume's racism remains part and parcel of his thought up until to his death in 1776, ahead of which Hume re-emphasises his racist thoughts that he had originally conceptualised between 1748 and 1754 in his essay *Of National Characters*.[61] It was at about the same time, when Francois-Marie Voltaire composed his racist notions, with which he became one of the central thinkers of polygenism in France and all over Europe.[62] I am deliberately jumping here in this very unconventional way from Enlightenment - not only with Hume and Voltaire, but

---

58   Cf. Smith, Adams: *The Death of David Hume. Letter to William Strachan*. November 9, 1776; Rothbard, Murray N.: *Economic Thought Before Adam Smith – An Austrian Perspective on the History of Economic Thought*. Aldershot 1995; Library of Economics and Liberty – *David Hume*.
59   Brown, Joel Nathan: *Kant, Derivative Influence, and the Metaphysics of Causality*. Dissertation. Syracuse 2012: p.16; Stanford Encyclopedia of Philosophy: *Kant and Hume on Causality*. 2013.
60   "I am apt to suspect the negroes to be naturally inferior to the whites. There scarcely ever was a civilized nation of that complexion, nor even any individual eminent either in action or speculation. No ingenious manufactures amongst them, no arts, no sciences. On the other hand, the most rude and barbarous of the whites, such as the ancient GERMANS, the present TARTARS, have still something eminent about them, in their valour, form of government, or some other particular. Such a uniform and constant difference could not happen, in so many countries and ages, if nature had not made an original distinction between these breeds of men. Not to mention our colonies, there are NEGROE slaves dispersed all over EUROPE, of whom none ever discovered any symptoms of ingenuity; though low people, without education, will start up amongst us, and distinguish themselves in every profession. In JAMAICA, indeed, they talk of one negroe as a man of parts and learning; but it is likely he is admired for slender accomplishments, like a parrot, who speaks a few words plainly." Hume, David: *Of National Characters*. Original text published in 1748 and revised in 1754. in: Library of Economics and Liberty – *David Hume*.
61   Cf. Chukwudi Eze, Emmanuel: *Hume, Race, and Human Nature*. in: Journal of the History of Ideas. Volume 61, No.4. October 2004.
62   Cf. Voltaire, Francois-Marie: *Of the Different Races of men*. in: Voltaire, Francois-Marie: *The Philosophy of History*. Original text published in 1766. New York 2007.

also with Kant's essentialisation of the "Negroe" and "white race"[63] in mind - and the use/misuse of Friedrich Hegel's Master-Slave dialectic, to Churchill's racist propaganda, in order to show the scope within which European racism as a discourse was built and propagated historically. It is important to keep this in mind, as it exposes how white superiority as a self-perception was not merely fabricated in the colonies in order to exploit land and accumulate capital, but rather how it had been theorised in Europe and become a system of thought deeply rooted in the European imagination. Most notably, it determined how Europe positioned itself towards the world.

This is vital because European colonialism targeted the African continent almost simultaneously with the beginning of Enlightenment, and thus needed this conceptualisation of racism for its project. However, it also had to turn racism into a more practical instrument that was necessary in order to create an emotional and social distance to undermine the settlers' ability to identify with the ones they had come to subjugate and displace, so that a discourse could be formed that rendered the brutality with which oppression was exercised as normal. Oppression of that "sub-human" or "non-human" did not have to be opposed or questioned, because it was not imagined as wrong. Colonialism as a project, in order to rationalise its concept of superiority, its occupation of land, its imposition of what it determined as valuable life, and its modes of production, needed to advance racist discourse to the propagation of scientific racism, releasing it to become attached to the settlers' imagination. Superiority from here on was rendered a scientific fact but at the same time remained an enduring desire.

---

63   Kant, Immanuel: *Of the Different Human Races*. Original text published in 1777. in: Bernasconi, Robert and Lott, Tommy Lee: *The Idea of Race*. Cambridge and Indianapolis 2000: pp. 8-22. This text shows how Kant thought of race particularly, and how in general, read together with Hume's text, the essentialisation of race and notions of purity that arouse out of enlightenment were articulated and framed at that time: „…Negroes and whites are clearly not different species of human beings (since they presumably belong to one line of descent), but they do comprise two different races. This is because each of them perpetuate themselves in all regions of the earth and because they both, when they interbreed, necessarily produce half-breed children or blends (Mulattoes). Blonds and brunettes are not, by contrast, different races of whites, because a blond man who is the child of a brunette woman can also have distinctly blond children…I believe that we only need to assume four races in order to be able to derive all of the enduring distinctions immediately recognizable within the human genus. They are: (1) The white race; (2) the Negroe race; (3) the Hun race (Mongol or Kalmuck); and (4) the Hindu or Hindustani race." pp.9-10, 11.

Interestingly, it was Hegel with his above mentioned "Master-Slave" dialectic, also referred to as "Lordship and Bondage" concept, who saw this desire as so great that it would arouse a "struggle to the death", in which the master neurotically imposes himself as the predominant and powerful over the slave, without recognising the impossibility of his desired lordship. Superiority in Hegel's concept is impossible, because those who are expected to acknowledge it are oppressed and therefore not free to provide for it.[64] Looking at exactly this desire for superiority, Coetzee also emphasises the comparison being made of *black* people and animals such as hogs, turkeys and cattle,[65] which is a different way of picturing the them as "savage", a label that I argue can be seen as the predecessor of the label "criminal", in that it serves the same rationalisation model, not in the sense of what it aims at, but how it is used to justify certain policies or economic decisions. If to label a people as "savage" served to justify the notion of superiority of the settlers' community on the one hand, and the physical violence that took the highest rank of imaginable brutality on the other hand; today, to label a social group as criminal, or potentially criminal, is used to discredit and to construct as undesirable in the face of its created paradox, that is conformity. The modes of argumentation in this process are informed by colonial classification and propaganda. Lalu explains in this regard: "The end of apartheid has been declared without a sufficient critique of colonial conditions of knowledge that enabled a modern system of segregation. The colonial process of disciplining subjects has not sufficiently shaped the critique of apartheid in the direction of setting the scene for an epistemic break from that past."[66]

Another emphasis stressed in white supremacist writing concerned the areas and social architecture in which indigenous peoples lived. After having tried to forcibly throng them into ways of living that were approved by Europeans, for example in terms of land cultivation, water aggregation, family structures, the construction of houses, as well as religious affiliation[67], complaints about what was perceived as their inability in this regard were spec-

---

64 Cf. Hegel, Georg Wilhelm Friedrich: *Phenomenology of Spirit*. Delhi 1998: pp. 111-119.
65 Coetzee, J.M.: *White writing: On the Culture of letters in South Africa*. New Haven 1988: p.12,13,15,16.
66 Lalu, Premesh: *The Deaths of Hintsa. Postapartheid South Africa and the Shape of Recurring Pasts*. Cape Town 2009: p.268.
67 Cf. Comaroff, Jean and Comaroff, John: *Ethnography and the Historical Imagination*. Colorado and Oxford 1992: p.200, 238, 272, 279.

ified in different reports and other texts and accordingly archived.[68] To provoke the constructed dichotomy of the "civilised" European and the "savage" indigenous, a whole - what we may name Architecture of Othering, was positioned against indigenous peoples' habits and cultural artefacts. European clothes, houses, furniture, commodities, churches, etc., served not only as objects of utility, but also as objects of that very othering.

This is not to oversimplify the plurality of forces and present the settlers community as a homogenous entity. Gender and class inequalities within the social landscapes of colonial society must not be ignored. The same applies for the different ruling camps within the colonial apparatus, distinguished by Comaroff and Comaroff into three separate groups[69] that were the British, with state colonialism as their ruling model; the Boer, whose model can be characterised as settler colonialism; and evangelists and other missionaries, who propagated what they called "civilising colonialism", a system of thought that was fixated on turning what it determined as "savage" into "noble" workers and believers. Each camp had particular approaches and interests, which often stood in direct contradiction to each other and later led to what is called the *Great Trek* of Boers into the interior of the country away from British rule and eventually to the Anglo-Boer wars.

That having been said, fixed sets of racially coded aesthetics were framed to build the common normative of the social and spatial, and any performance outside of this frame was determined as barbaric and inhumane.[70] Since the much-desired sameness as the core aim of the "civilising" mission was impossible to realise, otherness was demonised and presented as the unaesthetic, irreconcilable paradox that had to be subjugated. In addition, in the inspecting eyes of the settler, the *black* subject was always seen as a potential slave[71] and thereby as an object that now had to prove the extent of its usefulness.

---

68 Cf. Elphick; Richard: *Kraal and Castle – Khoikhoi and the Founding of White South Africa*. New Haven and London 1977: p.195, 203, 206; Marais, J.S.: *The Cape Coloured People 1652-1937*. Johannesburg 1962: p.80, 81; Coetzee, J.M.: *White writing: On the Culture of letters in South Africa*. New Haven 1988: p.19.

69 Cf. Comaroff, Jean and Comaroff, John: *Ethnography and the Historical Imagination*. Colorado and Oxford 1992: pp.198-207.

70 Cf. Coetzee, J.M.: *White writing: On the Culture of letters in South Africa*. New Haven 1988: p.22; Rhyne, Wilhelm Ten: *A Short Account of the Cape of Good Hope*. Originally published: Schaffhausen 1686. in: Schapera, Isaac (ed.): *The Early Cape Hottentots. Writings of Olfert Dapper, Willem Ten Rhyne and Johannes Gulielmus de Grevenbroek*. Cape Town 1933: p. 123.

71 Ibid.

In fact, the *black* subject was deprived of its humanity through being reduced to a sheer body without mind and consciousness. This is clear for instance in the statement by physician of the *Dutch East India Company* and member of the *Council of Justice* Wilhelm Ten Rhyne who argued that "...whoever wishes to employ them as slaves must keep them hungry, never fully satisfied..."[72] Further to this, distinctions were made between *black* peoples regarding their grade of obedience and potential assimilation. J.S. Marais writes in his racist account of what he introduces as the history of "The Cape Coloured People", that the colonial missionary Van der Kemp "found the Hottentots[73] much easier to influence than he had found the Xosas. The latter still had their Chiefs, and their tribal institutions were still intact. The Hottentots had already lost, or were rapidly losing, both. They were, therefore, ready to listen to the exposition of a new way of life and to accept the missionaries as their leaders."[74] This degrading narration, not as a random incident but as discursive practice, again nurtured the European's sense of superiority[75] and functioned as a truncheon with which *black* peoples could be reminded of their lesser value[76], always indebted to the colonists who brought civilization, believe in the right faith, are clean, hard-working, know how to make profit and how to create a liveable life.

Similar modes of argumentation are used today within the Urban Development Discourse, again serving to render low-income residents as undesirable, through pointing to their areas as neglected, unliveable and unprofitable neighbourhoods, while ignoring the historical formation of inequality whose material basis was produced systematically. To blame low-income residents for their living conditions and narrate the unequal distribution of wealth as direct consequence of their inabilities, is part of a historical discourse that applied the same argumentations to *black* communities. From the technologies of the archive, with the archive itself as their very nurturing base, dominant discourses learn how to silence in the face of what they aim to highlight. Absence as the antonym of memory comes to its full use in order to repress what

---

72 Ibid.
73 Racist and degrading term for Khoi and San people.
74 Marais, J.S.: *The Cape Coloured People 1652-1937*. Johannesburg 1962: p.144-145.
75 Superiority as a term for a concept that is part of the racialised regime through which colonialism and apartheid were possible, appears in many different writings of the colonial and apartheid era. Cf. for example: Marais, J.S.: *The Cape Coloured People 1652-1937*. Johannesburg 1962: p.264, 282.
76 Cf. Ibid.: p.107.

must not be said. Michel Foucault halts at this mechanism thoughtfully, when he stresses that "The manifest discourse, therefore, is really no more than the repressive presence of what it does not say; and this 'not-said' is a hollow that undermines from within all that is said".[77]

Residents of whole areas can be marked as superfluous and obstacles to the state of development that the area would take without them. The superfluous body, once appointed, can be policed, removed, replaced. The ways in which they are looked at, their living conditions interpreted and the reasons for their discursively constructed non-conformity are presented to the public, are direct descendants of colonial and apartheid narration, and archival presentation. The Urban Development Discourse, as many other discourses in the postapartheid, holds a genealogy that can be traced back to that very authoritarian condition. The production of knowledge inside discourse receives its validation through this verifying with the past. This recycling process of the colonial archive blurs the contours of time periods distinguished as the colonial past and the postapartheid, as they both present a homogenous epistemological material and discursive condition.

Imagining a third space

What else emerges through the nature of the relation between dominant violent discourses and the people who, affected by the violence of those discourses, create counter-archives? As we have seen, people affected by politico-economic violence[78] become Archivists of the Repressed. The reason is, as I have discussed under the section Forbidden Archives, that "the people" demand to be able to narrate their histories themselves. Counter-life, counter-archive, counter-narrative, all are concepts that evolve out of the necessity to access memory, narrate it through a tool (writing, filming, speaking, amongst others), and make it accessible to the public. Accessing one's own memory and analysing the ways in which discourse has been created historically, shapes

---

77   Foucault, Michel: *Archaeology of Knowledge*. London and New York 2002: p. 28.
78   Politico-economic violence I define as a category of violence that in itself entails various forms of violence. As long as it is politico-economically motivated, it can include physical violence, discursive violence, institutionalised violence, amongst other forms. Politico-economically motivated is all violence that serves to maintain an economic status quo, profit, or governmental interests.

our perception and analysis of the present and alters our imagination of how our future should look like.

At the same time, counter-lives, counter-archives, and counter-narratives lock the archivists - the ones who archive as a social response to what dogmatically categorises and defines them - into the mechanisms and dynamics of the dominant discourse. One might ask, and how does that take place? I suggest the answer is, through the fact that writing of one's own history becomes underscored into a sphere of discourse and anti-discourse, of dominance and opposition to dominance. Consequently, this reduces any possible interaction to the status of a response, rather than to an independent strategy that can stand for itself. This I see as a part of the "discursive violence" that Michel Foucault describes and tries to conceptualise, one that generates a perpetual captivity inside a sphere that includes us all, people affected by political-economic violence, archivists, artists, activists, and researchers.

What I then propose to include in one's approach in the context of critical humanities research, is to try to think of a third space. One that does not imperatively stand outside the sphere of dominant discourse and anti-discourse - because the authoritarian condition it has to relate to is real - but rather one that points towards a space that it determines as imaginable. The new imaginaries of method that are created this way, will still be influenced by the described duality, but they at the same time inhabit the opportunity to give birth to something new.[79] Having this serious challenge in mind, I follow Depelchin when he underlines that, "The question is how to move away from the

---

79 Works that inspired this book in relation to new imaginaries of method: For *Memorializing the Past*, an analysis of the discourses that are constructed through and with the South African Truth and Reconciliation Commission, Heidi Grunebaum created in a long-term process an archive of interviews, films etc, that she at the end refused to use for the final text. Without employing personal narratives of people, she decided to precisely concentrate on the evolution, use, and mechanism of the discourses themselves. Grunebaum, Heidi: *Memorializing the Past: Everyday Life in South Africa after the Truth and Reconciliation Commission*. New Jersey 2012. In *What is Slavery to me*, Pumla Dineo Gqola examines slave memory and its impacts on negotiating identity in present-day South Africa. She analyses contemporary artistic expressions that she reads as mirrors of a past that have not been dealt with in the official narrating of history. She does not use interviews or any text, photographs or films of the colonial archive. Instead, she treats art as statements and data, just as we will see in chapter five, V.Y.Mudimbe suggests. Gqola, Pumla Dineo: *What is slavery to me? Postcolonial/Slave Memory in Post-Apartheid South Africa*. Johannesburg 2010.

embedded practices of policing knowledge, how to prevent the sterilisation of knowledge (history), and instead to allow it to become emancipatory."[80]

Conclusion

Tracing back and analysing the creation of historical discourses and their relations to present-day conditions and policies, evolved out of a very material necessity. It is not possible to ask questions about politico-economic violence of the present, without looking at how this violence was made possible historically. Dominant discourses of the present that favour and produce unequal power relations between different subjects of society cannot be read without taking into account the archives that nurture them. The postapartheid archive could not set itself free from the colonial and apartheid archive. Whiteness as colonial and apartheid discursive practice lends many of its contents including framings, metaphors, and rhetoric to the Urban Development Discourse of today - one that is in turn facilitating the South African middle and upper classes in both government and business sector, with new old arguments and techniques. This is also one of the reasons why as a discourse, whiteness became perpetuated and functions as both a nurturing base for interconnected discourses, while at the same time standing on its own to form a complete and coherent discourse in itself. Further, the colonial archive operates as a source of rationalisation and justification of politico-economic violence; a use and manifestation through which the postcolonial condition inherits aggressive neocolonial features. Forced evictions of low-income residents in the Western Cape and the criminalisation and removal of people who become screened and determined as not holding the acquired social status from certain city spaces are as much unthinkable without the backing of the colonial archive's epistemological construct of superiority and inferiority, as the massacre of the striking miners in Marikana is without colonial technologies that were designed to force enslaved people, and later workers under apartheid, back to work under the most horrific conditions. Otherwise we would not be able to explain how the British *Lonmin* mining company could have been supported by the South African Police as well as by high ranked government officials, when before the killings its agents announced that all miners would be dismissed if they would refuse to return to work tomorrow. I am pointing

---

80 Depelchin, Jacques: *Silences in African History*. Dar Es Salaam 2005: p.1.

to this example only to explain why I conclude that the colonial archive and colonial technologies of power become reproduced through different governmental and non-governmental institutions, a manifestation that I marked as coloniality. But in order to render them an isolated social condition, forced evictions become dehistoricised and thus depoliticised. Collective memory is being navigated away from recognising the links between forced removals of the past and forced evictions of the present. We are as much facing a colonial condition of the postapartheid archive, as we are facing a colonial condition of memory.

But the absent documents on forced evictions are not non-existent. They are stored in the households of the people affected, always ready to become presented. It was the particular readiness with which Mrs. George, Jerome Daniels, and Faeza Meyer presented their archives that serves as testament that they did not create them not to forget, but rather to ensure that there will be access to their narratives on the struggle and the violence inflicted on them. And as put forward by Derrida, it is the political power that needs to control memory in order to maintain itself, as to control memory is to control the ways in which the links between history and the present become established. Aware of this relation between the political power that governs over them and the control of memory, even if they do not phrase it like that, people affected by forced eviction create their own, repressed archives, and readily share them with the public.

As discussed in the beginning of this chapter, the academy could not have been spared. The interconnectedness of the colonial project and the humanities was based on a reciprocal relationship from which both gained. Objectivity as the normative measure the study of the Other required and that determines the grade of scientificity of a work until today, derives from this relationship. Therefore, epistemology and in particular, method, must be critically revised and rethought as a constant process in humanities research that also allows for new methodologies to evolve. The limitation the duality of discourse and anti-discourse brings with must be thematised to enable ways out of this sphere. In this context, the comprehension of formations of forbidden/repressed archives can be central, as these archives form a tool to try and write one's own history towards a more inclusive reading of the past and the present and thus stand for themselves without necessarily forming a response to the dominant discourse. At the same time, and this is where that duality prevails, they oppose a violent discourse that uses an undignified repertoire in order to maintain discursive hegemony. The use of method in this regard requires high sensibility, since as much as the researcher's aim might be sympathetic; it is the research process itself that holds a capability to reproduce the violence inflicted on the subjects.

Chapter two

Policies of Displacement – Forced Evictions and their Discursive Framing

From my own point of view, the way that a concept like hope can be made useful is when it is *not* connected to an expected success — when it starts to be something different from optimism — because when you start trying to think ahead into the future from the present point, rationally there really isn't much room for hope. Globally it's a very pessimistic affair, with economic inequalities increasing year by year, with health and sanitation levels steadily decreasing in many regions, with the global effects of environmental deterioration already being felt, with conflicts among nations and peoples apparently only getting more intractable, leading to mass displacements of workers and refugees ... It seems such a mess that I think it can be paralysing. If hope is the opposite of pessimism, then there's precious little to be had. On the other hand, if hope is separated from concepts of optimism and pessimism, from a wishful projection of success or even some kind of a rational calculation of outcomes, then I think it starts to be interesting — because it places it in the *present*.

Brian Massumi[1]

Introduction

Policies of displacement in the Western Cape province cannot be understood without taking into account the interrelated histories of displacement and forced removals in the African continent, as well as present-day forced evictions that become continuously executed in all over Africa. Nor can the

---

[1] Massumi, Brian: *Navigating Movements*. Interview with Mary Zournazi. 2002.

politico-economic condition of South Africa and the many facets of neoliberalism and neocolonialism on the whole continent be factored out. Forced removals as an everyday practice of colonial and apartheid administrations were part of the technologies of power that were invented to appropriate land and take full control of the people living on that land. The study of present-day forced evictions in the South African context leads very soon to the comparisons many people affected and investigators of the topic make, between forced removals during apartheid and forced evictions of today. Mncedisi Twala was born and raised and still lives in the township of Gugulethu, Cape Town. From 2010 on, he became part of a broader organised anti-eviction movement in the Western Cape. In one of our conversations he took issue with the term "eviction": "They use the term 'eviction' to fool us. People created their homes in certain places for decades, and even those places they were originally forcibly relocated to. And because they want to make profit, they come in and forcibly remove people. Now, why is this term, 'forced removals', suddenly replaced by 'evictions'? To make it sound better and let people not be reminded to apartheid!"[2] But if this view is shared by many people affected by forced evictions, that forced evictions, as they are called today, are a continuation of forced removals and therefore of colonial and apartheid policies, how can this interconnection be defined?

In regard to present-day forced evictions on the African continent, in February 2015, the World Bank admitted to have funded a development project in the Gambela region of Ethiopia that led to the forced eviction of thousands of Anuak people. The manner in which the eviction was executed through the Ethiopian state included brutal technologies of power such as rape, imprisonment and torture.[3] Besides the World Bank's involvement, similar state-controlled land alienations were carried out all over Ethiopia and especially in different parts of Gambela. In Lagos, forced evictions of informal settlement residents have become an ongoing state practice. In February and September 2013, around 10,000 people were forcibly evicted from Badia-East in the Ijora area of Lagos, after a king had claimed ownership over the land. The king's claim must have suited the urban development plans of the city, as the Nigerian government carried out the evictions using the funds of a 200 Million USD World Bank financed project named the

---

2   Conversation with Mncedisi Twala. April 19, 2014.
3   Cf. Cultural Survival article: *World Bank Admits Link to Forced Evictions in Africa*. February 23, 2015.

Lagos Metropolitan Development and Governance Project. Senegal's Dakar is another example of an African metropolis interspersed with forced evictions. The evictions at the sites of Captage, Grand Yoff, Keur Mbaye, and Oest Foire, that left thousands of people homeless, are examples of an urban development policy that favours investment and profit over people. The forced eviction of about 4,000 Maasai people in the Kenyan Rift Valley, for the state to make space for the development of a geothermal project, is another more publicly known example. The World Bank's funding and henceforth complicity in this exercise of power is less known. The first evictions took place between 1982 and 1984, when the *Hells Gate National Park* was constructed and a US-American power company was authorised to drill dwells in order to generate power. At this point, the Maasai were closed in on a piece of land between the newly erected national park and Lake Naivasha. In 2014 they were expelled again. This time as a result of the new project that served the interests of a Kenyan state-owned power company.[4] Fouad Makki opens up the discussion about the World Bank's involvement and the determining of land as "terra nullius". He explains:

> "The Bretton Woods institutions, and the World Bank in particular, are today at the forefront of a thinly disguised narrative of terra nullius that is deployed to designate 'underutilised' or 'unproductive' spaces as ideal for large-scale commercial development[...]. A 2009 World Bank publication entitled *Awakening Africa's Sleeping Giants* posited the existence of a vast underused land reserve[...](World Bank 2009:175). A year later, the bank released a companion report classifying countries according to the criteria of yield gaps, defined as the difference between the attained and possible productivity of land. It found these gaps to be especially large for sub-Saharan Africa where no country appeared to be realizing even 50 percent of its potential yield (Deininger and Byerlee 2011:182)."[5]

---

4   Cf. Mariita, Nicholas O.: *The impact of large-scale renewable energy development on the poor: environmental and socio-economic impact of a geothermal power plant on a poor rural community in Kenya.* in: Elsievier Science Direct. Volume 30, No 11. 2002: pp. 1119-1128; IC Magazine article: *Maasai Protest Against New Land Concessions for Geothermal Extractions in Kenya.* July 7, 2014; Cultural Survival article: *Maasai in Kenya Go to Courts to Stop Evictions Caused by World Bank's Geothermal Power Project.* June 13, 2013; Cultural Survival article: *Kenya: Demand the World Bank Compensate the Maasai.* August 15, 2013.

5   Makki, Fouad: *Development by Dispossession: Terra Nullius and the Social-Ecology of New Enclosures in Ethiopia.* in: Rural Sociology. Volume 79, No 1. 2014: p. 93.

It is important to recall that the viewing of land as terra nullius originally began with the so-called discovery of unknown, blank spaces, that from the colonisers' perspective, had to be conquered, tamed and civilised. Today terra nullius are blank spaces in terms of the profit they yield, spaces that the capitalist imagination can project itself into, and upon which a practice of investment, development, and displacement can be incorporated.

Another example that is in accordance with this duality principle of profitable and non-profitable land has been the forced eviction of the BaSarwa people from their areas of residence in the Kalahari Desert of Botswana, their ongoing detention and torture through the state[6], and finally, their brutal marginalisation. Even though they constitute the last existing hunters community, their ejection from their historical living environment, that is a continuous policy since 1960,[7] emanates from that same logic of wildlife tourism and profit as authoritative over people.[8] The discourse that now has to rationalise, justify and normalise the eviction propagates the BaSarwa as a serious threat to the eco-system of the area. The fact that they are "real" hunters, which means that they truly hunt, makes them intolerable and superfluous. That they themselves are historically part of that same eco-system gets erased. Discursively framed differently, but falling into the same category of serving politico-economic interests, the eviction of around 20,000 residents of the Joe Slovo township that is part of the bigger township Langa, north of Cape Town, is the last example that I would like to point to in this introduction into the matter. As I will open up later, the 20,000 people were evicted from their shacks, for the government to surgically replace the aesthetic appearance of those shacks with new constructed social housing units. On a ground that lies right next to the N2 Highway, the same road that connects Cape Town's inner city with the Cape Town International Airport, the shacks were undesirable reminders of a society drastically divided by class. Most of the residents evicted were promised a unit once the construction project would be finished. But the rents of the new apartments were so high, that a majority could never afford to move back. The examples show that forced evictions are a politico-

---

6   Cf. Survival International report.: *The Persecution of Botswana's Bushmen 1992-2014.* November 2014; Take Part article: *Survival alert: Botswana's Bushmen arrested and tortured for hunting while tribal.* January 14, 2013.
7   Bolaane, Maitseo: *The Impact of Game Reserve Policy on the River BaSarwa/Bushmen of Botswana.* in: Social Policy Administration. Volume 38, No 4. 2004: p.413.
8   Cf. The Guardian article: *How the Kalahari Bushmen and other tribespeople are being evicted to make way for 'wilderness'.* November 16, 2014.

economic practice carried out in both rural and urban areas, depending on the aim and scale of the particular development project. It is important to keep that in mind as forced evictions might be associated less with rural and more with urban displacement, while they are an established practice in both spheres.

Karl Marx explains the ways in which capital, in order to maintain its ability to accumulate profit, has the obligation of constant disappropriation. He emphasises that originally, the capitalist elite obtained its property violently. This violent dispossession enabled the elite to invest in production and continuously increase profit. In this way, profit became permanently re-secured.[9] Rosa Luxemburg develops Marx's analysis when she examines capitalist land grabbing as the ultimate obligation of capitalism for it to be able to open up new markets and extract the profit that it cannot gather from its already established markets. In this vein, Luxemburg considers the capitalist mode of production as obliged to perpetually and violently access new markets, as it would not be able to maintain itself otherwise.[10]

To sum up this introduction into the matter, I pointed to a double-sided background that I suggest must be kept in mind and revisited during the whole process of researching forced evictions of the present in South Africa. One is parallel forced evictions in other African countries, and the encouragement to profitable development through international organisations such as the World Bank in the manners that are supported and advocated by these organisations. This aspect can be described as international assistance and advocacy. Second are forced removals as a preceding historical model that implicates the permanent question of interconnectedness to present-day forced evictions. The determining of land, irrespective of the life on the land, as terra nullius, implies ideas of worthless human life that are not only generated by capital interest and neoliberal urban planning, but also by colonial understandings of the human. This chapter asks the question of how this inflicted worthlessness becomes normalised and integrated in a discourse with its complex of signs, statements and practices that justifies the forced eviction of people today.

---

9   Cf. Marx, Karl: *Das Kapital – Kritik der Politischen Ökonomie*. Paderborn (no date): pp.529-532.
10 Cf. Luxemburg, Rosa: *Die Akkumulation des Kapitals. Ein Beitrag zur ökonomischen Erklärung des Imperialismus*. Berlin 1923: p335-338.

Despite its broad practice as an adapted, old politico-economic technology, to look at one specific area will help to understand the complexity of forced evictions. Capitalism and neoliberalism as systems of production and thought constitute a large share in the causes behind. But what combination makes forced evictions of the present so aggressive in the postcolony and in the case of this work, in Cape Town, South Africa? What does the condition of the postcolony implicate?

To particularise the theme and be able to unravel the concepts of thought and discourses behind forced evictions and the structures that function between government and business sector, this chapter aims to complete a very specific task. One part of it is to look at four present-day cases of forced eviction in the Western Cape, of which all were executed after 2009, 15 years after apartheid officially ended. I would like to know, what the arguments propagated by politicians and the business sector are that make evictions manifest as part of an everyday practice of what is called urban development. Source of analysis will also be the approaches, with which the takeovers of land through business companies and city/provincial governments are constructed, and their connections and co-operations with different levels of policy making. What are their constituent particularities and how do they relate to neoliberal urban planning? For this purpose, my approach here involved two types of conversations with the people affected. Informal conversations were part of many encounters on an everyday basis during the research period. They helped to understand the routines that evolved out of a life that had to endure eviction, relocation and criminalisation, how this experience destroyed the social networks that the residents had built over years, and how they now had to negotiate new concepts and sets of relation inside new and yet unknown structures. Recorded conversations evolved from the resident's desire to voice their story on the one hand, and on the other the need to travel through the details of what had happened, from the first eviction threat to the actual eviction, the demolition of the houses and the relocation. In all cases, residents would refer to a specific person pointed out as spokesperson or as the one who can present details of the eviction process more elaborately.

The journey of confronting present-day forced evictions starts in District Six – Cape Town's closer city centre. It continues in Symphony Way, Philippi, crosses over to Joe Slovo, Langa, and ends in Tafelsig, Mitchell's Plain.

The District Six evictions

In May 2013, Mrs. Magdalene George, Mrs. Victoria Bart, Mrs. Latiefa Edries and Mrs. Nadia Essop, were standing on the ruins of their former houses in Pontac, Nelson, and Aspelling Street, telling the story of their life as a community, the process of their eviction and the ways in which they tried to fight the eviction. Mrs. Bart's mother was seven years old when she and her family moved into one of the 17 rental houses, and one month short of a hundred years when she died. The tenants built a cohesive community, helping each other out, paying each other's bills if a family faced shortages, and taking part in each other's family celebrations. The houses were situated in District Six, ten minutes on foot to Cape Town's city centre. District Six is an acronym for the Sixth Municipal District of Cape Town. It was named as such in 1867, when the Cape Colony establishment was preparing the transition from a state of constant rotation between Dutch and English occupation and re-occupation, into a so-called self-governing state that at that point needed new administrational structures. 38 years after the different British and Dutch colonies united to the Union of South Africa in 1910, the National Party's takeover of power in 1948 also meant the beginning of official apartheid. In 1950, the apartheid government passed the first three laws that together formed the *Group Areas Act*. They included the segregation of municipal districts into *white, coloured, Native* and *Asian* areas.[11] It was the practical realisation of spatial segregation based on race concepts, which built the central column of the ideology of apartheid. People that were classified as *non-white* were now forcibly removed from the newly declared white areas. After District Six had been declared white area in 1966, the number of people removed amounts to over 60,000.[12] The small section of District Six in which Mrs. George, Mrs. Bart, Mrs. Edries and Mrs. Essop were living, was not declared a white area under apartheid. Mrs. George sarcastically speculated that "Maybe they forgot about us".[13] None of them thought that they finally would be evicted 18 years after the end of

---

11 The Group Areas Act. No. 41. Cape Town 1950.
12 Rasool, Ciraj: *Memory and the Politics of History in the District Six Museum*. in: Shepherd, Nick; Murray, Noeleen and Hall, Martin (eds): *Desire Lines: Space, Memory and Identity in the Post-apartheid City*. New York 2007: p.119; Swanson, Felicity: *District Six Forced Removals*. in: Field, Sean (eds.): *Lost Communities, Living Memories – Remembering Forced Removals in Cape Town*. Cape Town 2001: p.51.
13 Conversation with Mrs. Magdalene George. May 20, 2013.

apartheid. In 2004, the residents received the first letter from the *Essop Mohamed Omar Will Trust* that called upon them to leave the houses as soon as possible, as they were going to be sold in an auction by one of the eight brothers who own the trust – Omarjee Essop Mohamed Omar. For years the residents resisted moving out of the houses. They elected Mrs. George, who was 76 years old when I met her the first time in 2013, to their official spokesperson. Most of the people living in the houses were pensioners. "We fought with everything we had to stay in the houses", Mrs. George, Mrs. Victoria Bart and Mrs. Edries explained. They organised roadblocks, marches, and celebrations to raise awareness about the imminent threat of eviction. They corresponded with the lawyers of the trust, with the City, and with provincial government, writing letters after letters to prevent the evictions. Their struggle would last eight years, from September 2004 until February 2012, when the last evictions were enforced. Mrs. George recalled how another pensioner, Mrs. Charlotte Petersen, locked herself in her house on the very day of eviction. When the police broke into her house after two days, they found her unconscious lying on the floor. They took her to a hospital and from there to an old age home, where she died. "She was scared! She was 88 and she was born in that house! Can you do something like that to old people?" Mrs. George asked.

As in all other cases, the evictions were justified on the base of the *Prevention of Illegal Eviction from and Unlawful Occupation of Land Act* that was passed by the national government in 1998. Since the tenants are not protected by law in the moment of the houses being sold, they become "unlawful occupants" before the law, if they refuse to leave. The act claims, "...no one may be evicted from their home, or have their home demolished without an order of court made after considering all the relevant circumstances". In the District Six case, the judge of the Western Cape High Court argued: "I am satisfied that the respondents have all been given sufficient and effective notice to vacate the properties and that in disregard of such notice they have remained there unlawfully".[14]

But in order for the trust to sell the houses, they faced two main problems. First, the houses from which the residents were evicted were declared national heritage and lay under the custody of the South African Heritage Resources Agency (SAHRA). This meant that they normally could not be demolished by law. Second, the zone in which the houses were built was not

---

14   High Court judgment of May 11, 2010: *Essop Mohammad Omar Will Trust against Magdalene George, Latiefa Edries, Veronica Bart and others.*

specified as business or industrial zone, but as a general residential zone, according to the zoning by-law that was passed by the provincial government of the Western Cape in October 2004.[15] So to be able to sell the land to a business company, the trust had to convince SAHRA to exclude the houses from heritage status, and to negotiate the re-zoning of the area with the development officials of the provincial government. In May 2013, the trust succeeded with both proposals. The re-zoning of the area from residential zone into business zone is in process and SAHRA granted the permit to demolish and to build. The former residents asked SAHRA repeatedly, to do not give permission to demolish and build on the site. What is striking is the mechanism that leads to SAHRA being able to give permission to demolish by law. The City, together with the business developers and the Heritage Council, wait for the houses to disappear. In fact, every little material that is valuable and was part of the construction of the houses provides a source of income to homeless people, even though it might bring little earnings. All kinds of metal, wood and ceramic have been removed from the houses, so that one by another, whole walls and roofs disappeared.[16] In other words, demolition by attrition. This is also why one year before the permit was granted, ward councillor Brett Herron could summarise calmly that "In our view the application to have the buildings demolished will most probably be successful and, although they have some heritage significance, any future regeneration of the street block in this hostile context may not materialise".[17] Private security forces that are engaged by the district or the municipalities and the South African Police, visited and controlled the sites repeatedly. They were also aware of people living on the stoops and inside the semi-ruins. The picture was a paradox. The darkened glass of the almost affixed office park with the businesswomen and men behind, faced the remains of the houses that were inhabited by new people that were trying to survive. The same scenario happened in Coronation Road, one of the main streets in the area of Walmer Estate, neighbouring Woodstock and District Six. "These houses were heritage", explained the outraged Patrick and Elaine O'Connell, both living in Walmer Estate for almost 40 years. "Because they are not allowed to demolish the houses, they let them be demolished by people. After that, they make the argument that the houses are useless and grant the

---

15   Cf. Provincial Zoning Scheme Model By-Law.
16   Cf. also: Cape Argus article: *District Six: Our Street in Ruins*. April 30, 2012.
17   People's Post Woodstock/Maitland article: *Vacant houses now drug dens*. May 22, 2012.

permission to build."[18] A local newspaper reports, "A heritage building in the heart of Woodstock has been demolished after the majority of the landmark was trashed by vagrants and vandals".[19] Right after, the property was bought by Old Biscuit Mill and Woodstock Exchange owner, Indigo Properties. The applied strategy followed the above-specified pattern.

From the beginning of the eviction process, the presence of the huge office park, named The Boulevard, right next to the houses in Pontac, Nelson, and Aspelling Street, was striking. The residents had been almost sure that there was a connection between Faircape, the owning company of The Boulevard, and the decision of the trust to sell the houses. So it was not surprising when two years after the evictions, Faircape eventually bought the land. The Essop Trust had gained the re-zoning of the land as well as the permission to demolish and to build. There was no obstacle left for Faircape to acquire the land. Interesting was the way in which the official at the Built and Environment Unit of SAHRA in charge of the case of the District Six houses, responded to my questions during our conversation. The official did not mention that he/she would like to stay anonymous. Nevertheless, since his/her responses are crucial to the understanding of corruption within urban planning agendas, I prefer to not reveal his/her name. The person asked me three times to turn the recorder off, to then explain the relations between Heritage Western Cape that is accountable to the provincial government, and SAHRA, that is accountable to the national government. He/she illustrated how their unit at SAHRA had given the recommendation to keep the houses as a heritage site and do not give the permission to demolish, but that Heritage Western Cape had put them under pressure to withdraw their recommendation. He/she agreed with the residents that there must have been a connection between Faircape and the trust beforehand: "They most likely had an offer from the developer neighbouring the houses, because if you look at the form of the development, the land on which the houses were built are a nice missing link for this development to complete itself."[20] This would confirm the residents' assumption that when Faircape approached the community to compensate them for the damage that the construction of the office park caused on their houses and cars and agreed to paint the houses' roofs and pave the courtyards,

---

18   Conversation with Patrick O'Connell. June 1, 2013.
19   People's Post Woodstock/Maitland article: *Operation demolition*. December 19, 2013.
20   Conversation with a SAHRA official. April 17, 2014.

it was to cover their future plans and to secure an alibi in case of investigations. But what drove Heritage Western Cape to put SAHRA under pressure in an underhanded manner and demand the withdrawing of their negative recommendation? There are two possible answers. Either Faircape had a contact link inside provincial government structures, which was powerful enough to enforce a demolition permit. This would mean that there was clearly corruption involved. Or, provincial government had a clear policy of generally supporting business developers and paving the way if there were legal issues obstructing the developments. Both assumptions speak of a discourse that favours development over the needs and rights of residents, those members of society who have no say in the decision-making processes that take place between business sector and government.

The last time I met Mrs. George, she gave me the four pictures I referred to in the first chapter - each one a record of their struggle against the evictions. One picture remains most strikingly in my head: Mrs. George standing in front of her house, behind her a placard pinned on her front door, on it was handwritten this slogan: "Do not let history repeat itself."

The evictions of the Joe Slovo Residents

The Joe Slovo settlement defined the south-eastern section of the township Langa, with about 20,000 residents living on the site.[21] The number of shacks amounted a minimum of 4,386[22], of which the majority ranged in size between six and ten square meters.[23] When the National Department of Housing[24], the Western Cape Department of Housing and the City of Cape Town launched their *N2 Gateway* housing project in 2004, it was advertised with the aim of building homes for the residents of informal settlements, as those of Joe Slovo and of other parts of Langa. A large part of the completed constructions and of the constructions in progress is located along the ten-kilometre stretch on the N2 highway between Bhunga Avenue and Vanguard Drive. The

---

21 Constitutional Court of South Africa: Court Case CCT 22/08, [2011] ZACC 8. *In the matter between: Residents of Joe Slovo Community, Western Cape and Thubelisha Homes, Minister for Human Settlements, and MEC for Human Settlements*. Cape Town 2011: p2.
22 Ibid.
23 Community Organization Resource Centre (CORC) and Joe Slovo Community Task Team: *Joe Slovo Household Enumeration Report 2009*: p.22.
24 Renamed 'Department of Human Settlements' in 2009.

Joe Slovo settlement formed one part of the construction site and was also the first ground to start the development project on. The *N2 Gateway* project was composed of three phases. The first phase comprised the construction of 705 housing units in Joe Slovo.[25] The briefing of the project that was run by national, provincial and municipal governments, announced the project as a plan to "contribute to access for the poor through spatial restructuring, instead of contributing to their marginalisation through peripheral location".[26] The Social Housing Regulatory Authority, created by the Ministry of Human Settlement as a unit that assists with the strategic planning and practical implementation of the housing projects, issued the vision of the project as "To fast-track the eradication of shacks in the N2 Gateway Corridor area and to improve the living conditions of the community".[27] But the facts about the new living conditions of the appointed community prove the contrary. The residents had been forcibly removed without any economic perspective of moving into the flats built by the project. The removal resulted in most of the adults losing their jobs. The enumeration report of the Joe Slovo Task Team, which represents the community, and the Community Organization Resource Center that was finished in 2009, warned explicitly:

> "Most of the employed household heads currently find their workplaces adjacent to their community. Thanks to the proximity to the train station, about 57% of the households can benefit from relatively cheap train services. If the Joe Slovo residents had to devote a bigger portion of their income to transport the poverty cycle would worsen. Only 10.7% is spending more than R200 on transport at the moment. This already equates to a staggering 20% of the average household income. This will dramatically increase if and when people are relocated 20kms away. It is likely that many of the people gainfully employed at present will not be able to carry such an additional burden and will lose or even forfeit their jobs."[28]

---

25   The Social Housing Regulatory Authority: *Project Review Series – N2 Gateway – Joe Slovo.* Issue 3. Houghton and Johannesburg 2006: p.8.

26   A Joint Initiative of the National Department of Housing, the Western Cape Department of Housing and the City of Cape Town: *Briefing Document for the N2 Gateway Project.* Cape Town 2004.

27   The Social Housing Regulatory Authority: *Project Review Series – N2 Gateway – Joe Slovo.* Issue 3. Houghton and Johannesburg 2006: p.8.

28   Community Organization Resource Centre (CORC) and Joe Slovo Community Task Team: *Joe Slovo Household Enumeration Report 2009:* p.11.

The prediction proved true. The reason why most of the evicted residents could not move back to Joe Slovo and rent one of the new units was that the rents were unaffordable for the people removed. They ranged between R750 and R1100, amounts that the community members could not accomplish. This means that the result of the project, even though it was proclaimed differently, was the further marginalisation of the residents through peripheral location. Originally, the project's plan was to deliver 22,000 rental and ownership units, whereas as announced, 70% of the beneficiaries of housing built at the Joe Slovo settlement itself were planned to be residents of the same settlement and 30% to be coming from other parts of Langa.[29] After the construction company *Thubelisha Homes* was engaged by the project's officials to build the different blocks, the company, accompanied by the Minister for Human Settlements, and MEC for Human Settlements, applied for the eviction of the Joe Slovo residents. In March 2008, the High Court of South Africa decided in favour of the applicants and gave the order to evict. The judgment to the case stated among other things: "It is just not possible to rehabilitate and develop the land without first strategically relocating the occupiers of the informal settlement".[30] In order to express their protest to what the residents saw coming months before the court's decision, they organised a blockade on the N2 Highway itself that was violently smashed down by police. Over 12 people were wounded by rubber bullets. The government's strategy included the criminalising of the protesters, using false media reports in order to strengthen this discourse.[31] Sfiso Mapasa, then chairperson of the Joe Slovo Task Team, which was formed by the community, recalled a very detailed picture of police brutality in our conversation. "The polisi shot us like nobody's business. We hospitalised more than five people. Some of the leaders were arrested...During the whole struggle, they tried to criminalise us and make up cases. My brother was imprisoned, but he managed to get out. Many others were imprisoned as well."[32]

After the lawyers of the Joe Slovo Task Team filed an appeal, in June 2009 the Constitutional Court found, as the High Court did before, that the residents were "unlawful occupiers" and that the government officials had acted

---

29 Center on Housing Rights and Evictions (COHRE): *N2 Gateway Project: Housing Rights Violations As Development in South Africa*. COHRE 2009: p.8.
30 High Court of South Africa – Cape of Good Hope Provincial Division: Court Case NO: 13189/07.
31 ape Times article. Legassick, Martin: *Meet residents, Sisulu*. September 12, 2007.
32 Conversation with Sfiso Mapasa. January 28, 2015.

appropriately in seeking the eviction of the residents, as the project's aim was to promote more adequate housing compared to the existing housing in Joe Slovo.[33] But different than the order of the High Court, the one granted by the Constitutional Court included specific preconditions. Among other things it required the temporary residential accommodation unit to be at least 24 square meter in extent; to be serviced with tarred roads; to be individually numbered for purposes of identification; to have walls constructed with a substance called Nutec; to have a galvanised iron roof; to be supplied with electricity through a pre-paid electricity meter; to be situated within reasonable proximity of a communal ablution facility; to make reasonable provision (which may be communal) for toilet facilities with water-borne sewerage; and to make reasonable provision (which may be communal) for fresh water.[34] These preconditions emerged as a serious obstacle for the government to practically evict all the residents, as the relocation camp Blikkiesdorp, to which the officials had planned to remove the residents, did not feature the quality characteristics noted in the order. Therefore, the construction company had to continue the development with the remaining residents living on the site. What is not mentioned in the order is that about half of the residents were already evicted and relocated in the time period between the High Court order and the Constitutional Court order. Even after the order for eviction was discharged in a second decision of the Constitutional Court, because of government's inability to fulfil the court's preconditions, those who were evicted before had no opportunity to return. The ground they had lived on before was now set up with 705 apartments to which none of the Joe Slovo residents were relocated because the rents were unaffordable for them. More precisely, only one resident was able to rent one of the new flats.[35] The report of the Auditor-General that was commissioned by the National Department of Housing attests:

> "The households that were removed from the informal settlements adjacent to the N2GP and accommodated in temporary residential areas (TRAs) could not return to the rental units constructed in Joe Slovo phase 1 due to affordability problems. Although the average income of households in the region

---

33 Constitutional Court of South Africa: Court Case CCT 22/08, [2009] ZACC 16. *In the matter between: Residents of Joe Slovo Community, Western Cape and Thubelisha Homes, Minister for Human Settlements, and MEC for Human Settlements*. Cape Town 2011: p.3,4.
34 Ibid.: p.6.
35 Mail & Guardian article: *It's Our Duty Not To Be Silent*. August 24, 2008.

was approximately R1 200 per month according to the earlier versions of the business plan and communities had raised their concern regarding affordability, the actual tenant profile indicated that the income of 99,6% of the current tenants ranged from R1 500 to R7 500 per month. Consequently affordable housing was not provided for the target market identified."[36]

All these facts lead to the strong assumption that the government had planned to remove the Joe Slovo residents from the very beginning of the development project, and only let them return and move into the new flats, if they were able to pay the new rents, while officially claiming the opposite: "A better life beckons for the people of Joe Slovo informal settlement. The court has pronounced its judgment, and the biggest winners are the families who will soon put the misery of shack dwelling behind them."[37] It seems as if the "good end" that was promised and never achieved, was used as a justification to push the project forward with the aim of physically removing the Joe Slovo residents from the area. The government's purpose was an aesthetic upgrading of the space through the replacement of a poorer community by an economically better situated community, in order to render poverty invisible, respectively, and to relocate its visibility to a bigger distance from Cape Town. A 46-year old man who was evicted with his two children and three grandchildren (he does not want his name to be displayed), explained how the officials in charge of the project promised affordable rents in order for the residents of Joe Slovo to be able to live in the new buildings. During their first visits, residents would declare that they do not trust the government, neither the provincial nor the national one. He said, "Even at the time when they were saying, 'hello people, we are coming to build better homes for you', we knew that it was not us who were important to them, but the image tourists would have, when they would arrive at the airport for the soccer world cup, and would see our shacks on their right hand side, while driving towards the city." Depelchin comes to the same conclusion when he writes that "FIFA may not have stipulated that all efforts must be exerted to keep all and any signs of extreme poverty out of sight but the message comes through and RSA is doing everything to hide the offending communities away. It is not difficult to understand the reasoning behind this: people who come to be entertained by the soccer extrava-

---

36 Report of the Auditor-General on the special audit of the N2 Gateway project at the National Department of Housing. RP 177/2008: p.10.
37 Pambazuka News article: *Joe Slovo Residents Let Down By Court*. Issue 439. June 25, 2009.

ganza must not be disturbed by the sights of shacks".[38] Martin Legassick, the late writer, historian and old anti-apartheid activist who returned from exile in 1990, supported the Joe Slovo residents with reports and open letters. In his open letter about the politics of the Minister of Housing, Lindiwe Sisulu, he writes: "She (Lindiwe Sisulu) claimed she wanted to 'eradicate slums'. But what she is doing is merely moving the Joe Slovo 'slum' to Delft and installing better-off people in their place."[39] In a conversation we held, Legassick argued that "It is basically like apartheid. Capital wants workers, but it does not want to provide the cost to accommodate them. So you get evictions and violence."[40] The assumption of the man that was evicted together with his children and grandchildren, matches with a statement in the project's briefing, where it is emphasised that while the project has been initialised to address a zone suffering from poor living conditions including highly limited access to basic services and unemployment, it "has also been prioritised in light of its high visibility on the gateway corridor, linking the Cape Town International Airport to the main city."[41] The N2 Gateway Project has been taking over by the governmental Housing Development Agency which has since claimed to be more inclusive.

The evictions in Symphony Way

Three hundred families did not hesitate to occupy houses that were built within the framework of the *N2 Gateway* housing project in Delft, after Frank Martin, a City of Cape Town Mayoral Committee member, had sent them letters in which he granted the permission for the occupation and promised to take full responsibility for this encouragement. The occupation demonstrates the high degree of desperate people in need of a dignified place to live in. Not only the 300 families addressed, but about five times more families occupied about 1,500 houses in December 2007. Most of the occupiers were backyard-dwellers, people who lived in poor living conditions in little shacks that were

---

38   Depelchin, Jacques: *Reclaiming African History*. Cape Town 2011: p.45.
39   Legassick, Martin: *Western Cape Housing Crisis: Writings on Joe Slovo and Delft*. Cape Town 2008.
40   Conversation with Martin Legassick. January 27, 2014.
41   A Joint Initiative of the National Department of Housing, the Western Cape Department of Housing and the City of Cape Town: *Briefing Document for the N2 Gateway Project*. Cape Town 2004: p.2.

placed in backyards of other people's properties. The life of backyard-dwellers is marked by the highest grade of insecurity, because it means that their immediate future is uncertain. The main tenant or owner of the house can ask the dwellers any time to leave or cut off their electricity or water as he or she pleases. Many backyard-dwellers find their belongings dumped on the street, without being given notice to vacate the place in advance. As many others in South Africa, most families who occupied the houses were standing on the waiting list to receive a house from the government between 10 and 20 years. Michelle de Jongh, a 40-year-old woman with two children, explained why the life in the backyards was unbearable: "In the movies, the shacks we were living in in backyards are inhabited by dogs. Nobody wants to make a dog life for his or her children. Where we were living, we had no electricity because the landowners decided that we don't need any. Many times we moved from one backyard to another because the landowners suddenly asked us to leave. If you are going to live in a shack, then you want to at least know that it is your shack and that nobody can kick you out."[42] It turned out that the Mayoral Committee member Martin's encouragement had been an individual initiative that was not in agreement with the responsible units of the City and was therefore declared invalid. In February 2008, an Anti-Land Invasion Unit operation in which 20 people were injured and a three years-old child was shot three times with rubber bullets, ended the occupation of the houses and evicted all the people involved. On the same day they also loaded all the people's belongings, from pots and prams to bedding, furniture and electrical equipment, on their trucks and dumped them in places where the people could not find them again. About 500 residents, who did not have the opportunity to return to the backyard shacks they came from or move in with family members, decided to build little shacks on the pavement on a street called Symphony Way that is situated in front of some of the former occupied houses. The other residents either moved back to the backyard shacks, or moved in with family members, or accepted to live on a temporary site equipped with tents and daily hot food deliveries as well as outdoor water taps and portable toilets provided by the City. The camp in which they were placed was close to Symphony Way. The City only supported the camp with basic materials on condition that its residents would move to Blikkiesdorp as soon as the City would be ready for the relocation, whereas the allocation of responsibilities between provincial government and the City of Cape Town was

---

42   Conversation with Michelle de Jongh. May 2, 2013.

unclear. Those 500 residents who insisted to stay independent from provincial government and City officials did not trust the government and tried to resist their relocation to Blikkiesdorp.

Jerome Daniels, a community leader of the residents who remained on the pavement in Symphony Way, recalled in one of our conversations how Metro Police amongst others was deployed to threaten and frighten the community: "They came, they intimidated us with Law Enforcement, with Anti-Land Invasion, with whatever division they got, Metro Police, really they tried to intimidate us. To break our spirits." Then he explained how the police made up a case to imprison him and another resident, who was also very much engaged in the community struggle. He remembered the judge saying openly in court while reading his judgment that he will find them guilty to set an example, because they would be troublemakers from the Anti-Eviction struggle. He sentenced them to one year of prison and five years in suspension, of which they spent a total of three months in Goodwood and Pollsmoore prisons. Jeremy Vearey, Major-General, Mitchell's Plain cluster commander, and head of the anti-gang unit of the South African Police Service, agrees with Daniels that the City uses intimidation practices against people who face evictions and uncovers how Daniels' case was not an exception. In our conversation he explained referring to a similar case of eviction, "The City's Law Enforcement started harassing people and laid fake charges against people, resulting that I had to deploy members of the police to protect them from harassment by the City's Law Enforcement and by Metro Police. We said you don't touch people. If you touch any people here and we are not here, we will arrest you."[43] Vearey was very clear about the City strategically criminalising the people that it wants to evict, in order for the courts to rule in their favour and to discourage people and push them to agree with their relocation. The ways in which Law Enforcement, Metro Police and Anti-Land Invasion Unit intimidated the Symphony Way pavement dwellers, both physically and psychologically, but also their struggle and their organising of themselves as a community, one can read in the book *No Land! No House! No Vote! – Voices from Symphony Way* that they have written and edited themselves.[44]

Twenty-two months the community held out on the pavement in Symphony Way, before the Western Cape High Court granted the order for their

---

43   Conversation with Jeremy Veary. April 29, 2014.
44   Symphony Way Pavement Dwellers: *No Land! No House! No Vote! – Voices from Symphony Way*. Cape Town 2011.

eviction in October 2009. The majority of families had no other chance but to accept their removal to Blikkiesdorp.⁴⁵ A 38-old man, who, as Daniels, is now obliged to live with his family in Blikkiesdorp, expressed his anger in a conversation:

> "You will not believe when I say, that we preferred our shacks in Symphony Way, even though you would never know if its roof would resist the rain or if you would get wet at night, even though we had to learn how to deal with cooking on fire and collecting wood from the bush to make our own fire to cook, all these things. There, we had built our own support structures. We all learned how to share and take care of each other. We demanded our rights to housing, but they broke us and put us here, into these tin cans… They think we are stupid because we are poor. But we knew that this is not going to be a temporary camp. When we were living on the pavement in Symphony Way, they threatened us with this nightmare. We knew about people who were removed to Blikkiesdorp before, so we knew exactly what was awaiting us. I mean, look around, this place is scary… Apartheid, the same. They wanted to eliminate us and we thought we are resisting. And now, what is now? They still want to eliminate us."⁴⁶

After ongoing struggles and negotiations with the City, Blikkiesdorp and other Temporary Relocation Area residents are now waiting to be moved into RDP houses of different housing projects in Delft, some after twelve years of living in a TRA. The delays in construction and allocation has left most residents frustrated and doubtful.⁴⁷

The Tafelsig evictions

In May 2011, about 5,000 people, the majority of which were backyard-dwellers, occupied the two open fields Swartklip and Kapteinsklip in Tafelsig/Mitchell's Plain, close to the Kapteinsklip train station. The fields were distinguished from each other so that 4,000 people came to live on the one

---

45 See also: Cape Times article: *Symphony Way families move to Blikkiesdorp*. November 3, 2009.
46 Conversation. May 2, 2013.
47 GroundUp article. Lali, Vincent: *Blikkiesdorp residents frustrated by housing delays*. June 29, 2018.

field that was Swartklip, and 1,000 people on the other field that was Kapteinsklip. Before the occupation, they were living in shacks in Mitchell's Plain's backyards on other people's properties. Like the Symphony Way pavement dwellers, most of them were on the housing list for many years. The motivation and inducement to occupy the fields came from an organisation called the Backyard Dwellers Association. They took advantage of the desperation of people and even registered them for small plots of land against a registration fee of 10 Rand and handed out receipts and plate numbers. In the morning of the day after the occupation started, Anti-Land Invasion Unit and Law Enforcement entered the fields with trucks. They drove over the structures, then took the occupiers belongings and threw them on their trucks. This was an illegal vacation, as the City is only allowed to remove belongings of people during an actual eviction and according to the *Prevention of Illegal Eviction from and Unlawful Occupation of Land Act*, the eviction itself must be granted through a court order after all the circumstances of the residents were taken into consideration. After the City applied for their eviction, the first eviction order was granted on 1st of June 2011 by the Western Cape High Court. Many residents of the fields protested in front of the court against their eviction and their housing situation, accompanied by several hundred people from Joe Slovo, Gugulethu, Khayelitsha, Newfields Village and Blikkiesdorp, who came to support the occupants and show solidarity. Many supporters had experienced evictions themselves and demanded housing for the poor on placards. After the Anti-Land Invasion Unit and the Metro Police had realised the court's order and evicted the occupants from the fields, the evicted continued to return. They heavily refused to be relocated to Blikkiesdorp and referred to the relocation camp as a "death trap" or as a "hell hole". In stark contrast to the name of Blikkiesdorp that was given to it by its residents, the occupants of the Tafelsig fields renamed them New Horizon, a sign for people associating hope with a new life on the fields. "New Horizon" was standing versus "death trap" and "hell hole", such as independence and actively creating a new home versus the removal to a place where people would have no future prospects.

From the first eviction on, a seesaw began between occupants and City. People would return to the fields after being evicted again and again. They would build shacks and other structures to live in, being aware that the Anti-Land Invasion Unit or the police could remove them any time. As people would try to resist, both, the removal of the built structures and the eviction of people implied police violence and arrests. Verbal attacks were common practice during the vacations. But once the police removed the structures, the occupants would rebuild new shacks overnight. Law Enforcement would come mostly in the morning and remove all the belongings people had. One of the occupants and later community leader, Faeza Meyer Fourie, explained in one of our conversations how they tried to circumvent Law Enforcement: "Law Enforcement would come every morning around 6 o'clock or 7 o'clock, and then they would break our stuff down and take our things. And then we looked at it and said, this is a pattern, why are we not defending ourselves. And then we started to bury our stuff. We would get up at five in the morning and we would make huge holes and bury all our materials and close it up. And so they would come and be very frustrated because they are not allowed to come on the field at night when it's dark. So at night when they come there, they see all these shacks standing there and in the morning there is nothing."[48] Fourie also emphasised the negative role of charity organisations. They would come in and declare the occupation as one of their new projects. They would bring blankets and clothes and bread and make people stand and pose with the bags of bread or with the donated clothes on and take pictures of them. Often the bread would be rotten, but the organisations would list it as project expenses. The pictures taken would be displayed on the organisations' websites as tokens of their engagement. One example was an organisation called the Cape Charity Organization. Fourie was very determined about that if they had the knowledge of today, they would not have let these organisations abuse them and benefit from their struggle.[49]

Until October 2012, the court decided four times in favour of the City. After every eviction, the occupant's number on the fields dropped, so that at the end only about 150 people remained on the fields in resistance to the court's decision. After having resisted over a period of 18 months, and only after being evicted over 15 times, the remaining occupants had no other choice but accept to be removed to Blikkiesdorp. A 40-year old man, who does not want his name to be displayed, explained in a conversation: "It was illegal to evict us. We were living on an open field where they even don't want to build. We didn't disturb anybody. The court decided that we are illegal occupiers, but we didn't occupy anything but dry grass. The land belongs to the city, not to any private company or person. They could have let us live there." When I asked him, why so many people, who were removed to Blikkiesdorp do not want

---

48 Conversation with Faeza Meyer Fouri. March 20, 2014.
49 Ibid.

their names to be displayed, he explained: "You know, every single person who lives here hopes to get out of here. All of us are on the housing list for so many years. We are afraid to speak openly against the government. You always think, if I do this, or say that, will they kick me out of the list? I don't know. It's better to be careful."[50] It seems that before their removal to Blikkiesdorp, the residents of the fields had been highly aware of what would await them in the relocation camp. The same man explained about Blikkiesdorp: "When we were resisting the evictions in Tafelsig, we wrote a statement and declared that we see Blikkiesdorp as a concentration camp for the poor. We told them that we would rather continue living on an open field than come here. People die from hunger here or get murdered. They hanged a woman outside her house on the washing line. Another young girl was found stabbed lying on the ground. Look, here are no trees, no grass. Just iron and sand. In summer we boil inside these cans and in winter we freeze." I asked his wife, what drives people to start battling with the City for living on a field, knowing that the City might have the power to remove them sooner or later? She explained how desperation forces people to occupation of land: "Before we moved to the field we were living in a little shack in the backyard of other people. They didn't treat us equal and allowed themselves to talk to us in a very disrespectful way. We didn't see that place we were living in as a home. Actually, we did hate going back there every evening after work. Then we heard that some people were planning to go and build new homes in Swartklip and Kapteinsklip. In the situation, where you are totally desperate, you hold on even a very little spark of hope. We thought, what if we succeed? What if they leave us live there? Other people on the fields thought the same. We all acted out of desperation, because we had no place to call home." Her husband describing Blikkiesdorp as a "concentration camp for the poor" reminded me of a study I had read before about the criminalisation and marginalisation of homeless people in the city of Tempe/US. The "homeless campus" that the city created to relocate homeless people into a concentrated space was characterised by a homeless person affected as a concentration camp.[51] To call Blikkiesdorp a "death trap" or "concentration camp" might be an attempt to demonstrate and make tangible the effects of the restrictions and containment imposed on people. A

---

50 Conversation. May 3, 2013.
51 Amster: Randall: *Street People and the Contested Realms of Public Space*. New York 2004: p.105.

cry-out to say, look how we are made to live. Recognise the atrocities we have to endure. See us.

Blikkiesdorp

Since all the eviction cases I looked at are somehow enmeshed in Blikkiesdorp, as the evicted people were either removed to Blikkiesdorp or were threatened to be removed to Blikkiesdorp, I would like to provide a deeper insight into the structures and circumstances residents of Blikkiesdorp are living under. Blikkiesdorp, Blackheath, Tsunami, and Wolwerivier are so-called temporary relocation areas (TRAs) peripheral to the City of Cape Town (Wolwerivier's official status is that of a so-called Incremental Development Area). Of the four, Blikkiesdorp is the one to which many evicted people were removed. It was built by the City in 2007. Forcibly evicted people from Joe Slovo, Symphony Way, Tafelsig, from Spes Bona in Athlone, from Gympie and Cornwall Street in Woodstock, from Ruyterswacht, amongst others, were relocated to Blikkiesdorp, despite the fact that none of the evicted agreed to move there. Mrs. George, who was evicted from the District Six houses, remembered the day when their ward councillor came to make her that offer: "He said the council hasn't got property and the only property available to put us in is Blikkiesdorp. I said put your mother into Blikkiesdorp. I was so upset. I said just get out here. Don't tell me I must go and live in Blikkiesdorp. Go put your mother in Blikkiesdorp."[52] One of the main reasons why affected people would fight tooth and nail against their relocation to Blikkiesdorp was that they knew it would not be temporary. Most residents I talked to emphasised them knowing that the City did not plan their relocation as a temporary solution. This suspicion proved true as the relocated Symphony Pavement Dwellers alone just completed their twelfth year on the site. Others have been living there for fifteen years.[53] The relocation camp lies 30 kilometres outside of Cape Town and belongs to the municipality of Delft. Blikkiesdorp was named as such by residents who identified the place as "Tin Can Town" – that is its English translation. The City invested about 32 million Rand to build the about 1,600 one-room structures. The iron shacks are evocative of prison single cells, tide

---

52 Conversation with Mrs. Magdalene George. February 20, 2013.
53 Cape Argus article: *A place to call home*. April 30, 2014.

and dark. Each structure is inhabited by families between two and eight people.[54] To get to Cape Town city centre and back, residents have to pay a total of 30 Rand for minibus taxis. Daniels, who was removed to Blikkiesdorp from Symphony Way, emphasised in this regard that "For a person who is unemployed, who is struggling, I can tell you, to get hold of a ten Rand even, to get hold of five Rand, is difficult".[55] In and around Blikkiesdorp, no social activity is possible, as there is no park nearby, no opportunities to buy affordable food, no public space to gather. Most people who were forced to live there lost their jobs, as they were not able to pay the high taxi prices that they have to pay due to the lack of a train and bus network that applies generally to the city of Delft. The weak infrastructure implies that almost no opportunities remain to find informal work. The high amount of unemployment means that most families are already under a higher social and psychological pressure, which forces them to be much more concerned with securing food for their families than trying to build a bottom-up community structure that would create at least more social life. But despite the social and economic pressures of everyday life, residents have founded the Blikkiesdorp Informal Committee. Being offered emergency health care by the government, Eddie Swartz from the committee commented in 2009: "Things are very critical. Patients get anti-retroviral drugs from the Delft clinic but they don't have food. We have some help from NGOs but we need a container with 24-hour healthcare. Patients will die if there's no ambulance to fetch them."[56] The committee advocates not only the improvement of living conditions in terms of health care, unemployment, infrastructure and living facilities, but it also stands up for the purpose of public attention and awareness about the government's policy of removing evicted people to Temporary Relocation Camps that they see as a process of systematic exclusion. A former staff member of the Alternative Information Development Center, André Marais, emphasised that Blikkiesdorp does not constitute a dignified space to live in and that families should try and resist as much as they can being removed to the site. At the end of our conversation, Marais added: "Have you been there? It is a big graveyard. You cannot do anything else in Blikkiesdorp but die."[57] I assume that Marais' symbolic comparison to a graveyard derives from the reality of life in Blikkiesdorp

---

54 Cf. The Guardian article: *Life in 'Tin Can Town' for the South Africans evicted ahead of World Cup*. April 1, 2010.
55 Conversation with Jerome Daniels. March 27, 2014.
56 Mail & Guardian article: *'Dumping ground' for unwanted people*. October 9, 2009.
57 Conversation with André Marais. April 28, 2013.

that is living in isolation. Daniels used a similar rhetoric when he said that "it's not a dignified place to live and the reason is that people are dying". He was also very clear about the issue of isolation: "Spaces like Blikkiesdorp are making criminal. If you stay in Blikkiesdorp, you will see it in front of your eyes, because people got nothing to do. There is no jobs, there is nothing. So it makes criminal."[58] One will notice the factor of isolation at first sight, as the site is located in the middle of nowhere, in the sense that it is sandwiched in between sand dunes and roads with no facilities, not even a single shop or school. The fact that the shacks were built on demolition rubble and not on normal sand or gravel is quite symbolic, bearing in mind that many residents refer to Blikkiesdorp as a "dumping ground". In view of the high number of residents suffering from asthma only after they have moved to Blikkiesdorp, and of the fact that I started coughing every time I entered the space and the taste of dust that remained in my mouth between one and two hours after my visits, together with the community we decided to try to get the rubble examined by a laboratory that would have the respectability needed for the examination to be taken seriously by City officials. Together with Shaheed Mahomed, a Cape Peninsula University of Technology lecturer who engaged with the Blikkiesdorp community before, we approached the Council for Scientific and Industrial Research (CSIR) in Stellenbosch. Mahomed was able to activate some of his connections and so we got invited by the Council to present our case in Stellenbosch. The Council agreed to inspect the site of Blikkiesdorp and to meet with the community. After our first meeting at the site, they agreed to conduct the examination of the rubble, which filled the members of the community that were present with a lot of hope. But after this first inspection and a long conversation with residents, they never answered again any of our emails, letters or phone calls.

Fouri wrote in her diary that she kept during their struggle on the Tafelsig fields, entry of 25th of January 2012:

> "I spoke to William yesterday and said, it doesn't really matter how the City offers us temporary relocation, we have refused. We have decided to rather sleep on the sidewalk. What kind of mother in her right mind would sleep on the sidewalk with her children rather than a house with light with a door that locks, unless she is on drugs? That is how serious we are that going to Blikkiesdorp is worse than where we are now. I showed him a photo of

---

58   Conversation with Jerome Daniels. March 27, 2014.

my daughter, and said, there is nothing I can contribute to her future. Staying here is at least an opportunity to make her future better. Taking her to Blikkiesdorp would not be right, it would be putting my child in a hell hole! They said to us, if you guys come live here, I hope you don't have daughters because the gangsters come and take your daughters and you cannot go and fetch them! I am so scared for her. She doesn't hang out, she does her homework. I am so proud of her. Girls in this society and day are not interested in school. And she is – she wants to do something with her life. For me to take her to Blikkiesdorp would be robbing her of that."[59]

Conclusion

To conclude, forced evictions are an ongoing practice in the Western Cape. The low-income families who have been living for decades in the De Waal flats that belong to provincial government and are situated very close to Cape Town's central city, back dropped by Table Mountain with a fascinating view over the city and the harbour, have been threatened to be evicted and relocated to Pelican Park since the beginning of 2014. In 2015, 250 families were evicted from Skandaallcamp close to Tableview and relocated to Wolwerivier. The land from which the families of Woodstock's Gympie and Cornwall Street were removed from in 2012, was sold to *Swish Properties* whose plans to build a high-class luxury complex including 363 apartment units, a shopping mall beneath and a parking lot of 496 parking pays, were approved by the City's Mayoral Committee seven months after the evictions.[60] The families were relocated to Blikkiesdorp. The residents of Pine Road informal settlement in Woodstock face a similar future, as the City's plans to build social housing on the site will result in the removal of residents, none of whom qualify for social housing in the first place. The eviction order of 28 tenants in Bromwell Street, Lower Woodstock, to make space for a development project of the company Woodstock Hub, has been granted by the High Court in August 2016. The City now plans to remove the tenants to Wolwerivier, against which the affected

---

59 Conversation with Faeza Meyer Fourie. April 18, 2014.
60 https://www.capetown.gov.za/en/MediaReleases/Pages/CitysMayoralCommitteeapprovesexcitingdevelopmentprojectforWoodstock.aspx (seen on July 6, 2013). The City has removed the link from their website, but Property Wheel website has kept the City's statement on their website. Property Wheel article: *Exciting Development Project for Woodstock Approved*. March 9, 2013.

families appealed in court. The list of past and forthcoming forced evictions is long. Relocation camps like Blikkiesdorp and Wolwerivier imply that the people affected by forced evictions must not only endure the loss of home, of their social networks that they created through life, and in many cases of their jobs that mostly represent whole economic bases of families that were built through long years of personal effort and thus of their livelihoods, but also their removal to undignified sites of social displacement and erasure. With the displaced communities, their informal infrastructures and support networks get destroyed, leaving no prospects of being able to recover them. If Blikkiesdorp was situated next to a highway, it would obtain one of those huge signs installed by the municipality marking it as a "high crime area", asking drivers not to stop their cars at its edges. Exclusion and marginalisation are not only stable part of urban development, after the margins are created, they are also marked as danger zones inhabited by social rejects that the orderly city should circumnavigate. The warnings on those signs are more than any other political speech on the matter of discursive statements that intensify exclusion and compartmentalisation. As Daniels explained, places like Blikkiesdorp make not only criminal, but they make residents die a social death. The politics of off-city relocation is a practice that not only refuses to deal with questions of poverty and housing but obliterates these questions by placing low-income residents out of sight. Poverty becomes invisibilised so that orderly city life can produce itself as a patchwork of urban enclaves that do not have to deal with the disorders and dead ends of this system. They simply factor them out. Government officials are eliding the fact that the conceptualisation of forced evictions and relocation today borrows its technologies from the colonial and apartheid project. The postapartheid eviction of tenants from a part of District Six that was not declared *white* area under apartheid has a deep political meaning. The interconnectedness of this practice with the past gets silenced through referring to market forces over which the political sector would have no power. This rationalisation masks the fact that national laws and municipal by-laws are manufactured in favour of the market and its pushing for profit over people, not to mention that municipal authorities often grant eviction orders without the legally required court order, as was the case with the first evictions from the Tafelsig fields. This shows how the political sector has adopted the discourse of market-led urban development, without any frictions or contradictions between its own interests and the private sector. Especially the Joe Slovo evictions exemplify how the yearning for a world-class city status that is rooted in the capitalist imagination, determines the removal of thousands of people, while hiding behind false promises of upgrading for the residents' benefit. Jared Sacks, a journalist who continuously chases eviction cases in the Western Cape, describes it to the point: "After having seen many similar evictions for years and speaking to a range of legal minds on the subject, it has become clear that municipal governments all over the country take advantage of the inability of poor communities to represent themselves effectively in the media and access legal representation. They use this vulnerability to flout various constitutional safeguards when evicting shack dwellers and homeless South Africans. Municipalities then frequently go on to publicly assert the legality of their eviction by misrepresenting laws and lying about the facts on the ground."[61] Referring to a forced eviction case that took place in the beginning of May 2013 in the Philippi Township in the Western Cape, a government official stated that the eviction would have been conducted "in accordance with the *Protection of the Possession of Property Act*, which does not necessitate a court order". This was a surprise, as no one who has dealt with the subject of evictions before had ever heard of the mentioned act. Sacks investigated and found out that such an act does not exist. Experts at the Cape Town office of *Legal Resources Centre* assured him that "There is no such law called the Protection of the Possession of Property Act".[62] This means that on the one hand, the government tried to circumvent a court trial, and on the other hand criminalised the residents who resisted their eviction. The corrupt calling back of the Heritage Agency's report on the District Six houses further demonstrates how far the involvement of the political sector in this regard goes. It also shows that the open announcement of the judge in the Symphony Way case about him setting an example through the prison sentences against the two residents is not a coincidence but derives from a narrative of rightfulness as part of a discursive practice.

---

61   Daily Maverick article: *City of Cape Town makes up law to justify eviction of the poor*. May 6, 2013.
62   Ibid.

Chapter three

"Cleaning" the streets – Urban Development Discourse and criminalisation practices

"coincidentally Shoprite released its financial results on the same day as the so called 'poverty stats' were released by stats SA. Shoprite made super profits. (black) people are poorer. fact is many companies like Shoprite continue enjoying some form of Apartheid Dividend...companies that have always managed to sustain relatively consistent profits off the back of structurally low wages. the 'poverty stats' are relevant to this because in a country where more than half of the population lives in abject poverty there is bound to be massive distortions in labour market pricing. companies like Shoprite can continue to pay low wages and remain super profitable because they continue to enjoy this Apartheid dividend, which includes the compounded beneficial effects of a wholly inefficient labour market. if wages normalised many of these companies would still be profitable mind you. i'm rambling, but the tldr version is that not only is the whole get-up not fair but it's also not sustainable. which country can continue with the status quo when 55% of the population live in poverty? 55%. the related point here is that there is often an overstated contra-distinction between the efficiencies of corporate vs the inefficiencies of government. the simple fact is that when it comes to corporate SA, the distinction between meritocracy and structural privilege is often blurred. i'm rambling and i'm surprised Revolution has yet devoured us all."

Kholofelo Molewa[1]

---

1   Molewa, Kholofelo: Facebook post. August 22, 2017.

Introduction

After having delved into forced evictions that took place in four different parts of the greater Cape Town Metropolitan Area and the effects on the evicted people, this chapter aims to have a deeper look at the motifs and aims of the other side of the evictions - the business and political sector. What gets actively hidden behind the term "gentrification"? Can we speak of a specific project that aims to invisibilise and criminalise lower-class people behind the shield of the fight against crime?

In this chapter and the succeeding one, I will clarify why the term "the poor" is not useful for understanding politico-economic violence and its subjects. Kholofelo Molewa's statement above is to give an introduction into this understanding and to suggest thinking of new concepts when speaking about poverty and its subjects in South Africa. 27,6% of (official) unemployment[2]; low wages for workers on whom one can barely survive in the service sector, in the security sector, mining sector, industrial sector (metal, textile, shipping, fishing etc.), farming sector, public transport sector, and construction sector; outsourcing of workers by governmental institutions, by universities[3], and by the business sector among others; informal trade; social grants recipients; currently illegal industries such as the sex work and drug industry; pensioners; among other aspects – all must be taken into consideration to enable a radical analysis of what inequality means materially. Thus, it is crucial to consider that forced eviction, criminalisation, and marginalisation, are only three practices in favour of existing power structures and capital out of many others. Each sphere mentioned above contains various layers, each of which can become a field of analysis for the better understanding of the whole condition. But what matters in this chapter in particular is that in different ways and levels, all of these spheres are affected by and play a role in what this book zooms in at: The Urban Development Discourse.

In the introduction to this work, I clarified that I define Urban Development Discourse as an umbrella term for dominant government and business sector discourses on urban planning, on the role of the market, on the relation of the cities' inhabitants with the market, on housing, evictions, and socio-

---

2   Cf. tradingeconomics.com: South Africa Unemployment Rate (2017).
3   Insourcing of workers was and is one of the demands of the student movement. Cf. for example: Mail&Guardian article: *For real change to happen university students and workers must support one another.* May 31, 2017.

economic exclusion and inclusion. The emphasis here lies on "dominant", because using this umbrella term does not mean that multiple discourses within national, provincial and city governments do not co-exist. Already in 1995, one year after apartheid had officially ended, Patrick Bond spoke about Development Discourse in South Africa as in "the success of establishment development agencies - the World Bank, US AID, various UN bodies, international foundations and the like - in coopting progressive discourse while applying ineffectual policies inspired by neoliberal economic theory."[4] Ever since, many studies and writings deal with urban planning imperatives and their fostering of inequality in the country.[5] In this context of heated debates and conceptual controversies, especially within the ANC, competing approaches or at least differing views and debates on unequal space and access to life are depictable. Even within the more right-wing Democratic Alliance (DA) that has just won 20,77 % of votes nationwide and reassured its position as the ruling party in the Western Cape Province, serious discrepancies on social housing paradigms and socio-economic exclusion have developed over the years. In October 2018, Suzette Little, former City of Cape Town Government Councillor and Mayoral Committee Member for Social Development, Brett Herron, former Woodstock Ward Councillor and Mayoral Committee Member for Urban Development and Transport, Patricia de Lille, former Mayor of the City of Cape Town, Shaun August, former Chief Whip, and three other Mayoral Committee members and councillors, have resigned from their posts and their membership in the DA, due to, as they declared, racism and the blocking of land sales for affordable housing. Herron stated concerning this matter: "I cannot in good conscience sit by and watch the party lie to the public about this, nor can I continue to meet with communities and promise to deliver housing when it is clear that many in the party – enough to stop projects – are opposed to the provision of well-located affordable housing."[6]

---

4 Bond, Patrick: *Urban Social Movements – The Housing Question and Development Discourse in South Africa*. In: Moore, David B. and Schmitz, Gerald J.: *Debating Development Discourse – Institutional and Popular Perspectives*. Hampshire 1995: p.150.
5 Shepherd, Nick; Murray, Noeleen and Hall, Martin (eds): *Desire Lines: Space, Memory and Identity in the Post-apartheid City*. New York 2007.
6 Times Live article: *Flyaway Herron's talking rubbish, says Cape Town deputy mayor*. November 1, 2018.

The ANC on its side has drafted a so-called Expropriation Bill, which is currently online to be commented by the public.[7] The draft includes the possibility of expropriation of land from wealthy farm owners, in order to be able to redistribute that land to poorer families and communities in the respective area. Taking into account urban geographers who emphasise heterogeneity within government approaches towards urban development, Susan Parnell and Jennifer Robinson for example, speak of "competing voices within government" and distinguish between government protagonists with a "Reconstruction and Development Agenda" and those with a clear "neoliberal macroeconomic policy".[8] The diversified South African welfare system might be understood as direct product of these competing approaches. Disability, old-age and foster child grants are only three examples out of a variety of grants that low-income residents can apply for.[9] In addition, informal settlement upgrading as part of provincial and city governments' development policies can be seen as an effect of the developmentalist approach.

But despite heterogenous approaches towards access to houses and land within the ruling party and the DA, what matters to the analysis of this book, are the dominant discourses on urban planning and access to decent life; those discourses that have determined the status quo of South Africa's people up until now and continue to determine final decisions taken on public sector and business sector levels that have direct material impacts on the majority of the population. The fact that multiple approaches co-exist within both parties has unfortunately not changed the material condition of the majority in regard to housing, socio-economic inclusion and access to better living conditions in general. Access to physical and social death is provided overtly, whereas access to life remains controlled by a highly exclusive politico-economic system that favours profit over people. Official average life expectancy lies at 62,77 years, whereas Cuba, despite severe economic pressure of the past six decades, was able to reach a life expectancy of 79,74 years, more than a year higher than the United States.

---

7   Government Gazette. No 1409: *Draft Expropriation Bill 2019*. Department of Public Works. December 21, 2018.
8   Parnell, Susan and Robinson, Jennifer: *(Re)theorizing Cities from the Global South: Looking Beyond Neoliberalism*. in: Urban Geography. Volume 33:4. 2013: p.604.
9   Cf. Seekings, Jeremy: *The Broader Importance of Welfare Reform in South Africa*. in: Social Dynamics: A Journal of African Studies. Volume 28:2. 2002. pp. 1-38; GroundUp article. Kelly, Gabriele: *Everything you need to know about social grants*. April 7, 2017.

Against this background, Donovan Ward,[10] an artist with whose work I will engage further in the last chapter, emphasised in our conversation that city officials "speak quiet openly about cleaning up, when they speak of removals of human beings".[11] Having this statement and many other similar statements of friends and colleagues in mind, what I looked at is how the propagated aims of bringing profit, cleanliness and safety to the city/province collaborate with ongoing forced evictions. I also zoomed in on the ways in which a specific category of "the poor" is created. As a next step, I wanted to understand how this category relates to informal traders and why they are being criminalised and evicted. Here, it was most important to understand governmental decisions and the ways in which laws and by-laws are being applied. What then became clearer was how executive institutions as the metro police, law enforcement and private security companies that are engaged through councils on the municipal level, fulfil their tasks and rationalise them. I also wanted to know with which language and justification models, journalists mediate the laws and the discourse. Embracing the cities of the Western Cape and zooming in on their segregative structures and the actual implementation of related policies helps to develop a sense for exclusion and inclusion, for demarcation and comprehension. So, the central question in relation to urban development paradigms here is, whose body is welcomed in which space and whose body is attempted to be erased from certain areas?

Politico-economic violence and the coloniality of the present

"The legacies of colonialism and apartheid", "white supremacy", or "whiteness", are the expressions used and the links established between the former ruling systems and different forms of political and politico-economical violence that we are witnessing in present-day South Africa. Lalu asks, "How

---

10   Donovan Ward is a renowned artist who produces artworks since the 1980s. Besides exhibitions in South Africa and abroad, together with Paul Hendricks he also created the Gugulethu Seven memorial that commemorates the by the apartheid police murdered anti-apartheid activists who were all shot dead on March 3, 1986. As we will see in the last chapter, Ward is highly critical of urban development projects and the way they become implemented and rationalised. He opposes the fact that people with low income are being framed and displaced to make place for the desirable, design city marketed by business and political sector.
11   Conversation with Donovan Ward, May 30, 2013.

might we raise the stakes of the critique of apartheid in a manner that helps to unravel its institutional legacies and disciplinary regimes?"[12] This perspective puts itself forward for any researcher in the field but it is at the same time not an easy one to start from. In the initial phase of any research related to this question, it raises even more questions that, if not approached carefully, can also be confusing and disorientating. Looking at criminalisation and marginalisation as a political and economic manifestation, I also regarded the links between practices of today and the colonial and apartheid past as inextricable and undeniable. To enable the reader to fully understand this difficult position one resides in when asking the first more focused questions, here is a list of questions that came up and that were inevitable to answer:

How is it possible to seriously engage history in a matter like forced evictions and criminalisation? Asked differently, how is it possible to historicise present-day formations of politico-economic violence and theorise the relations between past and present? How can legacies of the past within current systems of violence be decoded and its events be processed as part and constituents of the present? What can be interpreted in the formation of city, suburb and township and the relations of domination between the three? What are the relations between forced removals during apartheid and forced evictions in the present? And what of the relations between the criminalisation of the *black* subject since the beginning of colonialism and the criminalisation of people today?

It was helpful to start with scholars, who see present-day forced evictions as a direct legacy of apartheid policies. Two examples are the conclusions of Martin J. Murray and Stephen Greenberg. Murray writes in his above mentioned book: "Forced removals have continued to take place after the end of apartheid, but paradoxically there is a kind of collective amnesia about the continuity between the past and the present."[13] Greenberg stresses the same point when he concludes that "In the face of a coldly rational model of planning, the horror of forced removals has not been consigned to history along with apartheid, but remains alive in postapartheid South Africa".[14] In agreement with the existence of this continuity stressed by both scholars, I would

---

12 Lalu, Premesh: *A Subaltern Studies for South African History*. in: Jacklin, Heather and Vale, Peter (eds.): *Re-imagining the Social in South Africa – Critique, Theory and Post-apartheid Society*. Pietermaritzburg 2009: p.283.
13 Murray: Martin J.: *Taming the Disorderly City: The Spatial Landscape of Johannesburg After Apartheid*. New York 2008: p.224
14 Ibid.

like to draw the attention to the system of thought and operation that was passed on to the postapartheid era. A specific relationship to violence was given free rein when the subject yet to be colonised was faced; a relationship that was characterised by the hierarchisation of human bodies on a scale from superior, to less superior, to less inferior, to inferior. The politico-economic violence of today should not be de-historicised. It must be seen in its historical context without being amputated from its past. As I see it, the overemphasis on human beings being superfluous and worthless stems from this constructed hierarchy of bodies in the past. It was the *black* subject that was set up as inferior during colonialism and apartheid. This relationship is part of a system of thought that was produced and established over a long historical period. The transformation of the political system does not include an automatic walking out of this discourse. It became reproduced and manifests itself today in an attempt to render the lower-class *black* subject inferior.

This imposing of inferiority does not remain an isolated ideological feature. It serves a specific mechanism that benefits the business elite of society. The power over bodies is the one that determines whose life is superfluous and whose is not, who must be silenced, displaced and rendered invisible and who is conducive to the desirable city that is placed on rivalry and competition for capital investment. This also applies to the dead, as the exhumations of an estimated number of 1000 enslaved bodily remains from a colonial mass grave show. The discovery of the human bones at a construction site in Prestwich Street in Cape Town's Green Point in May 2003 and the decision of the South African Heritage Resources Agency (SAHRA) to exhume, generated a whole movement of community leaders, Khoisan representatives, spiritual leaders, academics, and heritage sector NGOs,[15] protesting against, what Nick Shepherd, an in the movement involved archaeologist and lecturer, called the violence against the dead.[16] The opposition to the exhumations unified to become the *Hands-off Prestwich Street Ad Hoc Committee*. They pleaded for the converting of the mass grave at Prestwich Street into a memorial site, so as to acknowledge the pain and trauma related to the site, to not have echoed

---

15   Shepherd, Nick and Ernsten, Christian: *The World Below – Post-apartheid Urban Imaginaries and the Bones of the Prestwich Street Dead*. in: Murray, Noëleen, Shepherd, Nick and Hall, Martin: *Desire Lines – Space, Memory and Identity in the Post-apartheid City*. New York 2007: p.217.
16   Nick Shepherd in a conversation on violence and historical catastrophe, January 2012.

the apartheid regime's forced removals from the same area.[17] But this triple-level of violence, – the murder of the enslaved – the forced removals of *non-white* residents from the area during apartheid – and the removal of the dead without memorialising the brutality of their deaths in the postapartheid era, – was not of any interest of the officials in charge of the decision. The planned apartments were pre-sold and SAHRA took sides with the construction company in charge.[18] The bodies were boxed into containers and later placed in the so-called *Truth Coffee* café alias Prestwich Memorial. The commercial café-memorial was initiated by the City. It is constructed, designed and marketed in a way that commodifies the human remains, without involving any dignified memorialising element.[19]

The tuning up of Cape Town, Johannesburg and Durban to "world class cities"[20] goes hand in hand with agendas of neoliberal urbanism that is to produce an economically *successful* city subordinated to market rule, constantly being restructured with the movements of capital. Thus, the power of the market is the power to structure the evolution and "mental life"[21] of the city. The announcing of Cape Town as the World Design Capital 2014 and the consequences this entailed in terms of the related planning and conceptualising of the city must be read through this logic. The politico-economic violence is based on this subordination, but in addition, informed by the conceptual ground of the past that was inherited from colonialism and apartheid and carried into the postapartheid. The difference lies in the grade of visibility. With regards to the new subjects of criminalisation and marginalisation, the violence inflicted upon them is rendered invisible, whereas the apartheid system

---

17 Shepherd, Nick and Ernsten, Christian: *The World Below – Post-apartheid Urban Imaginaries and the Bones of the Prestwich Street Dead*. in: Murray, Noëleen, Shepherd, Nick and Hall, Martin: Desire Lines – Space, Memory and Identity in the Post-apartheid City. New York 2007: p.220.

18 Ibid. p.220.

19 Cf. https://truth.coffee/.

20 Cf. for example: Ndlovu, Cebo: *Turning Durban into a World Class City*. eThekwini Municipality article. November 18, 2013; *City and Carnegie Bring World-Class R78 Million Library to Khayelitsha Residents*. City of Cape Town government article. March 16, 2016; *Cape Town is a World Class African City*. Business Tech article. July 15, 2013; *Cape Town – A Real World-Class African City*. Rand Daily Mail article. July 1, 2016; *Thoughts on a World Class African City*. Future Cape Town article. August 21, 2013; *Cape Town's World Class Cruise Terminal*. Future Cape Town article. March 11, 2011; *Johannesburg a World Class African City*. LSE Cities Centre article. no date.

21 The use of this term is inspired by Tay, Eddie: *The Mental Life of Cities*. Hong Kong 2010.

was supported and maintained by highly visible forms of violence. Nothing could have been more penetrant than the geographical separation of people based on the concept of *race*. This visibility helped the rendering inconspicuous and unremarkable of the different violences exerted on the *black* subject. It turned the arresting of a *black* person in a *white* declared area to an ordinary situation. Something that is visible to such an extent cannot be anything other than legal and justified. These normalising effects of apartheid should not be underestimated as they continue to exist until today. It means that the criminalisation, marginalisation and rendering inferior of people is not only something engraved in the South African experience, but it is perceived as an acceptable method of social architecture within the majority of the profiting elite. The violence inherent to it is not acknowledged as such. On the contrary, it becomes trivialised by its executers and beneficiaries. This belittlement or intended oversimplification have become part of the Urban Development Discourse that in turn normalises the applied violence and secures the hierarchical self-situation of the social elite that consists of property, status symbols, ownership of prime land, access to infrastructure and public services, etc. This social elite does not use the terms displacement and exclusion but rather sticks to beautifying terms like gentrification and promotes it as evolutionary revitalising of areas that must be seen as necessary and inevitable urban renewal and progress. This discourse, saturated by rationalising arguments as "more safety", "more cleanliness", "more profit", "more liveability", keeps the hierarchic relationship between the urban lower classes and those who criminalise them intact.

The category of "the poor" and the disciplining effects of space

Urban planning is part of a specific politico-economic project that excludes and marginalises the majority of society and is not restricted to the material design of city spaces. Engineering becomes extended to the sphere of the public that uses and resides in the space. It means that not only buildings and streets are being designed, but also the fabric of people intended to avail themselves of them. Forced evictions are therefore not limited to the removal of residents from their homes. The eviction of informal traders and people that become screened and determined as not holding a certain social status from particular city spaces, is an established procedure of what is called city improvement. When Edgar Pieterse for instance argues, "that it is as plausible to build a conceptual model of the city from the perspective of the slum as it is from the perspective of the formal, concrete-and-steel city, as is normally done"[22], he refers to exactly these forms of exclusion and marginalisation. Many times, especially at night, one witnesses how security forces or the police, behind the shield of being given the task of observing suspicious behaviour, call upon a *black* person to immediately leave the area he or she is residing in. If one approaches to challenge the police officers or security agents, asking why they call upon the person to leave, as he or she has done nothing but walking or sitting, the same repeating answers come up, justifying that "Ma'am, we are trying to reduce crime" or "we want this district to be safe". An example of sources other than my observation is the video of a physical attack on the blind street performer Lunga Goodman Nono in the Cape Town CBD while he was playing the guitar. Several metro police officers beat him, smashed his guitar and forcibly evicted him from the place where he was performing.[23] The image of the eviction of a homeless woman who was resting opposite the Slave Lodge in Cape Town's city centre by guards of the private security company CCID (further explanation on the company see below) shows that the woman is clearly not obstructing traffic. [24]

The logic behind is interspersed with clearly classed, gendered and raced concepts of belonging. Spotting a *black* person after working hours, who in the eyes of the private-public security company guards most likely belongs to a certain social class, especially a lone *black* man or a group of *black* men walking the streets of Green Point, Sea Point or Camps Bay for example, brings up the question of their belonging and intentions for the authorities in charge. The city that changes its appearance after those who commute into the city - day workers, domestic workers and employees of the service sector have returned home, resides in this duality of rightful and integrated inhabitants on the one hand, and illegitimate, disintegrated visitors from the margins, on the other hand. In a conversation, Mthobeli Qona[25] described how he and his friends

---

22 Pieterse, Edgar: *City Futures – Confronting the Crisis of Urban Development*. Cape Town 2009: p.109.
23 See video of the eviction in SABC News report of 10th of July 2013: http://www.youtube.com/watch?v=b-fdeK2ADZA (last seen September 20, 2017).
24 Image by the Xcollektiv.
25 Mthobeli Qona is head of the Abahlali baseMjondolo shack dwellers movement in the Western Cape. He grew up in Khayelitsha township in Cape Town and has been part of several community struggles and protests. He is also active member of the Housing

"Cleaning" the streets – Urban Development Discourse and criminalisation practices   109

Image by the Xcollektiv

were asked by a police officer on the main road in Rondebosch about their purpose of residing in the suburb. Qona explained:

> "I have seen this several times. It happened to me. We were three guys walking in Rondebosch. We were working there, but we were just walking on the street and then the ADT security came with their car and they stopped us and said, 'Guys, what are you doing here?' And then I asked 'where?' They said 'here'. I said in South Africa or here in Rondebosch? They said, 'here in Rondebosch'. I said 'look, we are South African citizens. I think maybe you are mistaken to ask us, what we are doing here. Because this is our home. Our country. We were born here. We are Africans. We are not expecting you

---

Assembly, an organisation of people living in townships and informal settlements that fights for dignified housing for all (see chapter five).

to ask us, what are we doing here.' 'Ah I'm just asking, because we don't need people in the street.' 'Why? Why you don't need people in the streets? Why?' Because we want to see this district to be safe. The district must be safe'. And I asked him, 'Do we look, us three guys, like criminals?' 'No, I don't mean that.' 'But why are you asking us that question? Are we still living in apartheid here?' I said 'You must leave, because you cannot ask us. This is our country. We are living here. So we don't need those questions, please leave us.' And then he just drove away." [sic.][26]

Of course, Qona was aware that not everybody is prepared to answer with the same self-esteem. He underlined that it would be for this reason that workshops would be needed for people to learn how to react in these kinds of situations. Living in Khayelitsha township both today and through apartheid and as part of the *Abahlali baseMjondolo* shack dwellers movement in the Western Cape, Qona was a highly politicised person.

But how do normalisation and legalisation processes of this kind of direct exclusion and criminalisation function? In accordance with urban control policies of municipalities in the US[27], during the last 15 years, the City of Cape Town has passed several by-laws that allow police as well as different private security forces to evict a person from a certain area, if the person seems to not belong to that area; to arrest a person who is begging; to arrest people who live on the streets and are drunk; and to arrest people who are deemed by an official as standing or sitting in a public space in a way that is for any reason undesirable.[28] Public spaces include all city streets, paths and pavements that are not privately owned. In general, the possibility to pass by-laws is granted by the National Constitution for local governments to legally adjust their policies on particularities of the area over which they govern and warrant them legislative power.[29] In this way, by-laws can be progressive, because they can also be used to decentralise power and policy making and adjust regulations according to the needs of local communities. In most cases, they deal with

---

26 Conversation with Mthobeli Qona, March 15, 2014.
27 Cf. Kelling, George L.: *"Broken Windows" and Police Discretion*. Research Report for the US National Institute of Justice. Washington 1999; Memeza, Mzi: *By-law Enforcement in South African Cities. Centre for the Study of Violence and Reconciliation*. Cape Town 2015: p.7.
28 By-law Relating to Streets, Public Places and the Prevention of Noise Nuisances, 2007 (Provincial Gazette 6469).
29 Chapter 7 of the Constitution: *Local Government*. 156. – (2).

practical city management issues like air pollution, traffic, cemeteries and waste management for example. But they can also be used in favour of the private market and the governing powers. In the Western Cape, by-laws concerning safety of city spaces function as a tool to further control and regulate the people who use them and their relation to public spaces. The by-law *Relating to Streets, Public Places and the Prevention of Noise Nuisances*, a successor of a 2002 by-law, was passed by the City of Cape Town municipality in 2007. Section 2.(2) – *Prohibited Behaviour* – states: "Any person who blocks, occupies or reserves a public parking space, or begs, stands, sits or lies in a public place shall immediately cease to do so when directed by a peace officer or member of the Cape Town Metropolitan Police Department." Interesting to compare is also the City of Johannesburg's by-law that makes use of the term "loiterers", people that are classified as such because they "unlawfully and intentionally lie, sit, stand, congregate, loiter or walk or otherwise act on a public road in a manner that may obstruct the traffic".[30] What the formulations in the by-laws do not explain is the basis on which the decision is taken of who is allowed to sit or stand in a public space and who is not.

Criminalisation practices are not restricted to extra-legal discursive statements and police arbitrariness but are explicitly legalised by law. When analysing the city of Tempe's (Arizona/US) urban policies, Randall Amster refers to Jeff Ferrell: "…drawing on evocative images of filth, disease, and decay, economic and political authorities engage in an ideological alchemy through which unwanted individuals become [a] sort of 'street trash' [and which] demonises economic outsiders, stigmatises cultural trespassers, and thereby justifies the symbolic cleansing of the cultural spaces they occupy."[31] The legalisation of mechanisms of exclusion and marginalisation of individuals determined as "unwanted" presupposes its systematisation. This process is carried by a specific political decision that we can point to. It is therefore far from representing a structural condition, whose decision makers are not identifiable. Illuminating the systematic structures behind provides us with more clarity and helps to prevent the rendering of the process that is actually happening as non-specific and vague. This is equally true for the

---

30 City of Johannesburg Metropolitan Municipality: *Public Road and Miscellaneous By-Laws*. Chapter 2 – Paragraph 13; Cf. Bénit-Gbaffou, Claire: *Community Policing and Disputed Norms for Local Social Control in Post-Apartheid Johannesburg*. Journal of Southern African Studies. Vol. 34, No. 1 2008: p. 39.

31 Amster: Randall: *Street People and the Contested Realms of Public Space*. New York 2004: p.113.

statements of Suzette Little at the time when she still was City of Cape Town Government Councillor and Mayoral Committee Member for Social Development. What Little described as "work villages" to "rehabilitate and reintegrate homeless people and parolees back into society and to help them identifying their values", resembles what Foucault describes in *Discipline and Punish* as the last step of the judiciary system's development in the treatment of the criminal: "Of course, we pass sentence, but this sentence is not in direct relation to the crime. It is quite clear that for us it functions as a way of treating a criminal. We punish, but this is a way of saying that we wish to obtain a cure."[32] Little presented her suggestion first in a meeting with the CCID and JP Smith, Mayoral Committee Member for Safety and Security. In our conversation, she became more explicit and explained why she sees work villages as an adequate social solution.[33] In the implementation of the related by-laws, what is envisaged is a criminal being rather than a criminal action. The wording of the by-law *Relating to Streets, Public Places, and the Prevention of Noise Nuisances* explicitly speaks about the person who violates the law, not about the contravention itself.[34] Little, supported by the administrative order of the City of Cape Town, formed a specific discourse while she argued for the construct of a future work village designed for "the problem" of homeless life. Those excluded and marginalised are not only denied freedom of movement, a right that after apartheid is constitutionally guaranteed to all South Africans, but they also undergo a general denunciation that values them as a part of society not desirable enough to be integrated into urban life. Through this, they are denied speech/raising their voice and thus are silenced through a power that threatens to apply force if they do not accept being exiled to the margins. Referring to the 2010 Soccer World Cup, Depelchin points to this mechanism, writing that "2010 being just around the corner, South African officialdom, at least some of them, are implementing the most radical option in keeping poverty/the poor out of sight. In the process, these poverty/ethnic cleansers have affirmed, in various and modulated ways, that the poor are not worth listening to, that their voices do not count".[35]

The example of the by-law passed by the City of Johannesburg shows how much applicable the questions of this study could be to other parts of South

---

32 Foucault, Michel: *Discipline and Punish*. London 1977: p.22.
33 Conversation with Suzette Little, May 5, 2014.
34 By-law Relating to Streets, Public Places and the Prevention of Noise Nuisances, 2007 (Provincial Gazette 6469).
35 Depelchin, Jacques: *Reclaiming African History*. Cape Town 2011: p.45.

Africa. To strengthen this argument and to show how policies of displacement manifest in the South African political landscape, I would like to refer to Anna Selmeczi, who writes in her paper on the *Abahlali* shack dwellers movement in Durban: "I approached the City of Durban's and the KwaZulu-Natal Province's measures to dislocate the urban poor as their attempts to create the desirable milieu of the market. Surely, this entails favouring some areas over others, and requires that the movement between these areas be policed. For the circulation of people and things to be smooth, people, things and events perceived as non-conducive to the logic of market competition have to be moved out of its way."[36] Murray titles a part of a chapter in his book about the spatial landscape of Johannesburg after apartheid as follows: "Clearing the buildings and sweeping the streets: Driving the urban poor out of the inner city."[37] In its report that required four months of field work with the concerned people in Johannesburg, the Geneva based *Center on Housing Rights and Evictions* (*COHRE*) arrived at the conclusion that poor people are being criminalised and rendered invisible in Johannesburg.[38]

Lower-class life that is equated with criminal life is shaped by a powerlessness that is reflected in everyday situations we find ourselves located in. The internalisation of this powerlessness renders insecurity and thereby the reduced ability to respond to criminalisation and marginalisation as a constitutive part of one's own socialisation. The deep entrenched fear in a man's eyes when something like a remote control fell from under his blanket while he was walking and his shivering voice begging to believe him when he says he did not steal it, is only one example of what I perceive to be an internalised inferiority that seems to have mutated even the bodily posture of those who are being stigmatised as dangerous and undesirable and thus being criminalised. This power over bodies labels the lower classes with regimes of shame and dispensability. It zooms in on the body so as to be able to examine whether the person physically interrogated and scrutinised can be classified and registered as poor or not. A practice that is not only loaded with colonial and apartheid baggage, but that stems from the very inscription of the grade of value on the body that was used as a technology of all previous regimes, beginning with

---

36 Selmeczi, Anna: *Dis/placing political illiteracy*. Unpublished paper. Cape Town 2013: p.2.
37 Murray: Martin J.: *Taming the Disorderly City: The Spatial Landscape of Johannesburg After Apartheid*. New York 2008: p.223.
38 Center on Housing Rights and Evictions (COHRE): *Any Room for the Poor? Forced Evictions in Johannesburg, South Africa*. Johannesburg 2005.

colonialism. Its effects remain the same. The inscription of superfluity on the body and thus its heteronomy, draws off "the only reality we can possess",[39] that is the body itself as Prins asserts. The person deemed superfluous either accepts this loss or is obliged to constantly reproduce itself through dissimulating in every situation where it is observed as suspicious or as danger to "public safety" in order to escape further inspection. The constantly rejected body that is deprived of the right to inhabit itself and regarded as deviant, afflicted and shameful, always put in contrast with the "valid citizen", is more vulnerable to an inner and outward uptightness when facing the authoritarian other. This deformation of personality and body-hood unmasks the effects of the inflicted violence. It shows how the grouping of the lower classes to unworthy human beings, being denied their humanity and forced into a constant struggle for space, self-positioning and identity, makes their physical expulsion possible, an expulsion that reflects through situations as described above. Working with and through the echoes of these situations suggests imagining how the complex trauma of being declared inferior and undesirable within different regimes of racial oppression, multiplies itself in the moment of its re-experience, endured by the body of the lower-class *black* subject. However, thinking this multiplying effect further remains a challenge to the imagination of those who do not become exposed to this violence, as one can only assume the dynamic described here. To determine where to move and where to reside in and to act freely in the space of abidance makes a healthy relationship to human selfhood possible, a relationship from which self-esteem and the ability for self-determination arise. Metaphorically speaking, it is this ability to self-determination that constitutes the human home and bears evidence of an emancipated existence. It nurtures the self-confident relationship to the human self and negotiates the self-positioning in relation to the social outside. Through the violence inflicted, this emancipation and the possibility of belonging are rendered unreachable. The space in which one should move freely, which one should be able to personalise, own and create as a sphere of belonging, is once again turned into a colonised, subordinated and hierarchised space, more precisely, a space in which one human group is positioned

---

39 Prins, Jo-Anne: *Mediating Difference – Politics of Representation in Antje Krog's Chronicling of the Truth and Reconciliation Commission in Country of my Skull*. in: Duncan, Norman; Gqola, Pumla Dineo; Hoffmeyer, Murray; Shefer, Tamara; Malunga, Felix; and Mashige, Mashudu (eds.): *Discourses on Difference, Discourses on Oppression*. Cape Town 2002: p.356.

superior over the other, where self-determination and freedom of movement of the superior group implies the systematic exclusion of the group that is positioned inferior. This violence of space and the ways in which illegitimate beings are produced through space, can impose a certain kind of internal displacement.

Social justice slogans as in the Freedom Charter - "The people shall govern", "The national wealth of our country, the heritage of all South Africans, shall be restored to the people; The mineral wealth beneath the soil, the banks and monopoly industry shall be transferred to the ownership of the people as a whole" – were all buried with the end of the negotiations in 1994. These values of the liberation struggle were clearly erased to the advantage of market rule. The enormous political shift to the right mirrors in all city spaces. The public space that was supposed to be transformed from a policed and hierarchic space to a communal space in which public life and creativity can grow, has not been granted this transformation. Different than the imaginations about new spatial orders in a free South Africa that 100 years of liberation struggle had engendered, public space has been alienated from the idea of it as a tool for bringing people together, facilitating movement, accomplishing zones of interaction and allowing multiple narratives to co-exist. The postapartheid city remains a continuous site of exclusion, embedded in historical and contemporary experiences of humiliation, built on its unresolved histories, inspired by the exclusionary technologies and economic and racial compositions of its historical others, the colonial and the apartheid city. Noeelen Murray and Shepherd remind us: "...the most significant trope of space to emerge and grow was the space of the 'township', and it is this primary dichotomy within the post-apartheid city (between city, suburbs and townships) that characterises lines of wealth and poverty, access to resources, forms of exclusion, crime and violence, and many other aspects of life"[40]. This does not mean that in the analysis of this violence and exclusion one should ignore the mutual influencing of city and townships, facing each other as both conflicting spaces and defining features, or the liveliness, social energy, possibilities of improvisation and creative everyday tactics of survival, moments of joy and celebration that townships partly feature. Although they are imposed spaces, they are also collectively negotiated ones. Nevertheless, a decoding of the coexistence of immense wealth and misery and of the constellations that

---

40   Shepherd, Nick; Murray, Noeleen: *Desire Lines: Space, Memory and Identity in the Post-apartheid City*. New York 2007: p.6.

evolved between city, suburbs and townships, is necessary. The first step in revisiting the biopolitical moment of superfluity[41] in the postapartheid is to realise that what is determined superfluous life is boxed into enclaved zones that is the township space, tolerated in the traffic between townships and city, in busses, mini-bus taxis and trains, and disqualified in the moment of entering city spaces that are other than the determined margins and places of work, labour and service. Existence and movement of the constantly rejected bodies are allowed inside the township, but only in a relation of, in some cases, absolute non-belonging to the city, and in other cases, of a highly conditional belonging that depends on the grade of functionality of the worker or potential labour force. Creating this specific category of 'the poor', drawing on the lower classes that build the world below the cities – the underworld as in the trash heap of the world above[42], demonising it and placing it in permanent contrast and contradiction with the elite of society and its requirements, generates an ossified polarity that does not only nurture the Urban Development Discourse, but that is equally welcomed by the municipalities for the purpose of taking the easy way out when it comes to dealing with cases of violent crime. It means that the category created is held responsible for all kind of violent incidents, serving as a scapegoat whenever the elucidation of a case is a long time coming. Most people in Cape Town will not have forgotten that on the night of the *Red Hot Chili Peppers* concert in the Green Point stadium on the 5th of February 2013, a young woman was pushed down Signal Hill and died in follow of her injuries. Coincidently I was driving on the day after on the foot of Signal Hill, only to find all the different security forces united, busy with the forced eviction of some twenty people living at the foot of the hill in a small informal settlement. There was no connection made between the woman's death and the residents evicted, but somebody had to be punished and if the real perpetrator was untraceable at the moment, then the most vulnerable would have to serve as their compensation. This instrumentalisation becomes part of an epistemic system and thus of a larger ideological project

---

41 Achille Mbembe explains his notion of superfluity as follows: "To my mind, superfluity refers also to the dialectics of indispensability and expendability of both labour and life, people and things." Mbembe, Achille: *Aesthetics of Superfluity*. Journal of Public Cultures. Vol. 16, No. 3. 2004: p.374. In this study, I use the term in its very simplified and extracted meaning that can be described as dispensability or expendability.
42 Cf. Mbembe, Achille and Nuttal Sarah: *Johannesburg – The Elusive Metropolis*. Johannesburg 2008: p.22.

that has placed the category of *the poor* into a fixed position of invisibilised objectified beings easily subjected to a violence that remains unshakeable and inescapable. The here derivable relation of domination as an inextricable pillar of the politico-economic reality in South Africa produces contemporary silences, or as Depelchin would put it, paradigmatic silences,[43] that are difficult to break as they flow from seemingly privileged claims to justice and democratic processes of urban development.

A certain narrative is created that divides society into two groups: those who have worked hard and earned what they deserve, and those who do not want to achieve 'personal success', because they are either lazy or not believing enough in themselves or not motivated enough. Great emphasis is put on the motivation one would need to reach a higher social status. These were outcomes of conversations with Suzette Little and JP Smith.[44] It speaks of notions of self-produced and self-inflicted inequality, of taken or untaken opportunities and thus of a moralist reading of class differences. Little repeated several times that what has been missing in South Africa, would be a "debriefing", "making people to understand that everybody has the opportunity to live in Constantia or Bishopscourt", or "buy a house in Camps Bay".[45] This is a reducing of social inequality to mentality problems that could be resolved, if the people would attempt to "change their mind-set". Suzette Little used examples of dysfunctional families, as a five-year-old sitting at the family table putting together a gun to show how people are disoriented.[46] In this neoliberal argumentation that must be understood as part of a discursive practice, social issues are addressed through concentrating on the individual and expecting the individual to behave right, put more effort and be more motivated. It also implies that the majority of society is demotivated and lazy, a discourse I will also point out in chapter four.

Superfluous informal traders

To dwell on the criminalisation of informal trade as indicated above, city governments have the legal power to pass by-laws that apply to specific streets

---

43   Depelchin, Jacques: *Silences in African History*. Dar Es Salaam 2005: p.10.
44   Conversation with JP Smith, May 8, 2014; and with Suzette Little, May 5, 2014.
45   Conversation with Suzette Little, May 5, 2014.
46   Ibid.

in which informal trade is in progress. If they for example aim to prohibit informal trade on Longmarket Street in Cape Town's city centre, they can spontaneously pass a by-law that only addresses the prohibition of informal trade on that street. In Cape Town, Stellenbosch and Paarl, the eviction of informal traders are normalised procedures of what the local governments see as beautification and the creation of order. In most cases it overlaps with the private sector's interests in the area or in that particular street. A co-existence with informal traders is not what private business holders understand as orderly business conditions. Smoothness and the desirable city do not include low-income social profiles, stalls, and stuff being presented and sold on the streets. This picturing of how the city is supposed to look like, regulates who is allowed to draw income from it and who is not. The eviction of informal traders shows how the desired picture is being imagined by private and public sector. Informal traders do not fulfil the required aesthetics. They who already negotiate their livelihoods with a high level of instability, - since informality also means the constant reorganising of one's own locality, low income, and no secured access to health care and social benefits, - are also deprived of an equal access to the economy. It is especially the big supermarket chains like *Pick'n Pay* and *Shoprite* that benefit from this power relation. Many informal traders sell vegetables and fruits at much lower prices than the supermarkets. Their eviction, especially if they trade within walking distance of a supermarket, mitigates the competition for the latter and is therefore very much in their interest. In the duality of formal and informal economy, the informal has continuously been at the mercy of both private and public decision makers. In this relation, informal traders are turned into beggars who must plead for the maintenance of their businesses, facing arbitrary removal at any moment. So even if an eviction does not materialise, it is a permanent threat that overshadows the lives of the traders. Their trading activities are discursively framed as illegal. In places where they have not been evicted yet, they have only been tolerated, not welcomed. By being evicted from the places where they generated income and being removed to the city margins, the traders are rendered jobless, as the lack of customers due to marginal pedestrian traffic implies the impossibility of a further survival on the trade. With them, whole families face an uncertain future, as most traders support several family members, especially their children who often still go to school or enter university.

Out of the many conversations I held with informal traders in Paarl, Stellenbosch and Cape Town, three main issues were of significant concern. Most traders, regardless of which gender, emphasised that their trade was the key pillar of their families' support structures, providing for rents, food, electricity, money for transport, and school and university fees. Along with joblessness, they are now also facing homelessness, as most of them did not have an alternative income source that would enable them to pay next month's rent. Linda Radebe is an informal trader who I spoke to in Paarl in 2014. After her husband left her and the children in 2009, she is a single mother of two school children. She assured me: "I will be present in every protest that will take place against the evictions. I said to the others, what holds us back from protesting every day in front of the city hall until they allow us to go back to our tiny lots and continue with what we were doing for years? I have nothing to lose. I will even not be able to pay rent next month. What am I supposed to tell my children? Mummy is jobless and has no money for rent because the government wants the city to look nice? What am I? Ugly?!"[47] Some of the evicted traders held official trading permits that were granted by the Business Areas Management Offices of the cities. This also represents the second main concern the traders were raising. Frank Meintjies asks in an article about the new eviction waves of informal traders about the sense of approval processes if in fact the permits are worthless before the law.[48] Holding his permit in his hands, Khwezi Mabizela from Cape Town asked himself the same question: "Why did I run after this for three months if they planned to evict me another three months after?"[49] If a by-law is enacted targeting a particular street, it affects registered and unregistered traders equally. Trading fruits and vegetables, Mabizela now has to try his luck at some outlying intersections outside the city, trying to convince car drivers to roll down their windows and buy a bag of avocados or tomatoes. But even this new location is not a secure position to trade from. Trading at robots and intersections is prohibited through the in 2009 passed Trading by-law.[50] Rosheda Muller, the acting president of the *South African Informal Traders Alliance (SAITA)* and public relation officer of the *Western Cape Informal Traders Coalition*, explained in our conversation why the robot is an import location for traders:

---

47 Conversation with Linda Radebe, February 6, 2013.
48 The South African Civil Society Information Service article: *Time to Demonstrate Solidarity With Joburg's Street Traders*. November 21, 2013.
49 Conversation with Khwezi Mabizela. January 29, 2013.
50 See elaboration of the by-law and its functions in GroundUp article. Maregele, Barbara and Armstrong, Adam: *The Plight of Informal Street Traders*. June 26, 2014.

> "If you know informal trade, a trader is got to go where he makes his money. So maybe we come to the inner city or to the market and there is gonna be too many of them. So he sees the opportunity of the robot. He knows that at that robot he is going to sell 20, 30 packets a day. But maybe inside the market, competing with ten other traders of the same product, he is gonna sell two or three. So you have to understand that the informal trader has to go home with some money to put on the table, so there is food. So I would say that there is a message, that the hawker is driven by his anguish to survive and that makes him find a spot where he knows this is where I'm going to make money. And robots have been a spot which I sometimes find convenient, because if I drive and I see a bargain, you not gonna get a whole packet of tomatoes for five Rand in the supermarket, you going to pay five Rand for two, and there at the corner, you gonna get ten. So I think the service the informal trader supplies at a very strategic point of sale is important. And the informal trader is driven by his survival. And that is why you find them on corners and on certain spots. You can't go put a trader in an area, where it's a white elephant." (sic.)[51]

The third main concern pertained to the government's image making, presenting itself as being well-disposed towards informal trade, trying to make the public believe that it values informal trade as a positive contribution to the country's economy and acknowledges informal traders rights to the city, as it would employ almost one-fifth of economically active residents and produce a substantial percentage of the economy.[52] The alternative news agency GroundUp writes in one of its articles on the criminalisation of informal trade:

> "Last week, GroundUp witnessed law enforcement officers confiscating the fruit of two street vendors on the corners of Belmont and Main Road, Rondebosch. They are among thousands of informal vendors breaking city by-laws to sell their goods at traffic lights and intersections across the City in order to make their daily living. For two informal traders from Brooklyn, selling naartjies at a busy intersection in Rondebosch was not only a means of income, but also a way to reform from a life of crime. While the National

---

51 Conversation with Rosheda Muller. February 15, 2016.
52 Cf.: City of Cape Town's statement about informal trading: https://www.capetown.gov.za/en/ehd/Pages/informaltrading.aspx; City of Johannesburg's statement: http://www.joburg.org.za/index.php?option=com_content&id=3503&limitstart=4; and City of Durban's statement: http://www.durban.gov.za/Resource_Centre/Policies/Documents/INFORMAL%20ECONOMIC%20POLICY%20FINAL%20DOCUMENT.pdf.

Roads Traffic Act prohibits vendors from trading on the roads, the Constitution makes provision for the City to allow regulated informal traders at intersections. However, the City's Informal Trading By-law of 2009 clearly restricts vendors from obstructing sidewalks and creating traffic hazards. The vendors, who later identified themselves as Alex and Sean from Brooklyn, appeared accustomed to the process and without much protest handed all their stock worth nearly R300 to the officers. They were issued with a R500 fine. "I sell naartjies [tangerines] to stop living on the streets. Everything I was meant to sell is gone now. I used to rob people while living on the streets," said Alex, "but now I'm trying to change my life." Alex said it was still not clear how he would pay for the goods. "We work for someone else. The boss gets R10 and I get R10 from what we sell. They took all our stuff, I don't know what we are going to do because we sleep on the streets," he said. Alex and Sean said it was likely they would return to the same spot to sell fruit soon. The City's Mayco [Mayoral Committee] member for Safety and Security JP Smith said he was often subjected to hundreds of 'belligerent' calls from people complaining about traders at intersections."[53]

Most of the traders I spoke to saw themselves being used for the government's purpose of campaigning for itself. They assessed the governments statements about supporting informal trade as deceitful and dishonest, and as a strategy, "making them disappear little by little". One of the traders, nicknamed Aya, asked me to print for him the city government statements that I had referred to in our conversation after he had spoken about him feeling used for the government's self-presentation.[54] Remarkable statements on these prints were,

> "Through its local area economic development service, the City has assisted this sector through a city-wide informal trading policy..." (City of Cape Town government);

> "Informal trading is a key economic activity in the city. This informal trading programme is tasked with developing policies for regularizing informal trading in the city and to create opportunities for the informal trading sector

---

53   GroundUp article. Maregele, Barbara and Armstrong, Adam: *The Plight of Informal Street Traders*. June 26, 2014.
54   Conversation with Aya. Februray 14, 2013.

to share in the benefits of economic growth." (City of Johannesburg government);

"All work, whether in the more formal or more informal ends of the continuum, is to be valued, and especially when unemployment is so high..." (City of Durban government).[55]

These statements exemplify the government's benefit. Through officially pretending goodwill towards the informal sector, government's actual policies become neutralised, as it constructs the idea of a government that is willing to fulfil informal trader's needs and take special care of the issue. That way, the government's actions remain masked and unquestioned, unless one has a special interest in investigating the actual reasons behind the vanishing of the traders.

When I began researching the evictions of informal traders, I assumed that the evictions hit their peak before and during the 2010 Soccer World Cup, where even fishermen were forced to move from Durban piers as part of an "upgrade project" for the beachfront[56] and thousands of traders in Cape Town's Mitchell's Plain, Bellville, and the city centre, among other areas, were evicted without being offered an alternative trading location.[57] But soon I had to learn that these evictions were only the beginning of a new long-term policy that stretches out all over the country. Since a few years ago, more precisely, since October 2013, this policy has a name. The "Clean Sweep" initiative, sometimes also referred to as the "verification process", stands for the demolishing of thousands of trader's stalls and confiscating of their goods. The title chosen for the operation reveals the position the city governments ascribe to the traders in the hierarchy of human value. To openly announce that the city centre's streets must be cleaned of informal traders means that they are regarded as waste, superfluous disrupters of a discourse that presents the city as a first-class destination for investment and profit. The strategy of marginalising and consequently disabling informal trade, held an unofficial status until recently, but is now packaged as a written, official policy. Its accreditation started in Johannesburg and is since then being adopted in many cities and towns of the country. In 2013, 7000 traders were violently evicted

---

55 See footnote 235.
56 BBC article: *Durban fishermen cry foul over World Cup ban*. July 9, 2010.
57 Cf. Streetnet International article: Traders Evicted in Mitchells Plain Town Center. March 8, 2010.

in Johannesburg alone, registered and unregistered ones equally.[58] The initiative is set to "improve the liveability of the inner city" through a "coordinated crime and safety enforcement effort", paraphrased Johannesburg's (former) mayor Mpho Franklyn Parks Tau.[59] The characterisation of the initiative by the mayor might pose the question of the relation between informal trade and "crime and safety enforcement". Along with the initiative, the dynamics of criminalisation are in full swing. Through positioning them as the opposite of safety and liveability, Tau's statement poses a very subtle form of implementing the association of informal traders with crime. The police's practice to enforce the initiative suits this positioning very well. Durban city government and police are applying similar practices. In their report on *Street Vendors in Durban*, Sibongile Mkhize, Godwin Dube and Caroline Skinner conclude that police interventions are violent and government decisions highly hostile.[60]

Muller revealed criminalisation of traders as a systematic practice as part of a discourse in which they "are looked upon as criminals and second grade". Muller's personal experience shows that not only in everyday confrontations with police and law enforcement is criminalisation practiced, but that it also becomes applied strategically in situations where informal traders raise their voice collectively. In 2010, as part of the preparations for the soccer world cup, about 250 traders were evicted from the Green Point area, in which the soccer stadium is also located. Muller, who at the time was chairperson of the Green Point Traders, was arrested for trying to organise the traders: "I was even put in the back of the police truck and taken to jail and was arrested, because I was addressing the traders in the area where we trade. They said it was public violence." In the Johannesburg case, the traders won the court case. About six months after they were evicted from Johannesburg's inner city, the Constitutional Court declared the evictions as unlawful and a "degradation and humiliation" of the traders.[61] After this ruling, the traders were allowed back

---

58   Webster, Dennis: *The End of the Street? Informal Traders' Experiences of Rights and Regulations in Inner City Johannesburg.* Report for the Socio-Economic Rights Institute of South Africa. Johannesburg 2015: p.4, 35.
59   Daily Maverick article: *Operation Cleen Sweap: not just a clean-up but a purge of the poor.* November 15, 2013.
60   Mkhize, Sibongile, Dube, Godwin and Skinner, Caroline: *Street Vendors in Durban, South Africa.* Durban 2013.
61   Constitutional Court judgment: *South African Informal Traders Forum and Others versus City of Johannesburg and Others; South African National Traders Retail Association versus City of Johannesburg.* April 4, 2014.

to their original trading posts, knowing that the city government is desperately looking for legal opportunities to evict them permanently.[62]

The fact that the court ruled in the trader's favour does not mean that the city governments have changed their initial policy of "cleaning" the streets of informal traders. A Cape Town trader who did not want to be named described his experience of the police searching and scanning especially male traders, treating them as they would be criminals. Some traders testified that they were beaten by the police or had witnessed others being beaten when they refused to clear their place of trade, even though the Constitutional Court had ruled in their favour through a judgment that applies to informal trade on a national level. Muller confirmed that confiscations and evictions would be an ongoing practice in the Western Cape, especially if traders are not able to pay their permits which are due on a monthly basis. In fact, the permits must be renewed monthly, which also means that the decision about their approval is retaken every month anew. If it does not get approved for the following month, the trader loses his livelihood from one day to the other, which shows how uncertain the immediate future of a trader is. But it is also used as a means to put politically active traders under pressure. Muller gave an example of what that can mean: "At the moment, one of the executive members of SAITA, and a few of the leaders in the Northern Cape, they have been victimised. He has not received his permit to trade for months now, because he raised his voice on issues. And especially being a leader in the national level, you are looked upon like a troublemaker."[63] The lack of permits is only one reason for evictions. At the beginning of 2012 in Stellenbosch, informal traders were evicted from the place where they were trading for 17 years.[64] Muller explained: "For many many years, the traders were trading in front of a church in Stellenbosch in the main road. But they were not too close to the church. And the church allowed it. The local municipality collected R30 every day from them. They paid a fortune to the municipality. Then the church and the community decided, no, we don't want you here, you make the place look ugly. They were complaining, you are defecating and urinating, instead of addressing the issues, and say let's sit down and let's see how we are going

---

[62] Webster, Dennis: *The End of the Street? Informal Traders' Experiences of Rights and Regulations in Inner City Johannesburg.* Report for the Socio-Economic Rights Institute of South Africa. Johannesburg 2015: p.10.

[63] Conversation with Rosheda Muller. February 15, 2016.

[64] Cf. Streetnet International article: *Stellenbosch Municipality and Informal Workers Clash Over Evictions.* January 18, 2012.

to do this better. No, they were issued with their eviction."⁶⁵ The traders collected over R20 000 to be able to take the case to court, but they lost the case and were relocated to areas where they cannot make a living.⁶⁶ It shows how big groups of traders in clustered areas are targeted as much as the single, less remarkable trader. Muller gave an example of the constant eviction of a fruit and vegetable trader in Cape Town: "I know for example of a trader here. He sat at a corner with fresh vegetables and fruits, and the Law Enforcement will just always give him a fine. Now they confiscate your goods, it's fruit and vegg, it's soft, it's perishable, so now you must pay the fine and you must pay to get your goods back, but by the time you get your goods back it's rotten. So they make life so difficult."⁶⁷

The confiscation of goods until they become unusable is a frequent strategy to discourage traders. In Johannesburg during "Clean Sweep", physical violence against traders was used to frighten and discourage. Here was where among many other incidents of police brutality, a woman trader testified that she was beaten and thrown into a police van where police officers tore out almost all her hair after she had tried to record the beatings against other traders on her mobile phone.⁶⁸ Amongst other things, City of Johannesburg spokesperson Nthatisi Modingoane listed "illegal dumping", "public urinating", and "potential urban decay", as challenges that the informal trading sector would bring with.⁶⁹ The terminology used by Modingoane reveals the traders in a specific light. It inscribes on them characteristics of anti-socialness, dirtiness, and again dispensability, casting them as undesirable obstacles to urban upgrading and beautification. It is almost surprising how fluently the eviction of traders is assigned a position within the Urban Development Discourse, when Modingoane ends his press release stating that "…as part of ongoing initiatives to create a city that is clean, safe, resilient, sustainable, and liveable".⁷⁰ This was although the national minister of trade and

---

65   Conversation with Rosheda Muller. February 15, 2016.
66   Cf. Ibid.
67   Ibid.
68   Webster, Dennis: *The End of the Street? Informal Traders' Experiences of Rights and Regulations in Inner City Johannesburg*. Report for the Socio-Economic Rights Institute of South Africa. Johannesburg 2015: p.14.
69   City of Johannesburg press release: *The City of Johannesburg Announces Extension of the Informal Trading Verification Process*. November 12, 2013.
70   Ibid.

industry, Rob Davies, had at that time already started to work on an upliftment project that, as he puts it, would benefit informal traders, upgrade their working conditions, and develop their capacities to help them compete with the established businesses.[71] Davies introduced the new national strategy plan in 2014[72] that until today, although it was positioned as a multimillion rand project,[73] did not bring any practical change to the working conditions of informal traders. The plan was to start with the training of 1000 informal traders throughout all provinces.[74] But on the ground, the traders of inner-city Cape Town, Stellenbosch and Paarl, have never even heard of such a project being introduced by government. It shows that even if the initial 1000 traders have received training, how small the number is to represent a real and noticeable intervention. Muller herself was one of the traders chosen to attend the project. I asked her why no trader I spoke to had ever heard of the project. She agreed that it is not noticeable at all: "Because how many of us went? Ten! Ten in my organisation! You cannot measure it. One was from Bellville, one was from Parow, two were from Mitchell's Plain."[75]

The security sector and the production of fear

The above-mentioned examples demonstrate the large extent to which criminalisation and marginalisation practices are prevalent. Important is also to look at the organs that are employed to implement the policies related. Besides the Metro Police, Law Enforcement, and the South African Police Service, South Africa is quasi covered by different private and public-private security companies. Besides the approximately 140 000 police, about 400 000 people are employed by the private and public-private security sector that is almost one percent of the South African population.[76] Cape Town's, Stellenbosch's and Paarl's suburbs are the three spaces I studied to understand the market

---

71 National Department of Trade and Industry press release: *Minister Davies to Unveil the National Upliftment Strategy for Informal Traders*: March 10, 2014.
72 Ibid.
73 Ibid.
74 Vuk'uzenzele (national government bimonthly newspaper) article: *Informal sector gets help*. June 2015.
75 Conversation with Rosheda Muller. February 15, 2016.
76 Cf. Miraftab, Faranak: *Colonial Present: Legacies of the past in contemporary urban practices in Cape Town, South Africa*. in: Journal of Planning History. Vol. 11, No. 4. 2012: p.21.

of neighbourhood security and gated residential communities. These spaces are publicly adorned with "Armed Response" signs, security guard posts, and security guards patrolling by van, bicycle and foot day and night. The "Armed Response" signs belong to private security companies to which property owners must pay subscriptions if they want to become clients. Famous examples are the US American *American District Telegraph (ADT)* or the *City Bowl Armed Response (CBAR)*. In a conversation with John Brown, a lawyer who deals with the security industry and the new by-laws that provincial and municipal governments implemented, he explained what he sees as the complicity of the upper and middle classes. According to him, they would constitute one of the actors with a key function in the security business, because they are the ones who engage private security in order to keep the districts of their interests "clean" and "safe". Lower-income people would be criminalised for residing in an upper or middle class area and be permanently scrutinised and often forced by the different security improvement districts to leave.[77] Murray confirms this complicity pointed out by Brown when he writes that "Deprived of the segregationist statutes and racialist practices that kept the poor and impoverished black people at bay, the affluent middle classes have resorted to the power embodied in space to maintain their privileged lifestyles."[78] The main slogan of the Upper Woodstock Residents' Association is just a small detail of the whole picture, but is reminiscent of what Brown tried to explain: "Working together to unify, beautify, and create a safe environment in Woodstock."[79] Their goals proclaimed on their website mainly centre on crime prevention and counteracting what they call, and what we will later reencounter in the media analysis, "anti-social behaviour".[80] Parroting the discursive content of the Urban Development Discourse, safety is set as the objective that will lead to the orderly city.

The suburbs are arranged in a homogenised and obtrusive order. They are real and utopia at the same time. The house walls are topped with electric fences and razor wire, signposted by the "Armed Response" signs and the round the clock patrolling security guards who walk the streets and communicate via their walkie-talkies or sit in their cars and drive their rounds around the blocks. Equipped with the latest surveillance technology, CCTV cameras

---

77   Conversation with John Brown, March 19, 2013.
78   Murray, Martin J.: *City of Extremes: The Spatial Politics of Johannesburg*. Durham and London 2011: p.286-287.
79   Source: www.woodstock.org.za (seen August 3, 2014).
80   Source: http://www.woodstock.org.za/about-us/ (seen September 20, 2017).

that are installed in the central business districts and the affluent suburbs, the security companies claim, are the most effective deterrents. These defensive typologies of the suburbs' appearance created them as introverted spatial enclaves that are very certain about their agendas of inclusion and exclusion. One can ask the question of what the difference is between this form of creating protectorates whose barriers are already very physical and the building up of actual physical walls around the suburbs. Encapsulating themselves in the embrace of high-security settings, these artificial refuges are, in a qualitatively different way, as much spaces of confinement as the space of the township and informal settlements. The middle and upper classes are complicit in their own unfreedom, as the segregated city incarcerates them as well. Fear limits and does not allow ease. It creates a form of uptightness that is different from the uptightness of the inspected, interrogated, racialised body, but it is still an uptightness. It most notably means a withdrawal from public street life and from the possibility of inhabiting the street as a space of movement, leisure, and recreation. The securitised micro-worlds carve themselves out and cut any relationship to the street and all city spaces that are abandoned and left to their own devices. The outside is a space in between two gated places, as for instance between home and a shopping mall. Always approached by car, it is not of any use but to get from one place to the other, often from one enclave to the other. The car and the enclaves as places of residence build structures of disconnection and avoidance. Lower-class social profiles, as they are indexed, must be avoided because they cannot be controlled and are deemed to be dangerous. One time, it was a hot summer day in February 2015, I was walking on the coastal road between two bays on the Atlantic Seaboard in Cape Town to look at the security structures of those affluent neighbourhoods and at their gates and fences and the introverted architecture of the houses. Land Survey student Mahyar Bineshtarigh had previously made me aware of people living in caves in Clifton. I was just passing a water tap that is available for the public, when I saw a man behind the handrail from where I thought are only rocks and the ocean. I asked, "From which side did you come here?" He replied, "From my home". He then explained that his home was a cave embedded in the rocks and that there are four other caves were people live in. He offered to show me his home, he asked, "Do you want to see it?" So we jumped over the handrail, jumped over some rocks, and there we were. Five people were living in that one cave together. An older man explained that he was living in the cave for over 20 years. Some clothes were hanging on a washing line, on the floor some mattresses, blankets and small furniture. They then explained, "People don't want us here. They say we are dangerous and shouldn't be living here because we are not paying rent. They say we don't belong here. They even asked the City to remove the water tap, so that we won't have access to water. They want us out."[81]

To preserve affluent neighbourhoods and the benefits of insularity is to guard them against diverse publics and class heterogeneity and disrupters of the established comfortable yet defensive quality of life. Besides the fact that these enclaves have the infrastructural means and their inhabitants the resources to be connected to all the other privileged city spaces and can easily circumnavigate the disadvantaged ones, there is also no economic need to connect to the latter. The privileged city on the one side and the ordinary city on the other side do not contradict each other in the practical sense of the matter. They live two parallel city lives. The utopian orderly is created through the isolation of the disorderly and that which is real, and what is real has been perceived and presented as dangerous. In order to maintain the securitised and privatised enclaves, the image of the dangerous city outside the boundaries of CID guarded space must be kept up. Hysteria, paranoia, and fear are three components that are needed for the creation of this imagination. Cindi Katz points out "that the performance of security through objects, technologies and displays is meant to stage and foreground a pervasive sense of fear".[82] This also means that specific social profiles are set as scary or intimidating and are made to be perceived as a threat. I suggest that in this specific discursive setting, we can speak of a politics of fear that sets the ubiquitous possibility of bodily harm and loss of property as the reason for rightful separation and segregated city spaces. The promotional material of securitised residential units wallows in this fear and anxiety to advertise the properties as safe and defensible islands to which one can escape. "24 hour security", "CCTV cameras", "electrified fencing", and "biometric access control", are the keywords in property marketing.[83] Crime sells in the truest sense of the word. Its exploitation turns security into a lucrative commodity. The well-off minority is held in an angst-ridden relation to the majority of the population that is suspected of creeping around their gates. Crime as a discursive

---

81 Conversation with residents of the caves, February 2, 2015.
82 Katz, Cindi: Me and My Monkey: What's Hiding in the Security State. in: Pain, Rachel and Smith, Susan: Fear: Critical Geopolitics and Everyday Life. Hampshire 2008: p.59.
83 Cf. for example: promotional material of the Madison Place in Observatory, Cape Town, owned by Rawson Developers.

tool of generating segregation has replaced the colonial discourse of disease and savagery inflicted on the *black* subject, a threat from which *whites* had to be protected.[84] One example of the colonial public health discourse is the first removals of people from District Six, most of whom were dockworkers, that took place in the beginning of the 20th century. Accused and discursively framed as the main carriers of Bubonic Plague, the workers and their families were forcibly removed to Ndabeni township[85] and fear of the with disease infested was generated. Today, although racism as a discourse blurred into new discourses of belonging and social class, division and fear are still racialised. New and old discourses merge and become bounded. Urban space that was violently divided by group identity during apartheid, adjusted to be divided by social class in which *race* still plays a key role. Founded on historical ideals, this new configuration of division has also become the new idealised image of the urban elite. The compulsive focus on safety and security and the respective technologies and architectures applied, retains this condition to stay intact, and, as a historical déjà vu, restructures the present-day suburbs as spaces of authority and control. Seen from this angle and as I will delve further into in chapter four, the reclaiming of urban space as a main political challenge after apartheid has failed. The *Rights to the city for all* remained an idealistic slogan. In her research report on housing in South Africa, the architect Lindsay Blair Howe elaborates:

> "...the relationship between control and insurgency of the production of housing and delivery of infrastructural services is an integral descriptor of the 'right to the city' discourse that shapes such protests. These current events are a poignant reminder of the fact that our decisions as architects and planners directly affect lives and livelihoods. If we are to conduct a discussion of no-cost or low-cost housing, it must begin with uncovering and addressing the inequalities of urban development strategies, and how they are contested by the underprivileged collectively asserting their right to make and re-make the city 'from the fringe'."[86]

---

84 Cf. Miraftab, Faranak: *Colonial Present: Legacies of the past in contemporary urban practices in Cape Town*, South Africa. in: Journal of Planning History. Vol. 11, No. 4. 2012: p.15, 23.

85 Cf. Bickford-Smith, Vivian: *Mapping Cape Town: From Slavery to Apartheid*. in: Field, Sean (ed.): *Lost Communities, Living Memories – Remembering Forced Removals in Cape Town*. Cape Town 2001: pp.16-17.

86 Blair Howe, Lindsay: *City-making from the Fringe: Control and Insurgency in the South African Housing Landscape*. Zurich 2016: p.2.

So we are speaking of an aestheticised and normalised exclusion. Different than in Johannesburg where after apartheid the affluent classes drifted more and more north, in Cape Town, Stellenbosch and Paarl the urban elite did not have to withdraw from the city centre and from the more central districts to create their spatial enclaves. The locality of the lower-income majority in the urban periphery has been maintained. To guarantee the isolation of the disorderly, their entry into the guarded world must be controlled. This continuation with the past remains unquestioned and does not seem to disturb its beneficiaries. As Mike Davis points out, "...the defense of luxury has given birth to an arsenal of security systems and an obsession with the policing of social boundaries through architecture."[87] It conveys the feeling of being protected to its consumers and expresses metaphors of strength, stability, authority, and order. As part of this performance, the spaces are introduced as triumphantly safe – security villages that are taken special care of. But to an extent it is a simulated, hallucinatory safety and security. High-security settings in privileged city spaces cannot erase the social realities from which crime derives. Having never been dealt with and only ever blocked out, poverty conglomerates and explodes as crime - an omnipresent reminder of these realities, pattering down on all city spaces, including the privileged ones. This also means that the much-desired harmony within a bounded space does not materialise.

Today, most middle and upper-class districts have their own CID. It is short for private City Improvement District, such as the Sea Point City Improvement District, the Observatory Improvement District, the Central City Improvement District (CCID), and so on. It stands for both, the name of the security organ itself and the zone that receives the additional security service. Property owners of areas in which the majority can afford to engage additional security pay higher rates to supply for the CIDs budgets. This also means that urban governance has been privatised and subordinated to market rule. Areas where property owners cannot afford to finance a CID are not offered solutions to their urban challenges. Faranak Miraftab speaks about how this resembles colonial era urban governance where only the well-off proper-

---

87 Davis, Mike quoted in: Murray, Martin J.: *City of Extremes: The Spatial Politics of Johannesburg*. Durham and London 2011: p.216.

tied elite had a share in the decision-making processes regarding questions of urban planning.[88]

Private and public-private security guards come as the main performative expressions of triumph over the city. They are the visual spectacle of safety and security as discursive practice and the material demonstration of urban control. Their main practical task is by-law enforcement and related to that the prevention and deterrence of crime and streetscape maintenance. Let us look closer at the CCID's functions and approaches for two reasons. First, it represents a security organ which, because of the geographical centrality of its area of authority, most Capetonians deal with or encounter on a frequent basis. And second, the central city holds a historical significance as it was not only declared a *white* area (except for the neighbourhoods of Bo Kaap, Walmer Estate, and Woodstock) during apartheid but has been a site of several exercises of power such as exclusion and removal, ever since the arrival of the first settlers.

The CCID is commissioned by different business companies that are situated in the Cape Town city centre, and managed by a non-profit organisation called the *Cape Town Partnership*, an organ that is half private and half City-owned.[89] It is important to note here that generally, private corporations have the permission to initiate their own policing. They become the managing organ of city spaces, arranging their regulatory policies on the basis of their own profit. As urban management and the regulation of spatiality have increasingly become privatised, responsibilities and finding solutions have been handed over from the public to the private sector. This process has not unfolded as simple outsourcing. Although on the side of the municipality, this privatisation means that urban management is paid for by the private sector and not by City budgets, it is not a handing over of responsibility for the sake of simplifying structures and work processes. The takeover of urban management by the private sector is ordered by the sector's interests. It is the shaping of the cityscape to the advantage of capital and business profitability. This form of privatisation also means the handing over of policy making power to the private sector, which for instance includes the agendas through

---

88 Miraftab, Faranak: *Colonial Present: Legacies of the past in contemporary urban practices in Cape Town, South Africa*. in: Journal of Planning History. Vol. 11, No. 4. 2012: p.20.
89 Description of the Cape Town Partnership's founders from the website's section "About us" – "Who we are": http://www.capetownpartnership.co.za/about/.

which resources are distributed, or veto rights against City decisions that contradict business sector interests. Decisions are taken with the all-embracing objective to attract investment and to increase competitiveness, not to foster inclusivity.

Equipped with its own media organ, the CCID newspaper *City Views*, the CCID propagates its policies not only through its actions on the streets, but also through written text that it distributes for free to all inhabitants and business platforms of the central city, as well as the paperless format that is accessible online. To provide an insight into how it constructs discourse as part of the broader discourse at stake, I would like to start with an example of one of its slogans written on the front page of *City Views* issue of August 2012. I suggest it is a representative example because it matches the profile of these security companies that I am trying to characterise: "For a clean, safe and caring Cape Town." Using the same slogan on its website and having it placed on an image in which a woman and a man are hugging each other behind a well maintained flower bed, the next image that follows, rotating with the former, holds the slogan "Our CBD is open for business", impressed on a shot of the Cape Town Central Business District (CBD) from a bird's eyes view. The CBD is portrayed as the reflection of a desirable city, worthwhile to invest in. Besides safety and security, the increase of investment and attraction of global capital is also one of the main mandates of the CCID. More significant in terms of the discourse that is created are these lines, heading the website's section "About us" which also exemplifies how the discourse is phrased and promoted and how the social and economic overcoming of the central city's deteriorated condition before the swaggered "revitalisation" becomes simulated:

> "The power of widespread co-operation between stakeholders amplifies the effect of the CCID in its efforts to ensure Cape Town's Central City is a clean, safe and caring space that is open for business…The Central City is the core of the City of Cape Town's economy and the close partnership between the CCID and the City has seen the effective revitalisation of areas once in decline and is proud of its thriving social and economic centre…Cape Town's CBD is regarded by the South African Police Service as the safest in the country."[90]

---

90   From the CCID website's section "About Us": http://www.capetowncid.co.za/about/partners/.

With their permission to evict arbitrarily as soon as a person seems as unbelonging to an area, the CCID security officers are being handed over the force of law including the power to biopolitically abandon and therefore the power over bodies.[91] They regulate who is allowed to reside where, based on the grade of profitability of the presence of the person and of the compatibility of that person's appearance with the aesthetic standards of the guarded area. Safety is not public, as the imprint "public safety" on the back of the guard's green waistcoats claims, but private. Their mandate is to provide and secure a very clear portrait of Cape Town, a competitive, safe and smooth place to accommodate capital and invest in. Everything that is regarded as a disrupter of this portrait is at the same time perceived as a destabiliser of capital, irreconcilable with the profit seeker's imagination of a world-class city and must thus be removed, no matter how discriminatory the intervention might be. This second component of their mandate remains unspoken.

The eviction of undesirables is not a publicly announced objective of the CCID. It is only visible in the situation of eviction itself. The Urban Development Discourse with its by-laws and the production of a symbolic universe of space, needs to evict undesirables. At the same time, the eviction itself remains invisible and its traces become erased. The act of eviction is being executed in the same remote corners that are historically and systematically isolated from other city spaces. This isolation helps to not draw the attention of the orderly public. Profit, cleanliness, safety and security are the catchphrases with which their agenda becomes legitimatised. But despite the discourse of which they are an executive part, the outcome of many conversations I held with the security officers[92] shows how they themselves are dissatisfied with the content of their work. Most officers have been deployed by the City in the

---

91 This notion is influenced by Foucault's concept of the "Power over life" and the "Power over bodies". He illustrates how disciplining technologies that target the body have been developed historically and how the exercise of power over the body has changed in different time periods. Cf. Foucault, Michel: *Discipline and Punish*. London 1977; *The History of Sexuality – Volume I: An Introduction*. New York 1978. Here, I work with his concept in regard to spatial exclusion that becomes determined by the power over the social body (biopolitics), and to physical removal of lower-class subjects determined by the power over the individual body.

92 I held informal conversations with security guards in the inner city throughout the years of research between 2013 and 2016. For the data analysis, I relied on the notes that I took after each conversation.

past three years. They themselves belong to that major part of society that cannot afford to live outside the townships. Thus, they have grown up there, and still have to travel every morning long distances to their workplace. They will never be able to afford the spaces and lifestyles they are guarding. They have experienced and still experience inequality and highly separated city spaces based on class on an everyday basis. As security officers, they are deployed as robots who must do their work and then go home. They are only valued inside the framework of producing security. No social interaction between them and the clients whose businesses they are guarding is visible. They stay anonymous, with the number tagged onto their uniform as their only identification mark. After work finishes, they go back to the same disorder they are guarding against. To evict desperate people from the streets, often by force, therefore brings an ongoing conflict with their own social and political awareness about the condition the majority of the population is obliged to live in. But not only in relation to the eviction of desperate people like the homeless or street children, also in relation to individuals that they have to interrogate because they assume them to not be living or working in the district, this conflict becomes effective. The individuals scrutinised, interrogated and finally evicted by them could just as easily be they themselves, as in a situation where they do not wear their uniform, they could as much be categorised as ones who do not belong. To ask a group of *black* men or a lone *black* man about their reasons for being in an area and then evicting them is therefore as much a dehumanisation of their targets as it is a dehumanisation of themselves. This interconnectedness with their subjects of monitoring I assume is the reason why I could notice a general dissatisfaction with the policies whose implementation they are instructed to do. Some stayed cautious as they were doubtful whether or not they could trust talking to a random person who asks them questions and challenges their work. It also suggests a threat to their livelihood if they share their views. But even this caution and hesitation to express themselves spoke of a critical position towards their work that they retained and kept to themselves. Others would not stay reserved but explained that they also disagree but that this was their job and that they could do nothing about it. The fear of losing one's job does not allow provocation of conflict with one's employer. Some encouraged me to go and talk to their employers and tell them that not everybody agrees with their policies. But not a single security guard I spoke to agreed with or justified the practices of exclusion the CCID carries out. Only in the situation of eviction itself the respective guards would resort to the catchphrase of "Ma'am, we are just trying to keep this area safe."

In the previous pages I have shown how CIDs have become the executive authority of the Urban Development Discourse. Their mandate, entrenched behind the discourse of fear and safety and security, fosters exclusion, marginalisation, and spatial polarisation and upholds the continuities with the past in terms of maintaining conditions of segregation and the guarding of privilege and superior lifestyles. Spatial enclaves as the spaces of that privilege are the playgrounds of authority and control. There is where inclusion and exclusion are determined and exercised through high-security technology and institutions. The segregation at stake is less tangible than during apartheid, as it is not based on a state doctrine that deploys police to implement influx control, but on market forces that snatch urban spaces like octopuses and draw on inequalities that were generated by colonial and apartheid urban planning. Securitised and enclosed urban space are expressions of that power.

The business elite

The companies mentioned below are not chosen to illustrate the ultimate manipulators and propagators of the discourse. The aim here is not to portray them as evil and selfish forces thirsting for profit or to put forth any other kind of moralist reading. They are solely examples of how the interests of the business sector are framed, both discursively and materially, and how they get implemented. They provide an insight into strategies and rhetoric of the business sector and the grade of consistency with the framing of the issue at the political level and thus into understanding how Urban Development Discourse is a shared product of business and political sector.

The *Cape Town Partnership* is the managing unit of the *Central City Improvement District*. Before looking at its policies, it is important to understand the background of its initiation. The Partnership was formed as an agreement between private property owners and the public sector, to service and redevelop what they regarded as a "run down" CBD, interspersed with "crime and grime".[93] Not surprisingly, this meant that at a time when inequality and the

---

93 Conversation with Bulelwa Makalima-Ngewana, CEO of the Cape Town Partnership at the time. February 5, 2014.

remaining of the population's majority after apartheid in bare poverty became a certainty, the City government decided to treat the symptoms by focusing on how to eradicate them and to ignore where the symptoms originated from. To treat the body in its entirety that inhabited crime not as sheer crime or as an isolated factor, but as a manifestation of poverty, would have required the questioning of the postapartheid adopted political and economic system itself and was therefore unthinkable. In this effect, the *South African Property Owners Association*, the *Chamber of Commerce and Industry*, and the City of Cape Town came together to establish the Partnership as organiser and facilitator of, not poverty reduction but crime reduction, of marketing the CBD and every space of it as potential financial market, and of acquisition of new investors. So as the Urban Development Discourse required, cleanliness, safety and investment became the main driving forces of different initiatives that the partnership led. This course represented at the same time the core agreement between the political and the business sector. Sampie Terreblanche's conclusions in a conversation that we held in his house in January 2012, illustrate the way in which this agreement was installed historically. The late history professor, who was part of the first negotiations between the ANC and the apartheid government in England, explained how the business sector was the driving force that throughout the negotiations between 1990 and 1994, pleaded for the withdrawing of the ANC from its demands in the Freedom Charter and the adopting of a market driven neoliberal politico-economic model. Terreblanche's descriptions rang in my ears, when Bulelwa Makalima-Ngewana, at the time of our conversation CEO of the *Cape Town Partnership*, explained the Partnership's mandate and motivations, emphasising repeatedly, "we had to save the CBD".[94]

Today, 16 years after it was founded, the Partnership admits having made mistakes. Makalima-Ngewana explained how they were too single-minded about safety and security in the central city so that social questions had no place on their agenda. That the Partnership has come to this understanding it also proclaims publicly on its website. In the "about us" section it states: "But there have been unintended consequences to our exuberance and the rate of our success. We never saw ourselves as agents of gentrification, or thought of development as a tool for displacement. And yet that is how our work has been seen, and criticised, in some quarters…In trying to pave a road to our future, at times we lost sight of our past: parts of Cape Town might've transformed

---

94   Ibid.

in the last few years. But others are still living out apartheid-era realities of a life divided and disconnected."[95] Although admitting to have made mistakes in relation to the Partnership's whole orientation and strategies might be quite a progressive statement to make, the insights acquired through this belated realisation are not being put into practice. The CCID did not change their policies, as they are still evicting homeless people and, in their terms, suspicious people from the streets, not in order to help them but to make them invisible. At the same time, the CCID is the main organ of the Partnership that stands in direct contact with people on the central city's streets. If the Partnership wants to change its strategies, it will have to do it in the first instance through the CCID and a rethinking of the whole mandate under which the Improvement District acts. The same applies to the projects they run throughout the city. One of the projects that academics and community activists have intensively criticised[96] was a plan to upgrade a part of District Six. After the Partnership identified the area as economically run down, acquiring the lowest levels of investment compared to other parts of the central city, they commissioned project managers who drew up a plan on the basis of which they introduced urban design techniques that would trigger investment and a marketing strategy after which the targeted site was renamed "The Fringe". Their vision was to turn the area into a design and innovation district. In our conversation Makalima-Ngewana argued that the area needed a brand to make it more attractive for creative businesses to move in. She then admitted that the project had failed to address the many layers of history of the area and that it was not inclusive enough in regard to the disadvantaged groups that occupied the space. This should have made the partnership having to reassess its upgrading plans and methods. But these reconsiderations are not evident. The only component that visibly changed is the renaming of "The Fringe" into "the east city collective". The discursive framing of "The Fringe" project remained the same. The area mutated into the initially desired space for young creatives and small to medium businesses, many of them design related. As Ciraj Rassool puts it, "The Fringe is part of the way the market has balkanised the history of District Six."[97] Neither the history of dispossession

---

95 http://www.capetownpartnership.co.za/about/.
96 Cf. Farouk, Ismail: *Conflicting rationalities: post-apartheid spatial legacies and the creative city*. Cape Town 2013; The Con article. Rawoot, Ilham: *Cape Town: A City designed to forget*. May 19, 2014; Rassool, Ciraj: *District Six revisited*. Cape Town 2013.
97 Rassool, Ciraj quoted in: The Con article. Rawoot, Ilham: *Cape Town: A City designed to forget*. May 19, 2014.

and forced removals and the thousands of open land claims as part of the land restitution process play a role in the new formation of the area, nor inclusiveness of underprivileged groups. The new businesses are in full operation, the switch towards a design district for Cape Town is made, stylisation practices have been successful, and the CCID security officers are guarding the streets and the profit. In his critique of "The Fringe" and the specific concept of the creative city the project inserts, Ismail Farouk asks the question of, "How do contemporary stylizations of Cape Town serve to erase local histories, with the effect of re-entrenching historical injustice in the present?"[98] I would like to end this section with this question of his.

The next example is an excerpt of the advertising methods of *Remax*, a US real estate company that is also one of the biggest in South Africa. *Remax* depends on a franchise system, which means that the different offices that it holds worldwide, act semi-independent. On the website of one of its franchise partners in the Western Cape, *Bill Stymonds*, the caption, "Woodstock as a Wow Factor", titles the following text:

> "One of Cape Town's oldest suburbs, Woodstock, is set on the slopes of Devils Peak and enjoys views out to the harbour. Located within the City Bowl area, Woodstock also enjoys easy access to the Cape Town CBD.
> Typical of Cape Town suburbs, Woodstock is divided into two by its Main Road. Upper Woodstock has larger, restored Victorian semi-detached homes, while Woodstock proper, came through the times of the Group Areas Act as a mixed-race suburb associated with crime, litter and dilapidated drug houses.
> 'However', says Graham Alexander, Broker/Owner of RE/MAX Alliance, 'this image has drastically changed as urban renewal projects have gotten underway. Now there are a number of warehouses and Victorian cottages that have been converted into trendy spaces to encourage commercial investors and tenants. Young professionals are snapping up Victorian semis and taking advantage of these still affordable homes.'
> Adrian Goslett, CEO of RE/MAX of Southern Africa, says that since the Woodstock Improvement District (WID) received Cape Town City Council approval in July 2005, the positive results are becoming more and more apparent in the demand for property in the area. "Woodstock is rapidly regaining its

---

98 Farouk, Ismail: *Conflicting rationalities: post-apartheid spatial legacies and the creative city.* Cape Town 2013: p.4.

rightful place as a desirable place to live, work and play," he says. He cites examples of trendy new office, apartments and hotel developments such as The Boulevard Office Park, The Old Biscuit Mill, Buchanan Square, Durham Square and Upper East Side apartments and hotel.

RE/MAX Alliance currently has a unique Woodstock property on its books selling for R5,5-million. The home, which was originally built in 1904, is set on a stand measuring 800m2 with the space under roof approximately 300m2."[99]

The first two sentences of the text are aiming to advertise the District of Woodstock as a worthwhile site of investment. The expressions "slopes of Devils Peak" and "views out to the harbour" create a language that romanticises the position of the site. What the text names "Woodstock proper", Woodstock residents refer to as "Lower Woodstock", an area that is inhabited by lower-class families, embracing for example pensioners, families that comprise between six and twelve members living in one house and whose breadwinners are mainly nurses, construction workers, respectively low income workers, or retired residents with comparably low pensions. The text refers to them as "mixed-race", which means that it essentialises the notion of *race*, while it indirectly introduces the point of the inhabitants being *non-white*. In the same sentence, it mentions the suburb as being "associated with crime, litter and dilapidated drug houses". No evidence of the existence of poverty or disadvantaged households and no reference to the fact that this area was one of the few to survive apartheid-area forced removals is made. The structure of the sentence criminalises the inhabitants of Lower Woodstock, to then mark their circumstances in the next sentence as an "image" that "has drastically changed, as urban renewal projects have gotten underway." The residents of lower Woodstock are constructed as the polar opposite of the residents of upper Woodstock and again as the opposite of safety, that now has to be "converted into trendy spaces" in order to allure new investors. The "mixed-race" residents become replaced by "young professionals", who now have the opportunity of buying "Victorian semis and taking advantage of these still affordable homes". In the context of the ideological background and language with which the prior and the later of the area is portrayed, it is not surprising that the text celebrates "trendy new office, apartments and hotel developments such

---

99   Source: http://www.billstymonds.co.za/News/WOODSTOCK-HAS-A-WOW-FACTOR/498/ (seen April 6, 2014).

as The Boulevard Office Park...", uncritically, as they correspond to the form of what is thought as the uplifting of the area. They have been built to gain economic weight for the area. Discursively, wealth and smoothness are captured through them. It means that they do not only not disturb the development agenda of the City, but that they manifest ideal configurations of what the City wants to present as part of its world-class city narrative. As expected, the last sentence of the text is set to advertise a property that *Remax* presents for sale.

What is illustrated as "a desirable place to live", entails a practical exclusion of the historical residents of Lower Woodstock. The encouraging of "commercial investors and tenants" takes place pretending that the actual current residents do not exist. Their dynamics are much more urban because they have learned to survive the city on low wages and uncertain futures. They must put all their forces together and invent every day anew. The creativity needed for that fabricates urban practices that require high grades of interaction and connectivity and cannot be restricted to very narrow zones of operation. One such practice can be the redefinition of privacy, as in most cases spatial privacy does not exist. This can produce tensions but also very visible solidarities. Another one can be the developing of support structures built on various human networks. In addition, they are also enmeshed in the area historically. Engraved into the collective memory of the area are stories of the streets, markets, houses, schools, and shops under racial segregation and the ways they defined themselves in relation to the areas declared as *white*. To present the residents as insignificant is also to hollow out their urban power to take ownership of the spaces they inhabited for so long. As for the discourse at stake, lower-class life in Lower Woodstock is equal to the life of ghosts. In this quite recent process, its subjects only exist in the moment they constitute an obstacle to the next upgrading project, when ways are considered to get rid of them. The "young professionals" that are "snapping up Victorian semis" did not come to the rescue of run-down abandoned houses. Every house that stands empty represents a family that was either evicted and now lives far away at the city's periphery or was forced to move out as a result of unaffordable rental prices. The text erases any connection of the area's upgrading to this reality. It represents in compact form the arguments and verbalisation of the Urban Development Discourse. Among what is said, the unsaid shines strikingly through the lines. The whole package of the discourse comes compressed in one short paragraph. Erasure and promotion alternate. The discourse of the text invents itself through this interplay. Investment has come to mean something very specific. New developments like the Boulevard are set as the sites from which Woodstock draws its energy and thus as the sites through which Woodstock exists. Living space is created through them. Self-realisation and the forming of social networks navigate through them. The image without them is that of crime and decay, suggesting that new developments come to rescue the area. The way in which the materiality of the historical residents is presented generates a particular set of relation between them and the newcomers to the area. They are defined as being in stark contrast to each other, the one as a trendy figure of success and willing to play a part in the new designing of the area, and the other as a threat to the new order, a non-belonger living in non-places that have to be "drastically changed", and as the historical wrong of the area.

Unlike neighbouring District Six and University Estate, Woodstock had not been declared a *white* area under the Group Areas Act during apartheid. It existed beyond its houses and factories, drawing its liveliness not through physical sites but through the interaction of its people, through its multiple converging and parallel trajectories and its diversity in terms of income, religion, and language. It also exists in a long economic and spatial relationship to the Cape Town harbour with many Woodstock residents coming from generations of dockworkers, longshoremen, and porters. It is therefore an area that has a special relationship to the ocean, something that urban development projects totally disregard. The sources of this diversity and liveliness are very different to the new plans promised for the area, to create social life and the intensification of city life in general through massive investment in buildings, unable to think of the city outside of its material forms. Spatial expressions of this discourse are always those of capital, not of connectivity and human networks. The more gets accumulated, the more the area comes to life. Developers need to draw the public attention so much to themselves and to their narratives, until lines get blurry and the causal link between them and the displacement of people does not get established. If Woodstock had been declared a *white* area, urban renewal would have been bestowed with an already paved way to implement its projects without having to worry about the removal of residents from the area. Now that apartheid did not pave the way, the problem must be solved differently. To be forced to choose between either assimilating oneself or being removed, also involves a certain kind of colonial logic or is at least reminiscent of colonial power relations and practice. It reintroduces concepts of a polarised and segregated city based on the social status one inhabits, the very condition people live under in present-day

South Africa. The permanent threat of exclusion does not only mean that the residents are accused of being non-belongers, it truly prevents from feeling that the city belongs to them. The modes in which their exclusion is processed remain rather invisible. But it seems as if they have never really been fully adopted as rightful inhabitants of the area, but as if they have always in some sense been marginal and their existence in that particular space has always been temporary. Since they are not ranked as profitable enough, their living places have always been dominated by that threat and allocated for hunting by the financial / real estate market. Today, only the grade of intensity is different. But even when they are not portrayed as directly connected to crime and decay, they are being factored out. The City and the business sector pretend, as if the historical Woodstock residents have never shaped the urban landscape of the area. In the Urban Development Discourse of Woodstock, developers have come to build in a neutral zone without history. Woodstock historical residents' urban practices and the realities they inhabit go unconsidered firstly because they interrupt the new narrative of the city, and secondly because they are not valuable enough. Beneficiaries of this condition have the discursive power to determine the residents as such and take advantage of this position.

The kinds of future imagined for the area are futures of consumption and a mushrooming of developments through which capital becomes accumulated and new investors attracted. Within that new sphere and its restricted notion of belonging, residents will have been homogenised in the sense of their position in relation to the discourse. In this spirit, the new developments and upgrading projects can also be seen as expressions of power. The desired subject formation is clear. Exclusion and marginalisation are no longer perceived as socially negative. On the contrary, it is something that is welcomed. The new settlers to the area have come to adjust and replace the historical residents who the discourse treats as misplaced, low-income no-goods. This systematic replacement is the produce of long-term planning and marketing. The notion of what is socially just and unjust is being redefined. What follows are shrugs and the argument that the process of the economically more powerful replacing the less powerful is natural to urbanisation and cannot be prevented, away from the reality of displacement and the atrocities it involves. Segregated spaces are the normal way in which the city is understood. The removal of current residents is just another manifestation of this reality. Urban life is equated with jungle life, where the big eat the small and this is considered as normal. On the basis of this background it is possible to rethink the meanings of these urban development processes and draw on the notion of architectures and geographies of violence. Despite the metaphor of the jungle, whereas in some other cities of the global south one might assume a rather unregulated urbanisation, the one in Cape Town is deeply regulated, informed by the directives of the neoliberal project with the market as its driving force. Inclusion and exclusion and the boundaries between definitions of inside and outside are specified with such vehemence and in such a limitless manner that any kind of flexibility becomes unthinkable. To speak of architectures and geographies of violence might come with a certain absoluteness. But when we delve into the processes taking place and unpack them bit by bit, can we really continue to rely on terms like gentrification? The ways in which the new developments and upgrading projects are inserted into the city, allude to spatial regimes of power that aggressively perpetuate the nightmare of segregation and at the same time unburden the social elite through legitimising this process as rightful strategies of economic growth and spatial progress. They leave the city in a schizophrenic state that leads two personalities: Firstly, the monitored stylish city that easily accommodates the affluent middle and upper classes, where property and profit are guarded and where extravagant entertainment and spectacles in privileged sites and gated enclaves fall over each other and powerful interest groups are granted free reign to spatially order, manage and regulate urban space, and rearrange whole areas. And secondly, the city where one can lose all belongings from one day to the other, be removed to the urban margins and forced into an informal life in which survival means to circumvent social death.

Now let me introduce a third example of the relations between the business sector and the Urban Development Discourse and of the ways they nurture each other. Nick Ferguson, Jody Aufrichtig and Barry Harlen are large-scale property developers and the owners of Indigo Properties, Daddy Long Legs Hotel, Daddy's Deals, The Old Biscuit Mill, and Woodstock Exchange, among other businesses and properties. The Old Biscuit Mill and the Woodstock Exchange are both relatively large business complexes that are situated on Albert Road, the main road of Lower Woodstock and Salt River. They are quite recent redevelopments of an old factory and an industrial building and have been developed as spaces of enclosure that feature sterilised architectures and attract middle-class and upper-class consumers to go drink coffee, have lunch, buy wine, designer clothing, jewellery, and handicrafts, among other goods. The Woodstock Exchange consists of both, shops and eateries as well as ateliers and office spaces of different businesses. Down the road, the weekly *Neighbourgoods Market* draws thousands of visitors to the Biscuit Mill on Saturdays. Access to it is a matter of social status. The picture in front of the Mill on market days is symptomatic of what is happening in the whole area. Security guards scrutinise the people entering to guarantee a filtered and gated experience. Street performers and street children are kept at a distance. They are visible reminders of the contradictions the space seems to collapse under any time. Residents of Lower Woodstock, mostly working-class, are excluded from the visitors circle of the market, as the prices of the gourmet food in the wrapped up place are unaffordable for most of them. Indeed, as Murray has stated, "In these new postpublic spaces, affordability functions as a significant obstacle to wider accessibility where, strictly speaking, the barriers to entry are no longer racial, but financial. In such interdictory spaces, exclusivity is an inevitable by-product of the scale of control necessary to ensure that irregularity, unpredictability, and inefficiency do not interfere with the orderly flow of commerce."[100] Inside the complex, visitors experience what city marketers as the *Cape Town Partnership* display as a vibrant, creative and energetic Cape Town, one that has taste and is competitive and attractive at international level. Live performances bring in a harmonic atmosphere, people are standing or sitting together, eating and chatting or swinging to the music, one outfit more fashionable and colourful than the other. Inside and outside are two different worlds, so when the Biscuit Mill is referred to as a world class leisure spot by travel and business guides, when Western Cape Premier Helen Zille highlights it as one of the top ten things to do in Cape Town, and when travel guide Lonely Planet marks it as a "must see", it is not with reference to the pavement one steps onto when leaving the space.

In April 2014, together with members of the Xcollektiv whose work I will discuss in the last chapter, we filmed the eviction of street performers and street children from the street in front of the Mill by security guards. When going back the week after to speak to the guards and find out about their mandate, one of them explained that he is instructed to keep the inside of the Mill and the street outside pure. "If I don't, I will lose my job", he insisted. The notion of "pure" is significant for the articulations of power and the duality that is created. The market got all this attention by politicians and travel guides, one of the owners proudly mentioned in an angry response to an interview request of mine. In his email Nick Ferguson writes: "Sara, We have

---

100 Murray, Martin J.: *City of Extremes: The Spatial Politics of Johannesburg*. Durham and London 2011: p.216.

changed Woodstock for the better. You now see at the entrance to Cape Town International Airport a massive poster of the Old Biscuit Mill with Design Capital 2014 logos on it. We have recently been featured on television shows and have had a huge amount of positive press. It's a pity in South Africa if you do something positive that someone comes up with the inane attitude that it is displacing the poor."[101] In a theatricalising manner, Ferguson also attached to his email about 30 requests from journalists, all of whom praised the Mill and promised to write celebratory articles. This was also to communicate that the journalists understand and appreciate what the owners have achieved, but I, with my "inane attitude", do not. The aim of the developers was clearly to create an idea of creative space and make it become part of the middle and upper-class imagination of how the creative city is supposed to look like and through this, let it become one of the city's top sights. In order to maintain this idea, it needs to be reinvented over and over again. This needed reinvention is also why media coverage plays such an important role. Between the media hype, the imaginaries of a design city in which Woodstock Exchange and Biscuit Mill optimally fit into, and the plaudit of politicians, Ferguson misses to see the realities of Lower Woodstock life in whose centre his business developments are placed. In the absence of any relation with the area's residents, both spaces appear as bubbles, creating parallel worlds, one whose subjects are rejected from participating in the flourishing of their own neighbourhood and from merging with the new imaginaries of Woodstock, and the other that produces a concept of design and commodification, confident about the space it occupies and about the user group it targets. The Woodstock Exchange and Biscuit Mill have become places where the idea of design Cape Town is most fully generated. The hubs have long become role models for upcoming developments in the area, a scenery to be expanded. Just as we saw in the *Remax* advertisement, Lower Woodstock is presented as *the* place to invest in, promising every investor who helps the resetting of the area a booming business or rising property prices. Residents who have lived all their lives, through the Group Areas Act and the following decades of aggressive racial segregation in the area's houses, are now threatened to be evicted as rental prices are becoming unaffordable[102] or owners decide to sell their properties as they are offered large amounts of money. Tenants of houses in Cornwall

---

101 Nick Ferguson's email response, January 31, 2014. Before, he had sent that same email to political activist and journalist Ilham Rawoot.
102 Affordable Land & Housing Data Centre: Woodstock Transaction Data.

and Gympie Street, among others, have already been evicted and removed to Blikkiesdorp, after the owner decided to sell the houses and *Swish Properties* came in to build a nine storey complex including 363 apartment units and a shopping mall with an extra parking space of 493 parking bays.[103] City officials call it an "exciting development project for Woodstock" and community newspaper, the *People's Post*, celebrates it as "Woodstock's transformation from the bedraggled ugly duckling to a gleaming jewel on the cityscape".[104] In the discourse of regeneration and the uplifting of Woodstock, not only do exclusion and marginalisation get silenced, but also the perpetuation of historical legacies of spatial inequality. The interwovenness with this history is also one of the reasons why the term gentrification does not embrace the process happening. Behind the Design Capital logo on the Biscuit Mill poster at the airport, something gets hidden - something that Ferguson, the City and other beneficiaries of the discourse refuse to touch on. It is the relation between urban development and its "promotional efforts to sell the city",[105] and present-day exclusion that is embedded in histories of exclusion which are left untroubled. So when these world-class enclaves are gated against the impures and undesirables, they are also gated against their confrontation with these layers of history.

I pointed to these examples of an organisation formed by private property owners and the City that works under the mandate of safety, cleanliness, liveability and investment acquisition; of a real estate company criminalising the historical residents of Lower Woodstock for the purpose of justifying new business developments and the "uplifting" of city spaces at the expense of the excluded and evicted; and of developers Ferguson and Co whose business complexes represent implementations of the Urban Development Discourse and the commodification of notions of design Cape Town, nurturing new spatial dynamics of segregation; so as to exemplify the powerful role of the business sector in promoting and facilitating the Urban Development Discourse.

---

103   Cf. the City of Cape Town government website: *City's Mayoral Committee approves exciting development project for Woodstock*. Media Release No 1212 / 2013. March 8, 2013.
104   People's Post Woodstock/Maitland article: *Woodstock's star on the rise*. March 12, 2013.
105   Murray, Martin J.: *City of Extremes: The Spatial Politics of Johannesburg*. Durham and London 2011: p.xii.

Urban Development Discourse and media

There are many newspaper articles and short reports on present-day forced evictions, the relationship between informal settlements and crime, and homeless life in South Africa. The *People's Post* is a good example for the reproduction of the Urban Development Discourse in media that I will discuss in this next section. The work of journalists such as Nicole McCain and Tauriq Hassen, the way they look at urban development and the people affected by forced evictions, criminalisation and marginalisation, show how media is complicit in the propagation of the dominant discourse. The *People's Post* as a newspaper that gets delivered for free to all households of Cape Town's southern suburbs, the city bowl and the Atlantic Seaboard, envelopes a relatively large circle of recipients. It belongs to the South African media giant *media24* and its weekly readership comprises an average of about half a million.[106] It zooms in on the city, on its buildings, businesses, security forces, streets, public spaces, neighbourhoods etc., units that stand in direct relationship to marginalised and criminalised groups of society. It also tries to produce a specific idea of "the local". Residents in Sea Point do not read the same paper as those in Woodstock. Each area is defined as a community with homogenous interests and gets its own paper. The newspaper promotes itself as a community paper in which business is central. It advertises exclusively local small and medium businesses and is much more a business community paper than a community paper. At the same time, it draws on community as a concept to establish itself as a reliable source of local news. Its high grade of accessibility and its city focus formed the reason why I chose it as a source of analysis in this work. I included all editions published between the beginning of 2012 and the end of 2015 in the review. Since I mostly name the journalists who wrote the articles within the main text and since the respective locality within which the articles are written matter for this analysis, I have abstained from naming the respective journalists in the footnotes and highlighted the particular area into which the *People's Post*'s editions are officially divided instead.

As in the example of the removal and criminalisation of the informal settlement at the foot of Signal Hill, after the incident in which a woman died,

---

106 Readership numbers published on People's Post website weekly: http://www.media24.com/newspapers/peoples-post/.

Hassen suggests in a subtle way the engagement of the residents of an informal settlement neighbouring the Strand Street quarry, where a woman was robbed and killed the same day as the Signal Hill incident. While reporting on the case, he asks the question of the informal settlement's engagement in the robbery and killing without having any evidence of a possible connection. Under an illustration of the settlement in the same article he writes: "TO BLAME? The settlement neighbouring the Strand Street Quarry, known as "The Kraal", is a known destination for petty criminals."[107] The City and certain media share the criminalisation of informal settlement residents as a normalised practice, rendering them as embodiments of crime and as ultimate disrupters of liveability in the city. Regimes of disease and repulsiveness are inflicted on them. The media is needed in order to spread the rationalising arguments of the political sector. The ward councillor of Cape Town's city centre and Green Point amongst other areas (Ward 54) celebrates the eviction of informal settlers from an old military base in Bo-Kaap using these words: "The clean-up was successful and the local watches played a big part in getting this area sorted out. It seems as if this piece of land is finally on the road to recovery."[108] The evicted residents are presented as refuse that is now cleaned up; a disease that was combatted successfully and from which the land now has to recover. The ward councillor's statement remains unquestioned by Hassen. Different than Hassen and McCain, Andrew Ihsan Gasnolar challenges the dominant discourse on safety and underlines the systematic criminalisation of homeless people, the role of by-laws in this process, and the reminiscence of apartheid and present-day City policies. In his article, Gasnolar phrases key arguments of this book:

> "We need to focus our energies and effort to resist any attempt by Ward 54 councillor Shayne Ramsay to introduce draconian by-laws so that people can be managed with her own version of the dompas that was used by the apartheid regime.
> Last year, Penny Sparrow made her debut on Facebook and we all know how that ended. The truth is views like that are never isolated or simply exaggerated because of its publication on social media. Over the weekend, Shayne Ramsay, a Democratic Alliance councillor in the City of Cape Town, for Ward

---

107 People's Post Woodstock/Maitland article: *Fencing planned for quarry*. February 12, 2013.
108 People's Post Atlantic Seaboard article: *White flag raised at military base*. March 26, 2013.

54, which is broadly the Sea Point and Atlantic Seaboard region, took to Facebook against what she described as "grime and crime", although this was the usual attack on homelessness and poverty that we have witnessed over the years...We cannot deal with the issue of homelessness and poverty by using security and police but the City of Cape Town, the rise of groups such as the Central Improvement Districts, and private security are geared to police our spaces and to confine poverty to some far away place.

Shayne would like us to believe that homeless people are people too and that they can broadly be categorised into three categories – "criminals (who are in and out of overcrowded prisons), mentally ill or social outcasts, and those who are genuinely down on their luck"...After all, in Shayne's earlier version of this post, she would say, "our garbage bins are treated as buffet tables" but that would be expunged.

Frighteningly, the politics of fear, hatred and privilege comes through even more from Shayne and she confirms to her choir that she will be taking this fight to the Council chambers so that homelessness can be policed more effectively. Our Constitution is apparently too "liberal" and so "there is not much that SAPS can do to control vagrants" and so Shayne will be pushing her repugnant agenda by seeking to change the City's by-laws so that vagrants can be controlled as another category of people.

Tragically, the views of people like Shayne have been allowed to take root despite our past history of displacement, prejudice, victimisation, stigmatisation and fear." [109]

To complete this important parenthesis, committed journalist such as Gasnolar and Ilham Rawoot[110] have set an example for thorough quality journalism. This point is important for us to keep in mind, since certainly not all journalists in South Africa adopt the dominant discourse on Urban Development and "crime" in their investigations and writing.

Returning to the *People's Post*, in another article, Hassen portrays homeless people who live on the Cape Town Station deck and at the central bus

---

[109] Daily Maverick article. Gasnolar, Andrew Ihsaan: *Shayne Ramsay's politics of fear and hatred*. September 25, 2017.

[110] Cf. for example: The Con article. Rawoot, Ilham: *Cape Town – A city Designed to Forget*. May 19, 2014; Mail&Guardian article. District Six Fails to Rise from the Ashes of Apartheid. February 19, 2016; The Con article. Ilham Rawoot. *Cape Town's Pretend Partnership*. March 5, 2014; Dazed Digital article. Ilham Rawoot. *The Artists Taking on Gentrification in South Africa*. October 8, 2014.

terminal as filthy, obscene, undesirable, - one cannot put it differently – antisocial pieces of human trash.[111] Not a single reference is made to the reasons for homelessness and poverty or to the suffering that homeless life contains. Hassen interviewed a Cape Town local who uses the train and bus on a daily basis, who states: "We have plenty of tourists coming into this country and I'm sure some of them have been exposed to this vulgarity. I don't know how anybody can live like that." Then he includes the statements of the CEO of The Haven night shelter, Hassan Khan, who he introduces as having "further encouraged the City's Law Enforcement Unit to continue removing vagrants from the street". Then Hassen quotes the CEO: "That is their job, because we do not want to be faced with a situation where every public open space is being occupied by vagrants." Both statements Hassen uses create the homeless as highly superfluous entities, as aliens that have come to occupy public spaces and that disrupt narratives of a beautiful Cape Town loved by tourists.

The question of 'how can anybody live like that' suggests that people have chosen homeless life as a way of escaping effort and hard work. The homeless are the perpetrators and people who have to be exposed to them endure their vulgarity, their stench, and their pitiful sight, are the victims. The language that is used degrades them to the level of rats that have come to become a plague of which the legitimate belongers and desirables of the city must get rid of. It is this logic that drives journalist Tiyese Jeranji to write in an article about homeless people living on the banks of the Liesbeek River, "The homeless seem to be a headache for people managing the area and the river but they are not leaving anything to chance. They are working around the clock to make sure that the Liesbeek River maintains its beauty, no matter what challenges they are facing."[112] The words used evoke no other scene but the resolving of a challenging rat infestation. Constantly they are not only portrayed as an obstacle to safety but also to beauty. Ward councillor of Claremont, Ian Iversen, amongst other areas, speaks of homeless people as they would be a crumbling building ready to be demolished: "Vagrants camp out in this area, light fires and certainly litter the area in a big way. It is always an eyesore. Even though Law Enforcement and social workers have tried to intervene the vagrants just return."[113] With his statement in the last sentence he plays possum, acting as he would not know that homeless people choose certain areas to reside in

---

111 People's Post Woodstock/Maitland article: *Vagrancy – the big stink*. February 19, 2013.
112 People's Post Claremont/Rondebosch article: *Squatters invade river*. June 9, 2015.
113 People's Post Claremont/Rondebosch article: *A real plan of action*. April 10, 2014.

because it is easier to survive in them. However, this does not encourage journalist Astrid Februarie to ask further questions. In another article of McCain, the homeless become land invaders, when the chairperson of the Seapoint, Bantry Bay and Fresnaye Ratepayers Association complains about council's "apparent unwillingness to permanently remove them and their goods". The homeless "do not belong in an area where everyone is paying high rates. This may sound elitist, but the reality is that we are paying for services and they are not – yet they are residing where we all live. In our view this is a subtle form of land invasion."[114] As expected, the chairperson's statement remains unchallenged by McCain. Finding ways to survive and choosing an area because it might be easier to survive in become equated with land invasion.

It is no surprise that Suzette Little's old argument of the lazy homeless, unwilling to change their lives finds its way into a *People's Post* article about a survey of homeless people in Cape Town. Here she states, "We cannot force people to accept our offers of assistance and there are those who prefer to remain on the streets because it saves them from taking responsibility for their lives..."[115] This implies that all homeless who do not approach the City's social workers for help avoid taking responsibility and live an unconcerned life. Readers become introduced to the notion that people who live on the streets have chosen so because it is easier. The reader can stop being concerned about homelessness because it is homeless people's will to live like that. Once again, social inequality becomes reduced to morality problems and anti-social attitudes. In general, one encounters the term "anti-social behaviour" frequently being used in the articles examined on homeless life,[116] marking poverty and homelessness as behaviour caused by morality problems rather than a social condition. This kind of language, invoked by government officials and journalists, is being used as a means to pillory the homeless and flag their condition as individual failure. Through this, the issue becomes isolated from its background of historical exclusion and displacement and the social realities of the present that followed. Morality problems apparently also include those who came to the streets to make quick money. In one of the articles on homelessness, Little airs her view about the motivation of people living on the streets,

---

114 People's Post Atlantic Seaboard article: *Vagrants told to vacate.* December 19, 2013.
115 People's Post Atlantic Seaboard article: *City counts homeless.* August 11, 2015.
116 Examples: People's Post Atlantic Seaboard article: *Historic house of hassles.* September 18, 2012; People's Post Atlantic Seaboard article: *Gov rids Military Rd of settlers.* September 1, 2015; People's Post Woodstock/Maitland article: *Vagrancy – the big stink.* February 19, 2013.

stating that "...we have those who deliberately migrate to the streets because begging is considered profitable".[117] This turns the homeless into wily characters, having had the choice to work and have a home, but decided not to because life on the streets is more profitable.

Crime control and reduction is one of the main themes in the *People's Post*.[118] Obviously, crime forms a component of everyday life in South Africa and thus it being steady subject in media is not surprising. But it depends from which perspective it becomes highlighted. Although representing a community paper in one of the most unequal country in the world, in all the editions reviewed, there was not a single article on poverty reduction or social inequality. It is significant to understand that while even the politically powerful international organisation of the United Nations reveals in a 2017 report on the world's housing situation that South Africa has failed in its housing policy, the *People's Post* completely erases this fact. *The Guardian* refers to the UN report conducted by its special rapporteur for housing, Leilani Farha, as follows:

> "The "economics of inequality" may be explained in large part by the inequalities of wealth generated by housing investments. The impact of private investment has also contributed to spatial segregation and inequality within cities, Farha points out. In South Africa, private investment in cities has sustained many of the discriminatory patterns of the apartheid area, with wealthier, predominantly white households occupying areas close to the centre and poorer black South Africans living on the peripheries. That "spatial mismatch", relegating poor black households to areas where employment opportunities are scarce, has entrenched poverty and cemented inequality."[119]

In another article, *The Guardian* reports on the World Bank's inequality index:

---

117 People's Post Atlantic Seaboard article: *Fresh attempt to help homeless*. April 24, 2014.
118 Examples: People's Post Atlantic Seaboard article: *Business bid to beat crime*. September 23, 2014; People's Post Atlantic Seaboard article: *Speak up on fight against crime*. September 17, 2013, People's Post Constantia/Wynberg article: *Watch zooms in on crime*. September 17, 2013; People's Post Woodstock/Maitland article: *App for crime*. February 24, 2015.
119 The Guardian article. Foster, Dawn: *UN Report Lays Bare the Waste of Treating Homes as Commodities*. February 28, 2017.

"Using the most recent figures, South Africa, Namibia and Haiti are among the most unequal countries in terms of income distribution – based on the Gini index estimates from the World Bank – while Ukraine, Slovenia and Norway rank as the most equal nations in the world."[120]

But in the *People's Post*, inequality is dealt with as a policing issue that can be removed through an increase of law enforcement and security officers. The criminalisation and marginalisation practices of the political sector do not only remain unchallenged, they become underlined and propagated. Township life in Khayelitsha or Mitchell's Plain, of which big parts are not structured differently than the informal settlements on the other side of the mountain, does not get problematised. Informal settlements are only dealt with when they disturb middle or upper-class life, being marked alien to the rest of the area's facade. Sea Point has been a striking example of this mechanism. The *People's Post* regularly interviews residents and ratepayers' associations who call upon the City to permanently remove the homeless or squatters.[121] But they do not express where to remove them to. The issue of the homeless and of informal settlers is the issue of them residing in certain areas. If they would remain in the space of the township, the problem would be resolved.

When a journalist speaks to residents or members of an organisation, he picks from the things said what he wants to include into his article. Therefore, an unchallenged statement must in itself fit into the discourse the article aims to create. This is also true in the case of a neighbouring resident of an informal settlement in Bo-Kaap, who insists on the duality of hardworking taxpayers, a group in which she also includes herself, and lazy have-nots who disturb the middle-class life of the community: "We all work so hard to be able to live here. We pay thousands in taxes but have neighbours who are drunk and idle."[122] The journalist adds that she said these words "angrily". To multiply this anger, he includes voices of other angry residents who elaborate the statement of the first one. Criminalising tactics become unfolded when a resident accuses: "This property will continue to be invaded by squatters, most

---

120   Barr, Caellain: Inequality Index. *Where are the World's Most Unequal Countries?* April 26, 2017.
121   People's Post Claremont/Rondebosch article: *Vagrancy unsettles*. October 14, 2014; People's Post Athlone article: *Hope for Rylands' homeless*. December 18, 2012; People's Post Claremont/Rondebosch article: *Problems persist at plot*. August 20, 2013.
122   People's Post Atlantic Seaboard article: *Squatters make a comeback*. May 14, 2013.

of them being criminals..." His statement is left to stand for itself, no questions are asked, no elaborations of who the squatters are. Most noticeable, no squatter gets interviewed. They remain anonymous criminal disturbers to be removed. The criminalisation of homeless people and informal settlers has become perpetual part of the discourse. The absence of their voices contributes to it. Their voices would build a mirror in which privileged parts of society would be obliged to see themselves and to acknowledge to what price their privileges are being maintained. Listening to homeless and informal settlers' voices would confront them with what the dominant discourse tries to erase. Suddenly, the roots of poverty would have to be discussed and not only its symptoms. The silencing of their voices continues to be crucial for disengaging from radical questions and is also why a police spokesperson is left unquestioned when he states in an article on homeless people scavenging through bins in Green Point that "The criminals and vagrants are walking around, looking for an opportunity to commit crime".[123] Homeless people scavenging through bins is part of everyday street life in Cape Town. The act of looking for leftover food and objects that might be of use on the streets and thus trying to survive on other people's waste is itself contradictory to the strategy of securing life through criminal activity. But even when they try to survive differently, they are labelled as criminal and a threat to society.

In the past pages I have shown the normalising effects of a newspaper that is the most accessible in Cape Town. Policies that I have described in this chapter as violent because they criminalise, marginalise and displace people become propagated as right and smooth strategies to address the discomfort social inequality and poverty bring with. This does not emanate from the personal preference of the journalists mentioned, but their way of seeing and agreeing comes from a discursive practice in which they have been absorbed and through which they rationalise and justify the frames in which they work and the concepts they use. The permanent association of people affected by poverty with crime creates them as fearsome creatures with whom it is difficult to sympathise. The repetition of this linking anchors and stabilises this perception. It also generates a distance between them and other groups of society because interaction with them is propagated as dangerous. This mechanism mirrors in the fear of a Bo-Kaap resident to open her door for squatters who sought her help after Law Enforcement officers had walked into their structures in the middle of the night and pepper sprayed them while

---

123 People's Post Atlantic Seaboard article: *Cleaning up their act*. August 14, 2014.

they were sleeping.[124] The woman sympathised with the squatters and was disgusted by the officer's actions but was too afraid to help. Their demonization secures their exclusion. People who suffer poverty and their material living conditions must be rendered out of sight. Not their condition becomes problematised but their visibility. The social agenda changes. The question of, why do we have so many people suffering from homelessness or still living in informal settlements under unbearable conditions moves to, why are they living in our area and not somewhere else? The community paper tries to produce a sense of attachment and affiliation of middle and upper-class residents. Through emphasising locality and the particularities of each area, the districts become constructed as castles that need to be defended against crime, dirt, and everything that threatens their liveability and profitability. It therefore provides a different material environment and adds locality to the discourse. In this sense, media coverage that does not ask questions but obeys the decisions of government officials, influences the public imagination about how to tackle poverty and erases other possible ways of seeing the whole matter. It paves the way for the political sector to continue undisturbed with the implementation of their policies, trying to enforce them as accepted by the public. Its persuasive power is the central characteristic that makes this relation possible. Without its complicity in the creation and maintenance of the Urban Development Discourse, the relationship between the executive political sector and an agreeing and encouraging, or at least a silent and indifferent public, could not be established.

Conclusion

In the first part of this chapter, I tried to deconstruct how a certain category of the poor is created and how this category borrows from colonial and apartheid understandings of the human and the systems of thought related to hierarchies of superior and inferior human beings. I have argued that as part of urban development agendas, doctrines of desirable and undesirable life have been inscribed on city spaces and on the public that uses the space. These doctrines are being legitimised and legalised as part of a discursive practice in which not only the political sector but business sector, private and public-private security sector (as a common child of the political and business

---

124   People's Post Atlantic Seaboard article: *'Bergie beatings' in the city centre*. August 7, 2012.

sector), and media are complicit. Criminalisation of lower-class members are part of this practice, not as random policing techniques of individual security forces, but as a technology of power that attends to the body, zooms in on it, screens it and interrogates it. The bareness and powerlessness vis-à-vis this authoritarian condition affects the body and undermines the right to self-determination and an emancipated existence. Dispensability occupies a central place in the Urban Development Discourse, a reality the body of the lower-class subject must continuously reposition itself against. Similar criminalisation models are applied to informal traders. Praised in official statements of politicians as an important part of the economy, in reality they are being evicted with non-negotiable force. Limited spots of trade are allocated to them and even those can be taken away as soon as the municipalities decide differently. This permanent threat adds to the instability of informal traders' livelihoods. The criminalisation of informal traders seems inconsistent with the dominant discourse at first view, as they are independent, active and productive subjects who fend for themselves. This is the opposite of unemployed and homeless people who the discourse inscribes with labels like irresponsibility and laziness. But a deeper look elucidates that besides the business sector treating them as a threat to its own profitability, informal traders do not fit into the dominant imaginary of an orderly, smooth, and beautiful city.

Gated communities have been created to strengthen the borders that keep the majority of society in the determined margins. The ones marginalised are being discursively framed as lacking the right attitude, being demotivated and lazy and must be debriefed to put in more effort and be more motivated, as Little puts it. *Criminal* as the successor of the colonial label *savage*, is used to rationalise the hereby induced segregated city. Movement outside this frame is impossible. It might be possible to challenge segregation but not to circumvent it. All physical space is shaped by this material condition. In order to maintain it, an army of security guards is needed. Four hundred thousand of them released onto the streets of South Africa, guarding the desirable, investment-safe city and a lucrative job market. But when not at work and not in uniform, the guards themselves do not hold the required social profile to pass as a valid citizen. What they are guarding against is themselves – the *black* man from the township, the non-belonger to the city. The point Murray stresses about Johannesburg equally applies to the cities in the Western Cape. "The power embodied in space" has replaced racial segregation during apartheid. New practices of exclusion had to be invented to secure the parallel worlds in which the affluent classes live. The Urban Development Discourse and its practices facilitate the privileged lifestyles to remain intact. City improvement has become an imperious slogan under which urban control policies become implemented and justified. Safety, cleanliness, profitability, liveability, are all imperatives that are used to disqualify the disorderly determined resident from the orderly city. Media organs like the *People's Post* transmit these discursive contents. With the newspaper being distributed for free and the very large readership it reaches, an intrusion in the public imagination is guaranteed. On the street itself, CID's have become the executive institution of this discourse. High-security settings create affluent neighbourhoods as introverted spatial enclaves, with defensive typologies as their main characteristic. Crime sells as much as fear sells, and security that is needed to build structures of control has manifested as a commodity inseparable from the South African economy.

The business sector wallows in this discursive setting. Fully dedicated to the narrative of design, creative, fashionable, and hip cities, its role is to engineer the architectures and aesthetics of the discourse at stake. Upliftment and regeneration of city spaces have become profitable investment projects, not only materially but also with regard to the building of imageries in which urban design is envisioned. Within this frame, lower-class communities have been rendered a thorn in the flesh and their exclusion and displacement are a promise that real estate agents make to potential buyers and investors. Their removal has become part of an aesthetic practice through which urban design is realised. The uplifting of an area becomes not only presented as economically stimulating, but also as crime reducing as the narratives of the *Cape Town Partnership* and *Remax* show. The expression of turning an "ugly duckling" into a shiny piece of the city is an articulation of power that verbally claims the imagination of the recipient.

I tried to show how a membership of the dominant group presupposes complying with and becoming complicit in the reproduction of a culture of justification and witting ignorance that makes a relation of domination and the silences surrounding it possible, and thus becoming complicit in processes which maintain inequality and erase the realities of poverty, as otherwise the authoritative dynamics from which profit derive have to be questioned, thrilled and thus destabilised. Development sector profit making under the new urban image for which not only the business sector but also the political sector pushes, goes hand in hand with processes of exclusion that are presented as normal side-effects of economic growth and regeneration of city spaces. The gradual effacement of unwanted urban fabric is set as an endorsed aesthetic practice. The traces of displacement lead to the city's periphery and unveil evidences of the reinvention of the segregated city. Temporary Relocation Areas are the monuments of this condition. They are the material embodiment of the politico-economic power that is able to set them as sites of removal. Excluded from the imaginaries of world-class Cape Town, the displaced have other stories to tell. Justification and ignorance proceed at such length that the pure act and public appearance of removing/evicting the undesirable other does not function as a vehicle for remembering the tragedy of human displacement in the colonial and apartheid past. This means that complicity is only possible in the rejection to recall history and consequently in the de-historicising of present politico-economic practices. This rejection inscribes itself on the city and guarantees that, "long-standing socioeconomic inequalities and racial hierarchies continue to be durable and resilient features of the post-apartheid metropolis".[125] Passive acquiescence that was such a common position during apartheid has remained intact. It is this process that depoliticises the navigating social elite to the extent of a political opportunism that remains a thick wall between the lower classes of society and their imaginable progress towards a more equal South Africa. Behind the promoting and selling of the city, displacement processes take place without being critically reviewed against histories of forced removal and relocation. The creation of world-class cities as the new imperative makes this fading out of history possible.

---

125 Murray, Martin J.: *City of Extremes: The Spatial Politics of Johannesburg*. Durham and London 2011: p.xvi.

Chapter four

Architectures of Division

"So it rained yesterday, big news! It is truly sad that most people were praising Cape Town as the best in the world just this week. Very few people know or care to know, that this city is spatially designed along its natural geographic layout to be anti-black. The settlement of our people in the Cape Flats (pay attention to the language here) and the whites along the slopes (from Durbanville to Constantia) of the land is a masterful design. The torrential rains of this city run down the slopes in well-paved and furrowed neighbourhoods with well-maintained drainage systems. Where the blacks live, in the Cape Flats, are literally flat lands where the water running down the slopes of the white suburbs is bound to rise up and flood neighbourhoods without the infrastructural design and support of the leafy suburbs. This is the design of cruel, intelligent people who receive awards in town-planning while servicing the systematic killing of blacks in the ghetto by incorporating geography (the history already destroyed) in deliberate Acts of God. Did you know, that in a very windy city like Cape Town, there are wind-free neighbourhoods for the wealthy? Something has to go give..."

Sabelo Mcinziba[1]

Introduction

This chapter might appear as an unusual analysis. After it was written, I reread it as an interlude of walking and moving between interconnected points across the greater Cape Town area and the neighbouring town of Stellenbosch. The chapter's central theme is movement. Hiking, walking,

---

1   Mcinziba, Sabelo: Facebook post. April 23, 2016.

driving, thinking, standing and feeling, challenged my own understanding of how an analysis of segregated city spaces must be written. Movement is how the work of nature as well as architecture comes to life. Here, I animate that work through my own movement – moving through and above the city, along roads, through corridors, on top of a mountain or at its foothills, allowed me to inhabit the ways in which natural landscape and architecture are set to work together. Without claiming to be extraordinarily innovative, it is solely an attempt at committing to paper the physical spaces in which I actually perceived cohesions of landscape and architecture, in which I thought them, witnessed them, rethought them and conceptualised them. In the previous chapter, I analysed the silences in the dominant discourse of 'dangerous', 'crime-ridden', 'dirty', 'lazy', 'irresponsible' life, versus 'safe', 'clean', 'liveable' and 'profitable' life. Here, I would like to map unequal life, point to it and let it impact the ways I see and perceive the city and its people.

To map unequal life through movement provided me with a foundation for undoing mapping as a discipline of conquering space. Since spaces become first and foremost conquered through mapping, and as an unmapped space cannot be conquered, the history of colonial mapping and the urban planning of conquered spaces is particularly connected to aerial photography. This is why, almost subconsciously, I tried to circumvent aerial photography, as well as other tools of land survey, essentially the technologies of modern mapping. Only later, in the discussions that followed the actual work of confronting different city spaces, did the approach of moving through and above the city and painstakingly covering everything seen and thought become clearer.

Many of my observations and findings, enabled through moving in and above spaces, are of course not new ones. One only needs to look at the websites of the many unions', collectives' and movements'[2] and the texts they contain, to understand that the dominant discourse on unequal life is part of a bigger, historical, political and economic project of erasure in which the Urban Development Discourse, elaborated in previous chapters, plays a key role.

What I would like to do at this point of the book is to formulate what I encountered as segregated/divided city space. How did the engagement with the city from and in these specific spaces help me to frame and name what I

---

2   Cf. the National Union of Metal Workers South Africa (NUMSA), the Housing Assembly, the Xcollektive, Abahlali base Mjondolo, Ground-Up, Reclaiming the City, Tokolos Stencils, the Rhodes Must Fall and Open Stellenbosch student movements, amongst many others.

experienced as a segregated city? This question meant that for some periods of time, I had to move away from the immediate sites of forced eviction, temporary relocation and instant criminalisation. The study of criminalisation and marginalisation of the working-class/ low-income residents, or, as most of the people I talked to would say, of "the people", forced me to look at the dualities of 'ordinary' and 'extraordinary' life, of 'safe' and 'unsafe' space, 'developed' and 'backward' areas, 'clean' and 'dirty' streets, 'individually' and 'collectively' negotiated homes, 'depressed' and 'joyful' atmospheres, 'profitable' and 'unprofitable' people, and so on. I tried to find a way with which it would be possible to incorporate the city as a whole in the analysis of urban development, criminalisation and marginalisation. When I later read a conversation that Mary Zournazi had with Brian Massumi, I understood that movement as a way to approach the city had been formulated as an actual epistemological idea:

> "When you walk, each step is the body's movement against falling — each movement is felt in our potential for freedom as we move with the earth's gravitational pull. When we navigate our way through the world, there are different pulls, constraints and freedoms that move us forward and propel us into life. But in the changing face of capitalism, media information and technologies — which circulate the globe in more virtual and less obvious ways — how do the constraints on freedom involve our affective and embodied dimensions of experience?"[3]

For me to be able to connect what I was looking at with the broader structures of urban planning, with the discursive settings of the greater city, and with the histories of the spaces, it was necessary to once in a while leave the sites of immediate struggle and friction and separate from the pain that I had accumulated in myself. I knew that I had to acknowledge the pain, to face it, and to ask: what is it exactly that makes this city so painful and unbearable? While this type of analysis was a challenge to my writing habits (as I now had to develop my analyses from these actual physical angles without resorting

---

3   Zournazi, Mary: Interview with Brian Massumi: *Navigating Movements*. 2002. Online source: https://archive.org/stream/InterviewWithBrianMassumi/intmassumi_djvu.txt Massumi has become a leading voice in conceptualising movement of the body and the related sensations as a source of collecting data in humanities research. Cf. for example: Massumi, Brian: *Parables for the Virtual. Movement, Affects, Sensation*. Durham 2002.

to conversations or things said in other formats), the different perspectives from which this chapter is written provide actual data with which I could work. Each perspective allows me to disentangle broad and vague terms such as inequality or segregation and to define what it is exactly about space and architecture in South Africa that makes us use these terms.

When contemplating the civil and social engineering of South Africa's landscape, segregated space and unequal geographies is what remains the most striking aspect. The binaries of city and township, suburbs and township, working-class and middle-class areas, and the ways in which townships refer to the cities they neighbour, contain different layers of marginalisation, exclusion, hybridity, highly liveable and highly unliveable life, and complex encounters between city spaces and its people. This chapter aims to reflect on urban space in the Western Cape by moving in, viewing, thinking, and understanding the greater Cape Town area and neighbouring Stellenbosch from five different physical angles. Each coordinate and angle widens or narrows the dimension from which to look upon the city; depending on the specific coordinate it becomes unclosed and introduced from. The coordinates create the possibility for several engagements with the city, with its historic and present-day construction, with its architectures of space and cityscapes. They also allow to grapple with the city's present sites of exclusion and marginalisation. Each site is therefore double-loaded with meaning: As much as it stands for itself and unveils very specific dynamics and structures, as much it is a symbolic space that holds specific histories. I see histories of spaces as deeply determinative of their uses, shapes, landscapes and relations to other spaces. But how is it possible to revisit histories of spaces thoroughly? Why is it so important to unravel them? The last question can also be flipped– why and for whom is it important to silence the history of a space? Why should it not be put out there, publicly announced, pointed to and referred to? This chapter will formulate answers to these questions from five different perspectives to the city.

First coordinate: Table Mountain

"In Cape Town, South Africa, the city in which we reside and the country of which we are citizens, Table Mountain is a powerful focalizing metaphor symbolizing our shared histories and identities of oppression. Yet in the daily reality that informs the myriad perspectives on this mountain, we are confronted with the pain of continued forms of exclusion, denial and misrecognition. In the context of glaring socio-economic inequity that is overlaid by a public rhetoric of having overcome the pain of our history, imposed boundaries of colour and identity become ossified in the inter-personal encounters of daily life."

Heidi Grunebaum and Yazir Henry[4]

The first coordinate I would like to start with is one that has formed the Cape's character ever since its existence. Table Mountain's unique beauty and majestic character is a very ambivalent companion of Capetonian life that reflects on the entire city. Mirrored in the tinted window glass of the city's huge business complexes, it introduces a different perspective to engage with the city and its history. Being used as one of South Africa's main tourist magnets, it also poses questions of accessibility and affiliation. The flat part of the mountain range literary looks like a table, and especially so when embraced by white clouds- a sequence that has been called the *table cloth* in popular sayings. This part of the mountain range that has been portrayed in uncountable travel documentaries, travel guides and postcards, is at the same time the Central Table of the Table Mountain National Park. There are as many hiking trails as a person would need or desire for a lifetime of exploring, wandering, getting lost, and starting over again: Up from Signal Hill, to Lion's Head, across the Central Table, to Devil's Peak, across Back Table, to the Twelve Apostles, to Llandudno Corner, to Karbonkelberg, across Hout Bay to Constantia Berg, to Noordhoek Peak, to Chapman's Peak, down to Kalk Bay Peak, further down to Swartkop Mountain, then to Vasco Da Gama Peak, and finally to Cape Point/Cape of Good Hope at the very edge. For me as a mountaineer, or better yet, as a person who is truly in love with the mountains, several silences would pop up during the many hikes I took throughout the years. Those silences would raise question after question, some of which I would like to try and answer here.

The mountain range holds a unique geographic position, as it sits on the central strip of the Cape and divides the land into two halves. Due to this position, it constitutes on one side the very border of the major site of Cape Town's townships that apartheid architecture and its accomplished racialised

---

4   Grunebaum, Heidi and Henri, Yazir: *Where the Mountain Meets Its Shadows: A Conversation on Memory, Identity, and Fragmented Belonging in Present-Day South Africa.* in: Strath, Bo and Robins, Ron: Homelands: *The Politics of Space and the Poetics of Power.* Brussels 2003: p.268.

inequality has located on the imposed space of the Cape Flats, and on the other the middle and upper-class suburbs that reside in between the ocean and the mountain, namely the well protected districts of Sea Point, Green Point, Camps Bay, the City Bowl, Gardens, and Table View, amongst others. John Western describes a situation in which "an educated young Jewish woman from Sea Point, Cape Town, was astonished to hear that [he] was pursuing research on the Cape Flats: 'Ooh, how fascinating! And you go out there at night?!'" Western explains that the Cape Flats seemed as "exotic" for her, as the Ituri forest in the Democratic Republic of Congo, even though she lived only 15 kilometres away.[5]

Njabulo Ndebele continues this conversation when he characterises the "contemporary white South African suburb" as an area identifiable through "security fences, parks, lakes, swimming pools, neighbourhood schools and bowling greens".[6] In her extensive work on urban planning in Cape Town, Vanessa Watson illustrates how "patterns of spatial inequity and exclusion are persisting in the post-apartheid era, although they may now be attributed to income inequalities and poverty, rather than to legal racial barriers. At a general level, the clear divisions in Cape Town between wealthier areas and poorer areas remain, and have intensified."[7]

Looking down from the top of the Central Table, the actual shapes in which the suburbs were architecturally made become illuminated. Vredehoek, Sea Point, Betty's Bay, Clifton, Camps Bay, and Bakoven are engrafted in and embraced by the mountain range and its foothills. They stand there as if nature has rolled out a mountain carpet while synchronously pasting human suburbs into its patterns. The idyll is not interrupted, not in the view from up the mountain. Even the roads and drives connecting the suburbs shine, appearing as romantic routes that beckon the viewer. The reflection of the lighted ocean shimmers on the glass of the windows adoring the houses.

Depending on the time of the day and the weather, which brings clouds or draws them away, the suburbs evoke different images and feelings. From VIP-zones, to cosy coves, to boundless beauty – every one of these perceptions is possible. But if one's eyes are ready to perceive differently, to per-

---

5   Western, John: *Outcast Cape Town*. Minneapolis 1982: p.25.
6   Ndebele, Njabulo: *Fine Lines from the Box – Further Thoughts About Our Country*. Cape Town 2007: p.61.
7   Watson, Vanessa: *Change and Continuity in Spatial Planning – Metropolitan Planning in Cape Town under Political Transition*. London 2002: p.145.

ceive something other than what the dominant view on the suburbs dictates, the composition of houses, police stations, schools, shops, and churches, suddenly reveals something that gets hidden in the narrative of Capetonian beach life - the one that invites people from Europe and elsewhere: pensioners, exchange students, adventurists, entrepreneurs, designers and others to come to Cape Town and stay or spend a part of their lives. It is only from above that all the dimensions of the insularity of each suburb become uncovered. What becomes visible is the separateness from the rest, the unresolvable distance created through the insistence on the idyll, the social and political formation of seclusion. From the top of the mountain, the architecture of buildings, gardens and their fencing, their coverage with grass and plants, the streets and roads in between, their access to each other, and their claim for nature to embed them, form the bigger picture that is needed to understand how Cape Town's suburbs create their relation to the physical outside and what they fence themselves off against.

But that Other, the one that must be excluded not only from the physical space of the suburb but also from the narrative of what forms the suburb politically, socially, and economically, is not made non-existent by using the mountain range to cut the suburbs off from their counterparts. It exists and resides on the other side of the mountain. The question then is, what does the suburb not want to face? What is it that the narrative and the physical arrangement of the suburb exiled to the other side? I am asking this simple question because it is important to emphasise that those exiled compose Cape Town's majority. The answer to this question is not "the poor," but "the majority". Therefore, to fence off against the majority of the people, at least a mountain range is needed.

Other elites in cities with huge township populations might use other mechanisms to create guarded areas for themselves, but besides security control and the industry that comes with the politico-economic decision to create "secure" areas – a topic that I dwelled on in the last chapter – the mountain is made into a central device to create this setting. It supports the guarded areas not only practically through its actual position and massifs, but it also forms psychological support, something strong and massive enough to back the construct of the suburb. In between the minority and majority there lies a "massive" distance.

The use of nature as borders of segregated city space also means a repositioning of its social meaning - mountains or rivers gain a totally new relevance and function. They are no longer merely sites of joy and leisure but become discursive material of strategic use. Another aspect to nature other than its forming of borders is its unequal distribution. As adumbrated above, one particularity of Western Cape cities is that they are embraced by and interspersed with nature. In breath-taking sceneries, mountains, forests, waterfalls, wetlands, and the ocean come together, forming biologically one of the most diverse areas of the planet. Cape Town especially is located in an area of great biological diversity. Whereas most affluent suburbs are backed by the mountain and bounded by the sea, the majority of low-income communities have a different perspective on Table Mountain, as Heidi Grunebaum and Yazir Henri emphasise.[8] Placed on the margins of the cities, most of them are alienated from the physical space of nature. The lack of access prevents the chance to inhabit and personalise spaces of nature or create them as spheres of belonging. To reach the mountain from the Cape Flats can mean changing minibus-taxis three times before getting there. The high cost of public transport to go there and back prevents most people from making mountain hikes a regular undertaking. The part of the population that has easy access uses a hike up Lion's Head to do exercise, the paths of Newlands Forest for mountain biking, and the many beaches for family picnics or after work jogging. The incorporation of nature by those with access allows for them to relate to it through its personalisation and integration into their own everyday lives. Premised on unequal and segregated geographies that afflict nature as well, this relationship is limited mostly to occupants of the middle and upper classes. In this vein, the imposed exclusionary feature of nature adds a passive, brutal aspect to its beauty.

At this point, I would like to include an anecdote and reference camera footage that Prune Martinez took during a visit to Table Mountain with Ala Hourani and Tazneem Wentzel. The three had organised a drumming session with children and youth from Kalkfontein on top of Table Mountain. Most of the youngsters had never been to Table Mountain before. At that time, Hourani was a drumming teacher and worked with children in Kalkfontein and other neighbourhoods/townships. Kalkfontein is a small township on the outskirts of Bellville, enclosed in a triangular piece of land between Van Riebeeck Road, Kuils River Road, and Polkadraai Drive, just behind the

---

8   Grunebaum, Heidi and Henri, Yazir: *Where the Mountain Meets Its Shadows: A Conversation on Memory, Identity, and Fragmented Belonging in Present-Day South Africa.* in: Strath, Bo and Robins, Ron: Homelands: The Politics of Space and the Poetics of Power. Brussels 2003: p.268.

University of the Western Cape and not far from Blikkiesdorp. The *Kalkfontein Freedom Drummers* and Hourani, Martinez and Wentzel were drumming on top of the Central Table, when a *white* mountain guide started yelling at them: "Shut uuuuuup…..shut up you monkeys!". Martinez explains how the guide was repeating himself over and over again, insulting the children as monkeys. She filmed him yelling, but he would not calm down. "The guide was worried for the group of tourists he was guiding that they would not be able to see the dassies, an animal species that lives in between rocks in different parts of the Table Mountain National Park. A tourist of that same group sat down at one of the youngsters' drums, posing to be photographed by fellow tourists while pointing to the *Kalkfontein Freedom Drummers* in her background."[9]

Landscape emerges as an organising principle of a set of spatial dichotomies, of access and non-access, of comfort and alienation, of spatial power and spatial oppression. Millions of similar anecdotes sit on the city's shoulders — on its streets, in its buildings, on top of its mountains. Watching the groups of people that approach the Central Table by cable car reveals the social fabric of those who have the means to incorporate Table Mountain as a family destination.

Alienation from natural landscape has been produced and reproduced historically. Farieda Khan centres on exactly this issue:

> "The interaction of people with Table Mountain was determined by their race and class, which effectively meant that Whites used the mountain for pleasure while Blacks either enabled this enjoyment or used the mountain for survival purposes […]. Climbing to the summit of Table Mountain became a popular leisure activity among visitors to the Cape and upper class locals by the mid-to-late nineteenth century."[10]

At the same time, when pointing to the histories of alienation from natural landscape, it is crucial to keep in mind resistance to these legacies. Members of the *Cape Province Mountain Club (CPMC)*[11], formed in 1931, continue to organise mountain hikes and to create awareness around the use of nature and the various empowering relationships people can build with its many

---

9   Martinez, Prune: Conversation on August 25, 2017.
10 Khan, Farieda: *The Politics of Mountaineering in the Western Cape, South Africa – Race, Class and the Mountain Club of South Africa: The First Forty Years, 1891–1931*. in: Acta Academica. Volume 50. NO 2: p.57.
11 Cf. http://capeprovince-mountainclub.co.za/index.php/cpmc

facets. The club was founded as a response to the racist *Mountain Club of South Africa*[12], of which powerful political figures like Cecil Rhodes were members and in which no *black* and Jewish people were allowed.[13] The historically *white* Mountain Club was founded in 1830. Later, it deployed soldiers in the infantry brigade of South Africa in World War I.[14] Today, its main webpage slogan (Cape Town Section) states: "Welcome to the Mountain Club of South Africa – Cape Town Section"; next line: "Exploring and protecting our mountains for 125 years."[15] "Exploration" and "Protection" are popular concepts in both – colonial and postapartheid knowledge production. But appropriation, alienation, murder and displacement remain unspoken of, because they are four words that the Rainbow-Nation discourse cannot tolerate- not if they become commonly used. All of them would open up discussions on the past and the present. Colonialism and apartheid would become unveiled as huge survivors. The legacies of the past? Of course, they are spoken of, but under what frame and for the benefit of whom? The enslaved? The forced labourers? The Khoi and the San? "Runaways" living in the mountain? The people who knew the mountain, its waters, trees, rock formations, stones, animals, and medical plants, before 1652? The genocide of slavery has pushed them into books, poetry, performative art, various constellations of collective memory; but they must not occupy public space and discourse. Otherwise, established politico-economic structures become threatened. The question is: Who benefits and fears to lose, and who becomes silenced, excluded, and marginalised?

But at the same time as analysing this question, collective approaches that work to emancipate from these violent structures must be pointed out, too. The formation of *CPMC* alone bears evidence of a historical urge to personalise the mountain in combination with a deep sense of community that at the same time takes a clear political stance: It is against colonialism's, apartheid's, and the postapartheid's ability to alienate from nature and what rightfully should be inhabitable to all "people". In other words, this urge is against historical and systematic exclusion and marginalisation. Paul Hendrix, a long-time active member of *CPMC* explained in a conversation:

---

12   Cf. http://cen.mcsa.org.za/.
13   Cf. Ibid. and conversation with Paul Hendrix. August 24,2017.
14   Nasson, Bill: *Delville Wood and South African Great War Commemoration*. in: The English Historical Review. Volume 119, No 480. February 2004: p.71.
15   http://www.mcsacapetown.co.za/.

"I was working in the CPMC outreach or development programme with marginalised youth for some time. So much of what we did as a collective was to consider, through our activities, how we could reclaim the mountain as a historical and social space for marginalised youth who had been alienated from it since and even before the apartheid era given the history of segregation, forced removals, dispossession and dislocation. The social ills of gangsterism, drugs, crime and so on impacting black working class youth today and links to alienation and marginalisation has to a large degree been a driving force for our collective interventions, particularly through the Schools Environmental Education Project (SEEP).[16] SEEP actually has an organic link to CPMC as it emerged through the support of the club in 2000. This continues at present though both organisations are not particularly strong given their heavy dependence on social activism and voluntary contributions. For more information, I've attached a clip on CPMC produced in collaboration with the District Six Museum."[17]
Still standing on top of the Central Table and looking down on Camps Bay, the view to the Other[18] side is not a long walk away; one only needs to turn around, start off from the western side and head east.

On that Other side, wooden and iron shacks placed on winding roads, encapsulated in fenced areas with a few entrances, look at the mountain with questioning eyes and the mouth wide open. They have been marked as high crime areas that the orderly inhabitants of the other side of the mountain are called upon to avoid and circumnavigate. Some township areas that verge on highways are flagged by huge digital signs that warn the car driver: "High Crime Area – Do Not Stop Your Car", as is the case with Bonteheuwel and Langa on the N2 Highway. Since Ocean View township borders on a part of Noordhoek Beach, 'high crime' area signs are placed on its wealthy part, asking the beach visitor to not move more than 500 meters away from the sign. Townships and informal settlements were created as dangerous spheres of

---

16 Cf. https://www.facebook.com/Schools-Environmental-Education-Project-SEEP-213681591989576/.
17 Conversation with Paul Hendrix. August 24, 2017. The link to the video-clip he attached: https://vimeo.com/180298774.
18 This "Other side" is where the Cape Flats, that include the majority of Western Cape townships and at the same time the majority of Cape Town's inhabitants, are situated. An inheritance of colonial and apartheid spatial planning, they have remained the sites with the highest poverty rates.

non-belonging to the rest of the city. How must a person living here try to create equal relationships with the physical outside, or better, with that other, wealthy side?

The mountain appears to press down most attempts at starting to imagine oneself a person who will endure school, study hard, enter university, get a bursary, finish, find a job, and change sides.

Here, reflecting on divided city spaces is not synonymous with an absolute generalisation. Not every single individual living in a township or informal settlement becomes excluded, marginalised and criminalised in a manner that prevents him or her from leaving the township. Moreover, not everyone who leaves the township is thirsty to accept and inhabit the suburbs' logics, lifestyles, and discourses. This kind of assumptions would reinforce the binary of the colonial position, rather than disentangle the many complex layers in which the Urban Development Discourse has an impact. The aim of this work is under no circumstances to create townships and informal settlements as a homogenous entity or to reproduce fixed notions about township and informal settlement residents, but to specify how precisely the dominant discourse on townships, informal settlements, and other working-class areas, homogenises notions of space and people. The argument is that criminalisation and marginalisation of low-income residents/"the people", are solely possible through this discursive homogenisation.

But how is it possible to think and phrase this dominant discourse? Sunu Gonera's words, at an event organised by the Cape Town Partnership[19], ring in my ears: "As long as you work hard and don't give up, you can go to school wherever you want, let it be Bishobscourt or Camps Bay. I also lived in a township. I know how that is. But with the right will and motivation, everything is possible". Ilham Rawoot, a journalist and writer who attended that same event, quotes him in an article on the Cape Town Partnership:

> "Then there was the film director Sunu Gonera. The man has some good credentials – he was awarded a scholarship to a private school in Zimbabwe and now makes documentaries. He went on a long stroking session about how he has made it in Los Angeles. "One day I was talking to Clint Eastwood" ... "I go up and down between LA" ... "I have dinner with some of the best film directors in the world."

---

19 The Cape Town Partnership is a semi-private, semi-governmental institution (see chapter three).

He tells his story to 'boys at Bishops" and "boys in Khayelitsha", because he wants to show them that if he could make it, they can make it. That's motivating in theory, although it dismisses the fact that most of the children in Khayelitsha will not receive scholarships, because their classroom windows are broken and their teachers don't get paid much and many of them risk being stabbed for R10 on their way to school. Most of those children will not have the opportunity to excel in the classroom."[20]

Besides the narrative that Gonera and the Cape Town Partnership constructed in that specific event, even if that "everything" Gonera speaks about would be possible, what is it that one will have to leave behind? It is difficult to justify the changing of sides when it is you who made it out of hundreds of thousands. How does one refer then to the other side? Will it be like Makalima-Ngewana, former head of the Cape Town Partnership, who repeatedly said in one of our conversations, "I also have a brother in Langa. I know the township"? During the event titled, "How do we inspire a new generation of active citizens in Cape Town?" at which Gonera spoke, the question of responsibility was central. People must be responsible for themselves – it is people's responsibility to achieve personal success. This closely resembles the national government's request to South Africans that was formulated in a declaration released in July 2015. *Eyewitness News* singles out four quotes from statements made by 1) the ANC, 2) a political analyst, 3) a journalist, and 4) by the South African Communist Party that is part of the tripartite alliance with the ANC and the South African trade unions' umbrella organisation COSATU:

> "On Wednesday night, the ANC-led alliance released a declaration that also said communities must be taught that with rights comes responsibilities. Many economists have warned that government could soon run out of money because of what it spends on social grants and civil service salaries. Political analyst Nic Borain says this comment shows the ANC is coming face to face with the fact South Africa needs more money. 'The levels of expectations are unrealistic. You disempower people if you constantly give them the message, know it's your right and government will deliver it.' Econometrix economist Azar Jammine says this is a good move by the ANC. 'Because it's this kind of change of attitude and the direction that the alliance is now calling for that will start rectifying the structural weaknesses of the

---

20   The Con article. Rawoot, Ilham: *Cape Town's Pretend Partnership*. March 5, 2014.

economy.' The South African Communist Party (SACP) says this comment is a call to South Africans to stand up and develop themselves."[21]

Having arrived at the eastern part of the Central Table, I wonder, how did this become the official narrative? What political and economic structures, what systems of thought, and what discursive practices made this possible? Since apartheid has ended, Khayelitsha, Mitchell's Plain, Langa, Nyanga, Bonteheuwel, Hanover Park, Lavender Hill, Gugulethu, Kalkfontein, and many others; all continue to maintain their same economic status because of a lack of "responsibility". And the informal settlements in Woodstock and Bo Kaap? According to this narrative, people living in unofficial housing must be the most irresponsible, least willing to change their "attitude" and "develop themselves". Looking down from the top of the mountain I say to myself, "so Kalkfontein is an attitude".

The way responsibility is discussed in this official narrative also explains the discursive framing of crime in South Africa. Besides the specific notions of crime and criminal identities that are inscribed on Cape Town, Johannesburg, and Durban, and the titles given to them– such as "the most dangerous" / "the most murderous" / "the most criminal" / "the most violent city on earth" – the mountain holds a different position in this discourse. On the one hand, as I pointed to earlier, it serves as a practical and psychological assistant to the constitution of the suburbs, and on the other hand, it is portrayed as a terra incognita, a space where "bushmen"[22] and criminals gather, live in caves, come down to steal and to rape, having escaped the *civilising mission*. As much as hiking is advertised as a major Capetonian activity that belongs on every tourist's to-do list, it is the site of the undetected, one that invokes fear and produces sustained anxieties. As such, the mountain is a good example of how the polarity of minority and majority, of life and survival, constructs its own paradoxes and extremes.

---

21 Eyewitness News article. Grootes, Stephen: *Economists welcome ANC's policy shifts*. July 3, 2015.

22 The Khoi and the San later merged to become the Khoisan due to forced removals from the lands they inhabited, loss of their livelihoods, different forms of killings committed against them, and other violences inflicted by the colonial Dutch and British. They were given various derogatory names by the different colonial administrations, and by members of the settler society. "Hottentots" and "Bushmen" are two examples of thesesystematic attempts to create inferiority through naming. (see chapter one).

Driving down south, taking Boyes Drive short cut towards Muizenberg, arriving with the mountain behind and the ocean greeting from the coast down in Muizenberg, the hike up Ou Kraal trail is one of my favourite ways of accessing the mountain. The path is quite steep and hence takes one quick to the top where there opens up a surreal scene of rocks and Protea trees standing their chance to be circled by mist and sun at the same time. Yet every time I go alone, people's warnings, especially those of my landlords, ring in my ears: "It is dangerous. Are you mad going there alone? They will come and rob you and God knows what else." The mountain over Boyes Drive in particular evokes fear. "Don't go there! Can't you see Mitchell's Plain is so close?" Yes, Mitchell's Plain[23] is very close. Close enough that one can count a part of its houses and shacks from up Kalk Bay Peak and draw an imaginary line, one that suddenly connects Mitchell's Plain to neighbouring Kalk Bay and Muizenberg, two suburbs in Cape Town's south-east that are famous for their nightlives, cafés, restaurants, and wealth. Metaphorically speaking, one needs two strings, one leading from Kalk Bay to Muizenberg and halfway to Mitchell's Plain, and one leading from Mitchell's Plain halfway to Muizenberg, and a strap in which both strings can snap into. I imagine it to be like a curse, one that does not allow one to scratch Mitchell's Plain off the shoulders of Muizenberg and Kalk Bay residents as though it were an annoying fly. Muizenberg/Kalk Bay would have to face Mitchell's Plain and either keep shouting in its people's faces that they are irresponsible, lazy citizens – like people who repeat themselves being wound up in a specific imagination, too fearful to change their perspective -, or they would have to start to listen and ask themselves questions: What does isolated unequal life mean? How is it perceived, how does it become endured and survived and what are the views of the people living it?

But of course, there is no curse and without it, no politicians, economists, enough journalists, or residents of the other side of the mountain listening. What remains is the fear to go to the mountain. That fear of becoming a victim of "crime", is the only ghost that haunts all those that are not listening. It is almost impossible to think the mountain without that fear.

---

23   Mitchell's Plain is one of the biggest townships situated in the Cape Flats.

Second coordinate: Vredehoek Quarry

"Dear City of Cape Town...
My body remembers the history of slaves here, everywhere I go there are monuments in the likes of Jan Smuts - next to the Slave Lodge... This city is not built in my hearts desires, everywhere it hurts... My feet have callouses inherited from my mothers and her mothers mother... Here stand building tall and wide built by enslaved hands, here in the reconstruction I see black men layer brick upon brick to erect sky scrapers but still you refuse to reflect my hearts desires... the only history you allow is the one I see my body defeated and dead... no image of me celebrated... you are always asking me to die - AND I SAY NO! THE REVOLUTION MUST EMANCIPATE ME TO LIVE! NO MORE BLACK DEAD BODIES, WE HAVE DIED ENOUGH... #MVELO "

Khanyisile Mintho Mbongwa[24]

To most Capetonians, the quarry above Vredehoek is unknown. It lies at the bottom of Devil's Peak, the mountain peak that neighbours the Central Table on its north-west. One can easily pass the quarry without noticing it, as finding it would require one to walk through an old, run-down, half-hidden and dark tunnel made of concrete that leads to it. Outside, no indication of a quarry is visible. But if one pays attention, next to the tunnel there stands a very recently erected sign that refers to the quarry. It does not speak about the quarry's history, about when it was worked in or by whom. The sign is solely given a title: Murray & Stewart Quarry. Nothing more. Once one has walked through the tunnel, an unexpected scene is revealed. The quarry's high walls accentuate the massiveness of the stone. On the bottom of the quarry, a lake has formed that deepens the impression of insularity the place radiates. Its water mirrors the open stone, embracing all its different colours, taking me back mentally to the time before the quarry was abandoned. Revisiting the quarries and connecting their histories to the practices of exclusion today, opens up a different angle for reading the city.

Just as prisoners on Robben Island were forced to work in the island's quarries,[25] many other quarries were workplaces of slaves, prisoners and

---

24 Mintho Mbongwa, Khanyisile: Facebook post. June 5, 2016.
25 Mandela, Nelson: *Long Walk to Freedom*. Boston 1995: part 64; Worden, Nigel; van Heyningen, Elizabeth; and Bickford-Smith, Vivian: *Cape Town: The Making of a City*. Cape Town 1998: p.139.

forced labourers. Everyone who has read Mandela's *Long Walk to Freedom*, visited Robben Island, or has watched a documentary on the years of Mandela's imprisonment on the island, knows about the lime quarry and its white rocks whose reflection of light hurt the eyes and cause long-term damage. Most sources mention that political prisoners were forced to work in the lime quarry and general prisoners in the stone quarry.[26] But the quarrying on Robben Island had been initiated long before the island was turned into a prison. The first records of an enslaved person working at a quarry are those of a 30-year-old woman from Madagascar, whom the officials of the *Dutch East India Company* named Eva. She was brought to the Cape in 1654, only two years after Van Riebeeck's arrival. During her first years as a slave, she was deployed to serve Jan van Herwerden, a senior sergeant of the Company who had captured her in Madagascar. Later in 1657, she was sent to work at the Robben Island quarry, since the officials of the Company "considered her strong enough to carry the quarry stones".[27] The stories of the uncountable enslaved and forced labourers who extracted the very stone of which South Africa's cities are made, remain untold in the public discourse. The city of Cape Town is especially unique in this regard:

> "The point was that by the beginning of the eighteenth century slavery had become the basis of the economic and social position of a large proportion of the settler community. This was made inevitable by the establishment of extensive arable agriculture based on slave labor and the subsequent widespread incidence of slaveholding. As the colony expanded and diversified, slavery continued to play a key function both in its economy and in the social attitudes of its inhabitants. In the south-western district a group of farmers described as a 'landed-gentry' by several recent historians based their wealth on slave production whose local power led to a remarkably closed slave system. Meanwhile slave labour was becoming important elsewhere, especially in Cape Town during the eighteens century. The critical issue is the way in which an institution established by the VOC [Vereenigde Oost-Indische Compagnie / Dutch East India Company] developed in the context of local economic and social circumstances to produce a complex slave society."[28]

---

26   Mandela, Nelson: *Long Walk to Freedom*. Boston 1995: part 64.
27   South African History Online: *History of slavery and early colonisation in South Africa – The first slaves at the Cape*. April 2, 2015.
28   Worden, Nigel: *Slavery in Dutch South Africa*. Cambridge 1985: p.18.

The ocean was pushed back to allow more space between it and the mountain range. In order to enable this huge surgical intervention and to build the harbour, as well as mountain passes, streets, castles and other buildings, stone had to be extracted and processed.[29] The remnants of the later abandoned quarries recall that history, although nobody is asking questions, no institution deals with it, and no *Table Mountain National Park* signs commemorate that history. At some quarries, visitors find signs that record when the quarry was built and until when it functioned, but no indication is made of who created the quarries and who extracted the stone.

The quarries that are retraceable at the National Archives and whose remnants are still visible today, are the Robben Island lime and stone quarries; Vredehoek Quarry, also named Smit's Quarry or Murray & Stewart Quarry, whose stone was used for road material. Next to it stands Reid's Quarry, which has been turned into a shooting range. There is also, 700 meters further northeast, the Devil's Peak Quarry; then, Higgovale Quarry, Kloof Quarry, Lion's Head Granite Quarry, and Bellevue Quarry of which all four are located above Oranjezicht district. The latter was built to supply granite for the construction of the Cecil Rhodes memorial. The stone of Graaf's Pool Quarry in Sea Point was used to build the Sea Point railway line; Lakeview Quarry 1 and 2 above Boyes Drive delivered quartzitic sandstone and were worked already at the end of the 18th century. Kalk Bay Quarry's remnants lie in a private garden and are therefore inaccessible; its stone served the construction of the Huguenot Memorial Hall. There is also Delbridge Quarry and Glencairn Quarry in Fish Hoek; Simon's Town Quarry, and right next to it, Jackson Quarry, whose sandstone was used to build the Simon's Town harbour. The Lion's Rump or Signal Hill Quarries, also named the three Bo-Kaap Quarries in later popular sayings, are today known as Strand Street Quarry, Schotschekloof Quarry, and Signal Hill Quarry. Other sites in which slaves, forced labourers, and later contract workers worked were salt pans and different kind of mines.

This list of abandoned and retraceable quarries might be useful for anyone who decides to conduct further research on the quarries and the people who worked them. To identify these sites is also a starting point for the uncovering of the dynamics of slavery at the Cape. Other sites, like the quarry above Rhine Road/Sea Point, were filled in and disappeared once new vege-

---

29   Cf. ibid: p. 16-17.

tation covered them.³⁰ Close to the Rhine Road quarry, just above Glengariff Road, was another quarry, of which the only account in the National Archives is a 1961 denied leasing application to build a "Ladies shooting Club" named "Revolver Range".³¹ Barbara Beryl Scott writes about the Glengariff quarry in her *Memories of Growing Up* (in Cape Town), that "there was a small disused quarry on the hill near us and we would go there to play".³² Other quarries that remained unused and disappeared garnered the same degree of attention. These two records are the only documentations that makes the quarry above Glengariff Road traceable.

The documentation of quarries that were abandoned but not filled in and thus remained visible until today is not much more extensive. Except for the Vredehoek Quarry that was given a sign with a title, nothing indicates the quarries at their physical sites. No signs, no badges, no engravings on the stone. Most quarries are not even marked on the different maps of the Western Cape or Cape Town, also not on the extensively used Google Maps. It is as if they do not exist.³³ With this non-existence, their histories have been rendered non-existent as well. Robert Semple writes in his 1804 traveller's account: "...we soon came to the quarries at the bottom of the Lion's Rump, whence all the stone has been obtained, and still continues to be taken for building the town. In the principal quarry was a great crowd of slaves, which on approaching nearer we found to consist principally of Malays."³⁴ After his

---

30   South African National Archives – Cape Town Archives Repository: DEPOT: KAB; SOURCE: 3/CT; TYPE: LEER; VOLUME_NO: 4/1/11/124; SYSTEM: 01; REFERENCE: G6/3/11/37; PART: 1; DESCRIPTION: GENERAL PURPOSES COMMITTEE. CITY LAND. APPLICATIONS TO PURCHASE. MATTERS REFERRED TO PROPERTY COMMITTEE. OLD QUARRY AT TOP OF RHINE ROAD. 1948.

31   South African National Archives – Cape Town Archives Repository: DEPOT: KAB; SOURCE: 3/CT; TYPE: LEER; VOLUME_NO: 4/1/11/141; SYSTEM: 01; REFERENCE: G6/1/106/5; PART: 1; DESCRIPTION: GENERAL PURPOSES COMMITTEE. CITY LAND. APPLICATION TO LEASE.REFUSED. SITE FOR REVOLVER RANGE FOR LADIES SHOOTING CLUB.QUARRY NEAR GLENGARIFF ROAD, SEA POINT. 1961.

32   Account archived in The Church of Jesus Christ of Latter Day-Saints's family search website: https://familysearch.org/photos/artifacts/4008743.

33   The Land Survey student Mahyar Bineshtarigh provided me with a map that he created based on a data collection of the Geoscientist Doug Cole. Link to the map: https://www.google.com/maps/d/viewer?mid=1heIN5bWOiKB3YJuE39WgLLgYy1I&ll=-34.05641908089775%2C18.401702500000056&z=10.

34   Semple, Robert: *Walks and Sketches at the Cape of Good Hope- to which is subjoined- A Journey from Cape Town to Blettenberg's Bay.* London 1805: p.86.

witnessing of a cockfight inside the quarry, Semple continues to recount their way further up Signal Hill. This is it. Nothing more. A view from above the quarries, two sentences, and the journey continues. But what we can understand through this glimpse of Semple is the normality with which slaves were forced to work in the quarries. Nothing gets hidden; lifetime work in the quarries is supposed to be normal life. Just as normal as it is today that the city was built by someone, but no institution says by whom. Since I heard the story of the pushed-back ocean in different conversations with different people, I assume that it is part of general knowledge about the city. But it seems that there are no public accounts about the quarries and the forced labour. The story of who built the city remains untold. No maps, leaflets, signs, memorials, indicate that the city was built by slaves.

This also explains why I was surprised when an exhibition was put up in the Bo-Kaap Museum in early 2016, titled "Who built Cape Town?" But I was disappointed the moment I entered the space. The explanation on the museum's website claims that the exhibition is "dedicated to the slaves, convicts, and free workers who built the city". But what is actually exhibited neither really speaks about the enslaved, nor does it frame the exhibition in relation to the effects of the genocide of slavery. In a tiny room, four walls are covered with photographs, paintings, and explanations. One painting shows three people working on the roof of a building who may or may not have been slaves. The painting is without comment. In a photograph, a stone quarry and its workers are pictured, but no explanation is provided about the history of the quarry or about who the people were that worked in the quarry. The rest of the exhibition deals with the professions *black* people were allowed to occupy in the 20th century, the Cape carnival that was formed by slaves, and racial discrimination on Cape Town's streets. Through not speaking about the people who worked in the quarries and the forced labour associated with the building of the city, the exhibition, more than illuminating the history of slavery at the Cape, erases the proportion of hardship and violence inflicted on the enslaved. An appropriate title for this exhibition would be "Disremembering slavery at the Cape", or "Silencing those who built the city of Cape Town". It almost seems as if the exhibition serves as an alibi, to cover up the provincial and city governments' reluctance to create deep conversations about forced labour and how it relates to present-day questions. Even the Slave Lodge, the very museum in Cape Town's city centre that is fully dedicated to the history of slavery at the Cape, does not speak about the use of slave and forced labour in the building of the province's cities. Robert Shell, Sandra Shell and Mogamat Kamedien make this point very clear when they write:

> "...the people of South Africa are poorly served with the sort of public memorials and museum displays commemorating slavery which have appeared in West Africa, England, the United States and elsewhere. In Cape Town a Hitleresque statue of Cecil John Rhodes stands next to an un- marked slave bell which called the Lodge slaves to their urban plantation, now euphemistically called the City's Botanical Gardens. A solitary but well-hidden plaque commemorates the old slave tree in Bureau Street un- der which slaves were sold. South Africa's "door of no return"—the old en- trance, now rear entrance to the Slave Lodge on Parliament Street—is used only for rubbish removal. Iziko museums has made no formal attempt to establish the Lodge as a world heritage site despite much encouragement from Unesco and local researchers. Indeed, apart from the standing exhibition in the Lodge, the model of the slave lodge at Vergelegen and the memorial at Elim, it is hard to think of another commemorative site in the Western Cape. This memory gap is no doubt partly a result of underfunding, but one also suspects shame and denial."[35]

As a general observation of the place of quarries and forced labour in the public discourse on who built the city, it only remains to be said that the official presentation of the quarries cuts them off from their history. In the colonial imagination, the inscribed dogma of a people without history, these same people have been rendered a people that have never existed.

The only incident that disrupts this silence is when a mass grave is found. We have seen in chapter three how even the dead can be forcibly removed, how construction companies have the last say on whether their developments can be disrupted, how a mass grave with bodily remains of slaves must make space for luxury apartments to be built and sold. Looking at a different mass grave, Oddveig Nicole Sarmiento shows how the burial ground that lies underneath the University of Cape Town's Middle Campus, most probably underneath the Economics Department's building, has been neglected and never criti-

---

35   Shell, Robert; Shell, Sandra and Kamedien, Mogamat (eds.): *Bibliographies of Bondage*. Cape Town 2007: p.viii.

cally dealt with.[36] The dead, those who extracted the stone for the city, those who built the city, were nameless during their lifetime and remain nameless today. In contrast, this is not the case for those who enslaved them and who had come to inhabit, to own, and to oppress. The statues and memorials of Cecil Rhodes, Jan van Riebeeck, Jan Smuts, and Louis Botha are present in all over Cape Town. The inscription on Botha's statue that stands in front of the national parliament, celebrates him as "Farmer – Warrior – Statesman". Not only do the big figures of colonialism continue to be portrayed, memorialised, and celebrated, but the mountain side – the very space were the quarries have been abandoned and with them the bones of the dead –carries signs and metal badges that commemorate those who have been in charge of the construction of dams, trails, and quarries. For example, Thomas Stewart is commemorated; he is the engineer of the Woodhead Dam construction that is situated two walking hours south of the Central Table, right on the Back Table between Bakoven Bay on its one side and Kirstenbosch Botanical Garden on its other. The sign next to the dam that was mounted in 2008 claims:

> "International Historic Civil Engineering Landmark – Woodhead Dam – Built between 1893 and 1897, the Woodhead Dam was the first large masonry dam in South Africa. A regional water system with a major reservoir was a bold venture requiring difficult construction in a remote area. Innovative techniques, including an aerial cableway to carry materials, were needed. The dam's successful completion paved the way for sister dams that continue to supply water to Cape Town and environs and established young Thomas Stewart, the engineer who designed and managed the project, as a leading water engineer and reliable consultant. Stewart is known as the father of consulting engineering in South Africa.
>
> Presented by the South African Institution of Civil Engineering and the American Society of Civil Engineers – 1 August 2008."

The engraving of the year in which the dam was completed recalls:

> "The Corporation of the City of Cape Town – This the last stone of the dam was laid by HIS WORSHIP the MAYOR SIR JOHN WOODHEAD, JP, on the first

---

36   Cf. Sarmiento, Nicole Oddveig: *On Burial Grounds and City Spaces – Reconfiguring the Normative.* in: Haber, Alejandro and Shepherd, Nick: *After Ethics - Ancestral Voices and Post-Disciplinary Worlds in Archaeology.* New York 2015.

day of May 1897. Being the year of the diamond jubilee of her most gracious majesty Queen Victoria."

Similar examples are the sign next to the De Villiers Reservoir, about two kilometres south-east of the Woodhead Dam, and the plaque below the King's Blockhouse at Devil's Peak that commemorates the British forester Frank Jarman. What is important here is to look at what these signs reveal about the city, provincial, and national institutions' political engagement with the past of the city and thereby with South Africa's past. The question is, what is it that must be avoided and how does it relate to the city's present-day social engineering? There is meaning in fading out who built the city and instead commemorating single engineers of the colonial apparatus and other members of the settler society. Even if it is hard to prove that there is intention in this silence, that it is not only passive silence but an active suppression of the past, even if we assume that this past was buried in oblivion unintentionally on the institutional level, then still, this amnesia is discursively embedded in another, dominant narrative of the city. The dead of the quarries, of the dams, and of other sites of slavery and forced labour become alienated from the narration of the spaces through memorialising practices that silence their role in the landscaping of mountain sites and city, and which obscure the socio-economic conditions under which they were forced to live. What is supposed to be forgotten is the historical exploitation and the link between those who had no voice in the past and those who have no voice today. If those who built the city and the conditions under which they did so were to be emphasised, then the political and economic relations of the enslaved and their oppression with the marginalised and excluded of today would be established.

Inequality is a condition that has been produced historically. It is a manufactured product of colonialism and apartheid which has been maintained in the postapartheid period through capitalist modes of production, informed by colonial and apartheid discourse. Inequality has been embedded in the land ever since the beginning of colonialism. After the official abolition of slavery, other laws were implemented to systematise that inequality. The Master and Servants Act of 1856 that was "designed to enforce discipline on ex-slaves, peasants, pastoralists, and rural proletariat"[37] and to ensure obedience of servants to their employers; the Native Land Act of 1913 that allocated 93%

---

37   Simons, H.J. and Simons, R.E.: *Class and Colour in South Africa 1850-1950*. Aylesbury 1969: p.23.

of South Africa's land to the *white* population and prohibited the sale of land to *blacks*; the Native Urban Areas Act of 1923 that reduced access of *blacks* to the cities and forced them to carry permits to enter the cities at all times; the Industrial Conciliation Act of 1924 that declared strikes by *black* workers as illegal and prohibited them from forming trade unions while at the same time granting the right to organise in unions for *white* workers; the Immorality Act of 1927 that declared sex and marriage between *whites* and *blacks* illegal, and the Group Areas Act of 1950 that divided the land into *white* and non-*white* areas and formed the legal basis for forcibly removing non-*white* people from *white* grouped areas; are all examples of how inequality was theorised, legalised, and produced systematically over a long historical period. The silence about the past helps to obscure the link between social and economic conditions of today with those of the past and consequently between present and past violences. In particular, the personal – the names and faces of the people who have been masked out – is a serious disrupter of the narrative of a modern, stable, investment-ready, Cape Town. If for instance, fragments of the exploited of the past are revealed, what would hinder people from thinking of themselves, in relation to the exploited of the past? What would stop them from seeing that their condition is in a different way unbearable, and that, like their forbearers, they are put to work to serve the interests of the descendants of those who exploited them, and who still live in those secluded spaces that are inaccessible? I assume that long-term public debates about the relations between the exploited of the past and the present would touch on a suppressed consciousness of the reasons for people's socio-economic conditions today. It would help to create a public dialogue about accessibility, desirable and undesirable urbanites, segregated city spaces and the continuities of the past.

At the same time, since erasure is precisely an effect of genocide and of the colonial practice of pushing people into social death, most names, faces, and the histories related to them are forever erased and can therefore not be recovered. To speak of "recovery" does not take into account what genocide really means. But it means among many other things that generations of survivors have to live in the shadows of "no-names". This is the actual rupture and it is crucial to attend to it. The fact of public history not attending to this rupture does not mean that the ultimate aim should be public exhibitions which put up names, faces, and related histories. What I am speaking of is the unravelling of fragments that can be found and the naming and representation of exactly this process of erasure and genocide as part of forging a new public discourse of interconnected relations between past and present. To expand the discussion to the whole country, and maybe even to other related geographies, civil society has to take this huge task into its own hands.

Still standing inside the Vredehoek Quarry, I wonder how the quarry would act upon its visitors if its history would actually be presented uncensored and not as a dehistoricised and hence depoliticised part of the mountain that popped out of nowhere. Today, the rock climbers that use the quarry's stone walls for practicing, are completely set apart from the story behind the extracted stone. Rock climbing is also the only subject that links Cape Town's abandoned quarries to online-media platforms. But just like the official narrative of the city, these entries, which are predominantly photo essays, do not speak about how the quarries were created. On the combined business sector and city government side, the Green Point and Oranje Kloof Improvement Districts' joint website is the only source that mentions the quarries. However, the short article is concerned with the growing crime rate in the area of the quarries, not with the history of the place. Nevertheless, two introductory sentences touch on the past. The article opens with:

> "Many Capetonians will be familiar with the three quarries above the Bo-Kaap, and the growing concern about criminal activity that is linked to this area. What you probably don't know is that this part of Cape Town is also steeped in history, as stone from the quarries was used to build very early structures; and the diverse, rich culture of the Bo-Kaap stems from the Malay settlers who were based here."[38]

The next sentence crosses over to the actual topic of the article; the story of the quarries' past stops here. The stone that was used to build the city is presented as an abstract entity, removed from its political, economic, and social context. This active erasure becomes reinforced when the enslaved are rendered as "settlers". It is easier and less dissonant to portray the colonial era as a harmonious and quaint period. Erasure, then, involves not only the deletion of the historical practice of slavery and the modes of oppression and technologies of power applied in the colonial project; it also adheres to a directed romanticisation, oversimplification, and justification of the power relations

---

38 Green Point and Oranje Kloof City Improvement District: *City Secures Bo-Kaap Quarries*. October 21, 2015. Source: http://gpokcid.co.za/2015/10/city-takes-proactive-steps-to-secure-bo-kaap-quarries-and-provide-new-homes-for-residents/.

of the past. In the case of this article, two sentences show this complex mechanism at play. The first sentence silences the truth about the forced labour behind the extracted stone; the second sentence tells a direct lie.

The erasure of slave and other forced labour from the official narrative is supported by its erasure from the archives. There are no archival accounts that record by whom the city was built or from which parts of the world people were enslaved and brought to the cape. Malaysia, Indonesia, Mozambique, West-Africa, East-Africa[39] – who speaks publicly about the birth lands of slaves, about the fact that they were exiled, displaced, and forcibly kept under physical and psychological torture? Who speaks about centuries of torture and systematic humiliation? The Slave Lodge Museum prefers to put up costly temporary exhibitions about unrelated topics like the political character and career of Oliver Tambo.[40] The actual permanent exhibition on slavery refuses to speak about the social, economic, and political effects of slavery. In the National Archives, one has to treat it like a perpetual puzzle for which other accounts, for instance about the companies that were involved in the quarrying, must borrow marginal access to what one wants to know. All documents in connection with the quarries are of an administrative and regulative nature. Contracts with companies; permissions to quarry stone; applications for quarry licenses; contracts for the supply of stone; propositions for tree planting at old quarries; monthly progress reports; and permissions to sell a quarry— build the only archival evidences that the quarries ever existed. One document states, "that a gang of men be taken from the Quarry and employed in excavating the area of ground belonging to the Council...";[41] another one specifies about "...an Inquest touching the death of Paul Christian, and to give evidence regarding the safety or otherwise of the portion of the Strand Street Quarry...".[42] Some hints here and some traces there. Each document

---

39 Cf. Worden, Nigel and Crais, Clifton: *Breaking the Chains: Slavery and its Legacy in the Nineteens-Century Cape Colony*. Johannesburg 1994: pp. 100-101; 204.

40 Slave Lodge – Iziko Museums: *Oliver Reginald Tambo – The Modest Revolutionary*. Cape Town March 2013 - March 2014.

41 Extract from the minutes of a Council Meeting held on 6 April 1906. South African National Archives. Cape Town Archives Repository. KAB, 3/ELN, Volume 154, Reference 128/2.

42 Letter of the Court of the Resident Magistrate for the District of Cape Town to the Chief Constable send on February 8, 1911. South African National Archives. Cape Town Archives Repository. KAB, 3/CT, Volume 4/2/1/1/106, Reference 210/11.

stands in some relation with the question of who built the city and offers a small insight. The rest is non-existent.

This non-existence, the mixture of history falsification, of a general absence of public representation and of direct archival accounts, results in the erasure of the whole theme not only from the public space or the archive, but from memory. Collective memory about the way Cape Town was created and the people who were forced to work it, is rendered impossible. What remains is marginalised memory as in the memory of people and small groups of society who want the topic to be revived. The memorial space in which representations of history are distributed is being limited to a state in which asking questions about the past will not disrupt political and socio-economic arrangements of the present.

Third coordinate: Victoria Road

"The new [Cape Town] carnival references an existing set of aesthetic practices, while keeping the exclusion of these practices intact. So I would argue that within this discourse that is being created around the new Cape Town Carnival and the Creative City, Kaapse Klopse [the historical carnival organised by the enslaved and later by their descendants that is still held annually] is a sort of spectre that haunts the city. And I would argue that the new Cape Town Carnival accesses spectacles of erasure. It is an act of erasure or in other words, disavowing of local histories and presenting Cape Town as a place devoid of history where carnivals can be "invented" and 'imported' from places as 'exotic' as Rio. So space in this context is presented as a tabula rasa. As empty lines on a grid which echoes the colonial fantasy of empty space devoid of history and of people."

Oddveig Nicole Sarmiento[43]

I have been thinking about how to begin this section, since Victoria Road offers many different spots from which an introduction could start off. The discursive setting of the new Cape Town carnival[44] that this introductory note

---

43   Sarmiento, Oddveig Nicole: Talk at Thinking the City 2013 – *Public Space, Festivalisation, and Contested Cultural Expression*. University of Cape Town – African Centre for Cities. March 12, 2013.
44   Cf. http://capetowncarnival.com/.

by Oddveig Nicole Sarmiento speaks about, is a key example of how major business and media companies, and city, provincial, and national government institutions, dehistoricise and depoliticise space, architecture, cultural practices, natural landscape, and civil society. I am using Sarmiento's note as an entry into this section to make explicit how the curb and interior off Victoria Road are not just a product of colonial and apartheid architecture but remain the site of active erasure again as a discursive practice by the political and business sector in the postapartheid era.

Entering "Cape Town Carnival" in *Google Search* will lead one directly to the webpage of the new *Cape Town Carnival*. Its sponsors reveal the discursive foundation on which the carnival is built: The *People's Post*; *Media 24*; *DSTV*; *Coca Cola*; *Tsogo Sun*; the city government of Cape Town; the Western Cape provincial government, and the Arts and Culture Department of national government, among others, have all been listed one after the other.[45] The new annual carnival does not start in the historical quarter of the original Kaapse Klopse Carnival that was initiated by enslaved people in the Cape as a celebration of their only day off in the year. The new carnival starts in Green Point Main Road, the very road that leads down south towards Beach Road and Victoria Road and that is at the same time the same road that separates the central city from the Atlantic Seaboard.

Victoria Road itself is a beach road that provides one of the most scenic drives in South Africa. Beginning at Lion's Head's west-side, it is the dividing line between the ocean and the mountain. The wealthy suburbs of Bantry Bay, Clifton, Camps Bay, and Hout Bay, all start off Victoria Road. Only Bakoven and Landudno were built on hills underneath the road so that in their case, the road is not the dividing line between suburb and ocean, but the first main road to be reached up the hill. Passing Landudno heading south, the road eventually ends at Hout Bay's harbour. As in many coastal towns in the postcolony, the architecture and aesthetic of the houses that border the road is abruptly European; they represent architectural styles that mimic a fantasy of European architecture. No feature of the houses mediates between the two continents. Africa was to be Europeanised as much as possible, a mission that mirrors in the houses' facades and design. Driving up from Hout Bay towards Cape Town's city centre, this scene of Europe in Africa becomes as intense as nowhere else in Cape Town. As much as the region's wine farms comprise a very dense example of the European desire to recreate itself in Africa, as

---

45   Source: http://capetowncarnival.com/sponsors/.

much they are secluded entities at the very niches of suburban life that are separated from the rest of the suburb's architecture and infrastructure. But Victoria Road, as one of the main roads connecting Cape Town, bears a different value and symbolism. It is a long enough stretch to be representative of the commonalities between the suburbs, architecturally and socially.

As the density of houses increases from Bakoven onwards, their luxury features expand to swimming pool balconies, elaborately fashioned gateways, surrounding private palm trees, and the branding of luxury apartment blocks and villas with European names. The naming meshes with the street names departing off Victoria Road that range from Houghton Road, to Van Kampz Street, to Berkley Road. The building's names weave into these imaginaries of a European coastal town. They strengthen the Europeanising effort at the same time as they sketch the decisiveness with which it is fulfilled. Brighton Court, Sonnekus, Primi Sea Castle, Luna Blanca, La Corniche, The Bloemfontein, P Casa, Villa Del Capo, Dunmore Apartments, Aquarius, Villa La Perla - have become social objects that make a specific statement about the past and the present. The houses and their names perform Europeanity. They represent the embodiment of the idyll that cannot be created without pasting Europe onto the alien soil. And in case the names are not highly European, they play with words that emphasise the idyllic and romantic features of Europe in Africa. From Bakoven Sunsets to White Cliffs, up to Oceana Residence, all these names bring Europeanity to perfection.

Still driving north towards Cape Town city centre, the naming intensifies the moment Victoria Road becomes Queens Road, which then merges into Beach Road. At this point, Sea Point has just unhitched Bantry Bay, and one luxury apartment block after the other competes to have the better European name. Costa del Sol, Shoreham, Worcester, Winchester Mansions, Norfolk House, Atheneum, Knightsbridge, Bordeaux, La Camargue, Riviera Suites, Lido Court, Costa Brava, Queensberry Court – most of these buildings have been built in the late 1970s, the 1980s and the 1990s. Their names borrow from small towns in the United Kingdom, to residential districts in London, coastal enclaves in Spain, French cities and regions, and ancient Greek heritage monuments, amongst others. To name the buildings in this way is to rename the land and hence to change the city's scenery, a powerful ideological exercise to appropriate and claim it. These are words that float amidst the space, reconfirming Europe as the starting point of everything that would be built and created. Hence, as much as they represent an archive, they also appropriate the future of the space, establishing how it can be envisioned. Ngugi wa Thiong'o describes this procedure as the erasure of memory through naming.[46] It appropriates the future through framing how the city can be imagined and through discursively presenting the city with words for legitimate imaginaries.

Africa and the peoples that have been enslaved, forcibly removed, and dispossessed, have been hidden away behind these architectures of erasure and their ornaments. At the same time as these architectures erase, they are also exhibits of what is made absent, exhibits of a lost world. The appropriation of the land and the project of familiarising it to the degree of indistinguishability from an idea of European homeland, is also a project of the alienation and removal of the African subject from the aesthetic scenery. Conquest is being restored architecturally, aesthetically, and spatially. Through the architecture, spatial engineering, aesthetics, and the names given, the European vision of how to recreate oneself has been steadily manifested in the cityscape and therefore, in the ways its inhabitants imagine how a stable, profitable, liveable, and valuable city must appear. The colonising mission must therefore be seen not only as the colonisation of land, but also of aesthetics and imagination. Victoria Road and Beach Road hold such a heavy dose of the imprint of Europe, that it makes it seem as if all other Europeanising surface has expanded from here. No other place in Cape Town delivers as much symbolic imagery of and in favour of Europeanity as these two roads. Their message is one of erasure, materially and discursively, of the past, as well as of the present. Notions such as a progressive, harmonic, and romantic settler society become discursively framed through this setting of space, architecture, and aesthetics. Memorialisation of the past thus becomes manipulated not only through silencing processes, but also through this spatial and aesthetic frame. The city speaks to the memories of its inhabitants. In this dialogue, Europe in Africa is underlaid with all possible positive connotations.

The conception of buildings and spatial design represents not only the actual physicality of wealth, but also the very sphere these conceptions are guarding against. As the buildings harmonise with each other, they perform exclusion. In drawing from romantic and nostalgic images of Europe, meaning is applied to the past of the space, its past is constructed through the exclusion of the realities the space was developed in. In a conversation, Sara Abbas emphasised that they represent "also specifically bourgeois images, so

---

46   Wa Thiong'o, Ngugi in several speeches. Cf. speech in Cape Town. March 3, 2017.

this is an imagination that sees the European ideal in wealth and status and empire, and erases working-class European aesthetics and imagery, too."[47]

Deprived of its history of displacement and exploitation, the space remains untroubled by questions of belonging and power. The buildings and their names triumph over the bays and the ocean, demonstrating that the way the past is represented was chosen purposefully to set signs. The spatial, aesthetic, and architectural composition transmits a clear statement about the history of the space. The buildings physically isolate the inhabitants of the Cape Flats and other working-class areas. Those are created as non-belongers to the space, alienated through their own exclusion and that of their past. Their perspectives have been written out of the historical narrative that manifests itself through the conceptual design of the space. This erasure creates them not only as non-belongers, but it pretends their non-existence, whereas it is at the same time a very stylised silencing that hides behind fashion, leisure, and romanticism. The historical and social meanings Victoria Road and Beach Road are underlaid with mirror this erasure. And as much as this erasure, this illusion of the non-existence of those who are unwelcome in the space has been socially constructed, as much it has become a material reality that reproduces segregated city space and unequal living conditions. Segregation and inequality have become an unquestioned part of the elite's identity, with manipulated representations of the past delivering the necessary ground for rationalisation. Self-assertion is negotiated against the loss of memory of those oppressed and excluded, and against constructed memories of progress, brave explorers and pioneers. The power to maintain this position of denial and illusion reflects in the everyday performance of the buildings and their names and the spatial concept they are built upon. The buildings have become a metaphoric body. This engineered sterilisation helps to subvert the lived realities of the excluded within that contained zone.

Here come the limits of suburbs that swim in this limbo of a sterilised past and present, because every protected space will have to face its unprotected counterpart wherever there is the opportunity for confrontation. The dominant discourse on crime totally erases this fundamental aspect of the criminal event and drives the focus from the socio-historic constellation of the suburbs to a constructed morality in which township and other working-class residents are portrayed as lazy, deceitful, and ruthless cadgers. The

---

47   Abbas, Sara. Conversation on September 2, 2017.

urban practice of exclusion does not become problematised. Crime as a confrontation with the elite's ignorance is not spoken of. Europeanity pictured in the discursive ornaments of suburbia perpetually reconfirms itself through this discourse. The buildings, their spatial arrangement and their names are a physical translation of this reconfirmation and the historical claims of right to the land. The desire to establish a vertical power relation to the displaced and dispossessed must be read against this historical discourse whose architecture has become a main pillar of its maintenance.

Fourth coordinate: Imizamo Yethu

Image by Johnny Miller/ Unequalscenes

Before Victoria Road ends at Hout Bay harbour, it splits into two, with one branch of it running straight into the informal settlement Imizamo Yethu. In as much as the buildings and the spatial logic of Victoria Road represent the architecture that has been part of the historical discourse of rightful conquest, so can Imizamo Yethu be seen as an example of what has been factored out of the design that the discourse manufactured. The view from above unveils the details of the difference between the suburb and the informal settlement.

Whereas the suburb is a green oasis with uncountable trees surrounding its well protected houses, Imizamo Yethu is built on gravel, with barely 20 trees lining its roads. Most eye-catching is the difference in colour. Hout Bay gleams green and lush and Imizamo Yethu's reddish brown reflects the dusty dryness that it has to withstand, since it is enclosed by the suburb's trees, buildings and posh streets and thus rendered an isolated enclave provided with a few entrances – a space that is supposed to remain as it is. The trees are also set as the dividing line between suburb and settlement, even though if one were to throw a stone from Imizamo Yethu's north-eastern border aimed at the suburb, it might hit one of the swimming pools that many houses feature. The contrast between the houses on Victoria Road and the rest of the suburb, and the structures in Imizamo Yethu, has been normalised historically. Informal settlements and townships are where South Africa's working-class / low-income residents / "the people" live. The way domestic workers undertake to get to the houses on Victoria Road and Beach Road is the same way they take to get back home. The buildings with their European names are their spaces of work, not of social activity and belonging. This relation remained untroubled in the postapartheid, but in the absorption of the romantic and idyllic picture of the architectures of power and conquest, the scenery of Imizamo Yethu forms a disrupting space, something that dazzles in the eye of the beholder, until one withdraws one's gaze.

I have seen no other place in Cape Town where an image becomes so abruptly interrupted, where the idyllic world becomes so visually unsettled. In the middle of this contrast rolls in the red double-decker tourist bus from whose upper deck tourists stare at the informal settlement and its residents. The bus takes a left at the circle and drives into Imizamo Yethu, to then stop at its very beginning for the bus driver or the tour leader to explain, "Here we are at an informal settlement. The settlement counts round 35,000 inhabitants...".

The dominant touristic imagination about how 'poor people' live is being offered as a live comparison. Common-sense understandings of how an informal settlement is supposed to look like are being re-injected into the middle and upper-class narrative of 'poor people's life'. The tour has not been organised to reposition the receiver's thinking and perception of the city and the distribution of space. It also does not contribute to the creation of a public discussion about the binary of informal settlement and suburb or at least ways of critically viewing the space. The history of the political setting that produced this binary is also not spoken of. No alternative approach towards the encounter between tourists and residents is thought of. In between this silence, the tourists' cameras click on. The scene of poverty now turns into a photographic subject. The photo-taking is a way of capturing and reproducing tourist imagination about 'poor people's life', to be able to exhibit its outcome in their private spaces, pinned to the fridge or other places of display in their homes, to reassure themselves that they have also visited sites of poverty and not only of leisure when they were in Cape Town. Or, to be able to utter that famous sentence, "When I was in South Africa, I also visited a township". The photographs narrate the desire to express this fulfilling experience. By entering the informal settlement, an illusion of a direct relationship with those parts of Cape Town that have been inaccessible, crime-ridden places of potential danger - too dangerous to enter before, becomes created. Now they can view the space from above, looking down from a safe and stable position. This is the frame many working-class communities have been set up with, when middle or upper-class adventurists aim at them as they would aim at an undiscovered curiosity, romanticising their subjects and hunting 'authentic' images of shack dwellers life or of what they imagine as essential Africa.

How much this voyeurism derives from a position of power is clear. This position does also explain why the bus route is at the same time a trajectory of legitimisation. The incorporation of imagery of life, and with it the romanticisation of life in informal settlements and townships has become hegemonic narrative that is also discernible from the many township tours that different tour operators offer and the uncountable postcards that portray township life as a way of presenting authentic parts of South Africa. Township tours and postcards are set to appropriate inequality discursively, to paste townships and informal settlements into that very hegemonic narrative and to rearticulate and recreate them as objects of discourse in an accommodating image. The tourism industry has thus become a discursive economy that defines ways of seeing and perceiving South Africa. In the setting of the bus stopping in Imizamo Yethu, no questions about the possibility of changing the living conditions of the settlement's residents are asked, not by the tourists, not by the bus driver and not by the tour guide. As the bus passes Hout Bay harbor and its surrounding villas, and as it stops at its next destination that is Imizamo Yethu, the gaze of the tourists has a confirmative, reinforcing function. Rendered an exhibit of urban poverty, steadiness and inflexibility become inscribed on the settlement. The object that becomes exhibited is not supposed to change.

Through driving from Hout Bay into Imizamo Yethu and presenting the different living conditions, the bus becomes a factor in re-segregating the space and thus, part of the structure that dominates Imizamo Yethu's landscape and the landscape preceding it. Within these landscapes, Imizamo Yethu has a specific socio-economic role that the tourists' gaze is reaffirming. The fact that turning Imizamo Yethu into an exhibit is possible, makes the tourist bus a key characteristic of the space. It is through understanding the meaning of the bus driving into Imizamo Yethu that the way the informal settlement relates to its outside can be understood. Whereas Imizamo Yethu's residents occupy its space physically, another form of occupation is taking place simultaneously. It is the occupation of an imaginary, a clear idea of the way the socio-spatial should be constructed. The idea of the elites of where the working class is supposed to live manifests in the act of turning Imizamo Yethu into a tourist destination. This condition forms a link to the larger understanding of the position of the township and informal settlement and the way these spaces are thought of on a political level. Within the sphere between Imizamo Yethu and Hout Bay, the struggles of Imizamo Yethu's residents do not occupy any space, or at least not visibly. Returning from work, they are expected to disappear into the streets and structures of the settlement, the only space that is really allocated to them. Their subjectivities are not supposed to become inscribed on the landscape outside the settlement and not be narrated in any other way.

The binary of Hout Bay and Imizamo Yethu shows that a combination of districts does not necessarily represent a city as a socio-geographic unit. It requires certain social ingredients for single districts to coalesce into one city. Part of that composition must be fluidity of the boundaries in between and a brisk and equal interaction between the districts. In Cape Town, spaces like Imizamo Yethu form fully separated units that are isolated from the wealthy suburbs and middle-class districts, even though they stand in the immediate vicinity. And however networked the inside of a settlement is, until now, it hasn't been able to form a challenge towards the constellation of segregated city space it is built into. This I suggest is also readable from the look on the face of residents of Imizamo Yethu the moment the bus stops in front of them. This is not to suggest that township and informal settlement residents cannot also be subjects of resistance. How much this is possible we have seen in chapter two of this work, when we delved into how residents struggle against their forced eviction from their homes. In the past three years, Imizamo Yethu residents have struggled uncompromisingly against the threat of relocation and especially against the lack of services after fires had destroyed parts of the settlement and killed several people. During the protests, several residents were killed (see Appendix). But it means that the powerlessness towards the endurance of inequality, even if temporary, and towards the bareness in front of the tourists' eyes, reflects in the way the residents encounter the bus and its passengers.

The landscape underneath the visible remains untouched for the tourist who is unable to see beyond its surface and to reveal the inner world of the space. Once having entered the settlement, tourists imagine themselves to have penetrated the space, to have uncovered something knowable. But Imizamo Yethu's significance is not reducible to its built form. Its architecture and spatial order are not the end of what it tells. Social relations built on everyday modes of survival, creating new forms of collective living, and high amounts of creativity shape the socio-economic conditions of the informal settlement. The fact that these relations and structures remain impenetrable for the tourists and suburb residents preserves an entity Imizamo Yethu residents truly possess solely for themselves: their lives, which remain unseeable and untouchable for most outsiders. The meanings they give to their lives, their social interactions, the ways they fill their days, what they deem routine and what is extraordinary, the ways different people relate to each other, and the stories they have to tell - all remain in possession of the residents, not extractable and not removable. Public scrutiny is disabled. The exhibitable images that the tourists have come to possess can only be of parts of the space, not of people's subjectivities, their stories or anecdotes. This is self-inflicted as in this setting, the residents are rendered voiceless objects on display, exoticised and homogenised to the category of 'informal settlement residents', and especially, to the category of 'the poor'. The tourists have come to see real human subjects and the truth about their lives, but what they get is only a scene, mostly empty of any mutual encounters between them and the residents. Imizamo Yethu, as the other thousands of informal settlements and townships, remains to narrate itself, its struggles, its inappropriable memories and visions for the future.

Fifth coordinate: Main Library, University of Stellenbosch

My first physical encounter with South Africa was the encounter with the town of Stellenbosch. I went there as an exchange student during my master's studies. The small university town, situated in the middle of the Cape Winelands - the second-most popular image in tourist brochures after Table Mountain - is

Left: Enwrapped Cecil Rhodes statue at the University of Cape Town Campus - Image by Rhodes Must Fall student's movement (March 2015). Right: Students' gathering at University of Stellenbosch's main library - Image by Open Stellenbosch student's movement (April 2015)

famous as one of the most, if not the most, segregated town in South Africa. Holding a showpiece status in the Afrikaner nationalist narrative, it reflects the desire for seclusion during apartheid by the powerful elite, away from the turmoil around transitions to new orders. The negotiation of a new identity after apartheid, a process many spaces of the postapartheid went through, does not mean that their transformation and in parts reinvention has made them more equal spaces. In this process, Stellenbosch has insisted to remain the same. In the introduction to this study, I used the *Coca-Cola* signs of the massive Khayelitsha township as a metaphor to explain how my perception of the Rainbow-Nation discourse became interrupted at the very first moment of entering South Africa. One of the reasons why driving past Khayelitsha by the university's shuttle car was an interruption of that dominant discourse, is an aggressive spatial paradox that intimidates body and mind immediately. The airport can be approached by two roads: Borcherds[48] Quarry Road and the N2

---

48   From P.B. Borcherds, assistant secretary of an "expedition" from Cape Town to Lattakoe in 1802; commissioner and resident magistrate of the Cape 1834-1852, later chairman of the Central Road Board of the Cape Colony. Cf.: P.B. Borcherds: *An Auto-Biographical Memoir*. Cape Town 1861; Van Riebeeck Society Cape Town: *William Somerville's Narrative of His Journey to the Eastern Cape Frontier and to Lattakoe 1799 – 1802*. Cape Town

Highway – its other official name: "Settlers Way". One end of this road leads directly into Cape Town, passing Bonteheuwel, Langa township, and Langa's Joe Slovo settlement, and the other end leads over 2000 kilometers south-east, through the Western Cape province to the Eastern Cape, through the Eastern Cape to KwaZulu Natal, and finally, arriving at Mpumalanga province, ending in Ermelo, close to the borders with Swaziland and Mozambique. Twenty kilometres right at the beginning of this N2 Highway (that leads from Cape Town International Airport all the way to Mpumalanga), lies Stellenbosch, or rather, the exit to Stellenbosch.

After arriving at Stellenbosch from its 'neat' side, moving through the town, walking its streets onto its university campus, entering its university department buildings, institutes, alleys, gardens, river walks, small corridors, church squares, markets, sports clubs, and dormitories – the first question that came to my mind was: "What the hell is going on here?"

The wealthy part of town claims the neatness and organisation of the past and projects it into the future. Each beautiful building and tree perform this obsession of securing the past. Each street repeats the narrative of the previous one, with a specific insistence to uphold the picture of the perfect idyll. The town's cafés and restaurants have all been built with romantic features in styles like farmhouse, rustic, or more vintage designs that pretend to be material remnants of the past and that melt into the image of an ideal world of cosiness and pleasure. But everyone who has been to Stellenbosch knows about the idyllic town and what it wants to surgically remove from itself: the townships Kayamandi and Cloetesville, the very spaces that do not fit into the story Stellenbosch wants to tell. The whole town performs as if it has always been in that space or as if it has been built peacefully and in harmony with its environment. No signs exist that point to the forced removals of Khoikhoi people that followed the establishment of farms by settlers, through which so many tragedies were made, or of the forced and indentured labour that was used to build the town.[49] To highlight the past of the town and its surrounding farms would call into question the present and consequential debates about the socio-economic realities the town is embedded in, something that must be avoided if the distribution of wealth remains as it is.

1979: pp.6-7; Mc-Call Theal, George: *History of South Africa Since September 1795*. First published in Cape Town 1908. Cambridge 2010: pp.44-45.

49   Cf. Du Toit, André and Giliomee, Hermann: *Afrikaner Political Thought: Analysis and Documents – Volume One: 1780-1850*. Cape Town 1983: p.35.

Inequality becomes highly visible in the segregative constellation of city centre, suburbs, surrounding townships and informal settlements and at the same time, in the different university departments, their structures of personnel, the university dormitories, the sports clubs, the divided social life of the town that follows clear racial lines, and the historical inequalities that determines the students' socio-economic backgrounds. The town has remained an exhibit of apartheid ideology. To understand apartheid spatial planning does not require a visualisation of the past. The past is on display in every corner of the town. Stellenbosch is still a tale of two towns. Segregated space has not only been reproduced through the perpetuation of the specific distribution of wealth, but also in the way the university relates to the town and its inhabitants. Security guards are placed on the main streets surrounding the campus. They ensure that students can walk home safely without being disturbed, not even by a person who would ask them for money. In regulating the space, the guards are the main icons of safety in the town, because despite all the tensions and polarisation that inequality brings with it, Stellenbosch needs to maintain that it is a safe place if it wants to uphold its image. The guards are therefore also escorting the idea of the idyll. The tensions and polarised social positions might also be the reason why the town possesses no real public space in which residents can build collectivity and interact with each other outside frameworks of work and duty. The town is built for every social class to live in its own parallel world, walking past each other, without having to engage or explain anything to each other. Apartheid had always also been about the erasure of any common ground between the *racial* groups it distinguished. In Stellenbosch, nothing has been done to alter the architectures of division that were fabricated. This does not exclusively apply to Stellenbosch. As I pointed out above, many spaces in the postapartheid remain highly divided. But because Stellenbosch insists on safeguarding the idyll, a romantic place where residents live in harmony with each other, what is erased becomes even more striking.

The university's library is situated in the central part of the main campus. Around it, security guards move in a circle, making me ask myself what exactly they are guarding against. Standing on top of the stairs that lead down to the library, I wonder why books need to sit underground, in a library without daylight or any other welcoming element. It seems like a metaphor for the repression of questions never asked and of avowals never made. The library's mechanical and impersonal interior adds to this perception. Walking down the stairs and looking up from the library's entrance door, the university campus appears massive, expanding to besiege the town and showing off with its powerful and unshakable structures and social position. The metanarrative of stability and resoluteness of the town is backed by this performance of the university's architecture.

Twelve years ago, the stairs leading down to the library became also the place of an intrinsically anecdotal scene. A security guard had rolled a newspaper and was hitting a visibly homeless or poor person, who had come to campus to ask students for money. While the guard was hitting the man, groups of students who sat on different spots of the stairs started laughing. The loud laughter and giggling was accompanied by a sharp voyeurism, a gaze that was interspersed with silence and arrogance at the same time. Being confused with how to classify the laughter, as an exercise of power or as a nervous manifestation of insecurity and perplexity, I truly wanted to know how it would be possible to turn that laughter and silence upside down.

The first set of questions that came to my mind were reproachful. How could a whole town uphold a parallel world of strongly visible wealth and the portrayal of a picturesque idyllic world, a world of wine farms, of *Cape Dutch* architectured houses with their rounded gables and whitewashed walls, of green streets picturing Oak, River Red Gum and Bottle Brush trees; that had no connections to the workers and unemployed of the farms and neighbouring townships except for the work of the workers itself? And since students represent a significant part of the population of any university town, how come there were no protests or organising around questions of ongoing segregation? And if not protest or concrete political organisation, must there not be debates that address those questions? And where were the lecturers? Would they address socioeconomic relations in Stellenbosch in their seminars and lectures? The second set of questions addressed more the practical. How is it possible to organise against that silence and laughter? If that silence was historical and inscribed into the logic of Stellenbosch student life in the sense of students having gotten used to condoning and not striking back at injustice and the normalisation of power, how could this silence be encountered and challenged? Would enough people come together to work against it collectively? What could the first steps be of a joint action? A counter-narrative of the town, the university, and how they relate to the inhabitants of Stellenbosch and to questions of historical inequality needed to be produced. The town and university had to be turned into transit spaces in which all social structures and positions could be suspended and new ones formed. As silence was embedded in the town's structures institutionally, it was clear that any initiative had to come from those who had endured that silence for so long and thus from the marginalised and excluded themselves.

Walking the streets from one of the students' residencies in Banghoek Road, crossing over towards the centre of town via Bosman Road and taking a right into Victoria Street, I was thinking of the many students who saw themselves socially and economically alienated and who had to negotiate university life every day anew. Then, feeling alienated myself, although from a much more privileged, middle-class position, my mind would not stop here but think in circles. Township residents and farm workers – the most subaltern in that relationship as they had to endure one of the most unequal urban conditions in the world that excludes a majority of the population from any access to better life – were straying and alternating in my mind with the heaviness of Stellenbosch's performance.

The town was a portrayal of silence in its most obvious architectural, spatial, and academic manifestation. As much as the visibility of that silence was striking, nothing had seemingly changed when I went back in 2011, nor in 2012, 2013, 2014, or the beginning of 2015. But looking at the town, it was clear that it was impossible for it to stay like that. Even though the power relations of town and university seemed very much set in stone, one prediction would pop up regularly: something is going to happen. This prediction proved true. After the *Rhodes Must Fall* movement started in March 2015 at the University of Cape Town (UCT), Stellenbosch students joined the movement and organised themselves as *Open Stellenbosch*. The movement vowed to fight against white supremacy, institutional racism, and unequal access to education. Its first achievement was the official removal of Cecil Rhodes's statue from the campus of the University of Cape Town (UCT), which followed many protests and debates. The movement then reorganised itself as *Fees Must Fall*, bringing together students from Stellenbosch, UCT, University of the Western Cape (UWC), and Cape Peninsula University of Technology (CPUT), amongst other universities in other provinces. It was breath-taking to follow up the student movement and the simultaneous farm workers' strikes, since the years prior had made Stellenbosch appear as a forgotten town, in which no questions concerning social justice would be raised.

The complicity of academic research projects in the perpetuation of this condition complicated that silence and made it less tangible. One and a half kilometres away from Stellenbosch's centre, Kayamandi and Cloetesville townships had been constituted as the town's historical counterparts. Their people who were either unemployed or employed as domestic workers, cleaning personnel, road construction workers, traffic workers, shop assistants, scavengers, garbage collectors, security guards, drivers, transport workers, taxi drivers, etc., were living a life under spatial and economic segregation with no prospects for an unsettling of those conditions. Even more marginalised and economically oppressed were the farm workers, who continue to live and work on the prestigious wine farms for salaries that will never allow them to leave or to imagine improved living and working conditions for their children. The township's residents and farm workers were rarely subjects of claims and coalitions for social justice, yet they were often the subjects of academic research. Psychologists, sociologists, anthropologists, just to name some launched projects to zoom in on living conditions in Kayamandi, Cloetesville, and on the farms, reaching from the particularities of the spaces to universalising statements about township and farm workers' lives, to then formulate their research outcomes in academic papers and theses.[50] I remember a conversation with Sabelo Mcinziba in which he argued: "White people should stay away from our townships. I am sick and tired of students that want to know how the toilet and electricity systems in townships are functioning."[51] The *exotic* township resident and farm worker, whose life is expected to be easy to examine, open for any scientific inquiry, is again being narrated by externals who have come to make profit, even if that profit is not of short-term material gain. Just as the business sector and politicians continue their development plans that exclude township residents and farm workers from any kind of participation in shaping their futures, academic research defines funded work frames through which the needs and lacks of its subject of study become determined, without rethinking what self-determined collaboration of residents and workers with researchers could possibly mean. In this vein, competition and rivalry between academics has become the most striking example of how neoliberalism's values are adopted uncritically, even though the subjects of research are the very direct sufferers of that same mode of economic production, policy making, epistemology, and knowledge production.

---

50   No reference to particular academic works is made, as the aim of this article is not to focus on specific research projects but to point to a general approach in the humanities. But searching the key word "Kayamandi" or "Farmworkers Stellenbosch" in a search engine for academic journals will offer more specific insight into the titles and work frames under which projects become realised.

51   Mcinziba, Sabelo. Conversation on March 9, 2014.

Conclusion

In this chapter, the different angles and perspectives from which the city spaces were analysed have facilitated an x-ray of the city, a zooming in on the spaces, their functions, but also on their suppressed histories that lie underneath and still have to be recovered. Without claiming to have uncovered all unequal spaces of Cape Town and Stellenbosch, this chapter was an attempt to write the city differently. Without allowing for the different perspectives to evolve and to produce their very own analysis, it would have been impossible to reveal the paradoxes of the spaces. How else could it have been possible to explain how the mountain is used to practically and psychologically support the secludedness of the suburbs, while at the same time showing how it is a sphere that generates fear and insecurity for the middle and upper classes? My aim was to show how, as much as the suburbs' security is unthinkable without the mountain, the mountain is unthinkable without that fear.

In regard to the brutal aspect of nature I have pointed to, this chapter has come to the conclusion that a discourse is needed that confronts two issues. One is the alienation of low-income inhabitants or "the people" from natural landscape, the ways in which it is experienced psycho-socially and psycho-geographically[52], and ultimately its re-personalisation. The other is the dominant discourse on the use of nature, propagated by institutions like the World Bank, that treats natural landscape as a market and its use as a mere source of income and/or recreation.[53] A possible future discussion about the democratisation of the natural landscape should not fall into these categories and epistemology, but urge the re-imagining and re-shaping of the relationship between people and nature along lines that are reciprocal and re-creative.

Later, in viewing the city from Cape Town's abandoned quarries, the silencing of who extracted the stone and built the city unfolded. In the entire city, no public sign about slavery at the Cape exists, while at the same time, the big figures of colonialism as well as colonial engineers are memorialised. Not only are the slaves not spoken of, but also the quarries themselves. Most quarries whose stone served to build the city are not retraceable anymore,

---

52   Cf. Psychogeography. For example: Debord, Guy: *Psychogeography – History and Techniques*; Janicijevic, Aleksandar: *Psychogeography Now - Window to the Urban Future*. in: urbansquares.com.
53   Cf. Aylward, Bruce A. and Lutz, Ernst (eds.): *Nature Tourism, Conservation, and Development in Kwazulu-Natal, South Africa*. Washington 2003 (World Bank Publication).

not in the archives and not in any public account. With their disappearance from public knowledge, the forced labourers who worked them disappear too. Through this discursive practice of silencing the past, the links between forced labour in the colonial past and the living conditions of the socio-economically marginalised of today become erased. Inequality as a historically produced condition remains unspoken of. The dead of the quarries and the living of today are prevented to being put into context.

Victoria Road performs a different kind of erasure. The architectures of space and the names of the buildings reconfirm the power relations between suburbs and townships. Power is not only a hierarchical relation, it also becomes stylised and fashioned in a certain way. Europeanity is the embodiment of the elite's desire to reconfirm and endorse itself and to perform their claim of a rightful position – in regard to both history and the present. This I suggest is what Khanyisile Mintho Mbongwa points at when she says: "the only history you allow is the one I see my body defeated and dead… no image of me celebrated… you are always asking me to die". Victoria Road and Beach Road mirror this show of force and the advertising of settlerism as a romantic and just project. In this vein, to own the land and to transform it into new landscapes is to rename the land, which is why the naming of the buildings is not only a social act of a specific social group, but a discursive practice and an exercise of power that manufactures the dominant narrative of the suburbs.

The turning of Imizamo Yethu into a tourist attraction is the logical counter piece of this discursive setting. Imizamo Yethu is not supposed to change. As no critique towards inequality is being raised, the tourist bus driving into the informal settlement presents the distribution of wealth between Imizamo Yethu and Hout Bay as a static condition. The unequal landscape becomes normalised and colonial and apartheid ethnographic logics persist. The only public attention spaces like Imizamo Yethu receive, is when the tourist's gaze has come to exoticise their residents and to fulfil the tourist urge for adventurism and for memories of a troubled space. The regimes of thought that legitimised apartheid engineering are strongly embedded in this gaze. It might go too far to say that this gaze and the laughter at the stairs leading down to the University of Stellenbosch's main library are linked. But it is a discursive condition that enables the tourist bus driving into Imizamo Yethu and the laughter at the stairs. It is inequality that has become affirmed so that it can constantly establish itself in every corner of the urban. It is a state that remains unchallenged and is at the same time omnipresent. This omnipresence normalises and reconfirms apartheid regimes of thought in relation to how city spaces become imagined and what residents expect from them. Until today, a security guard hitting a visibly poor person is normal; informal settlements being exhibited to satisfy the tourist's voracity for adventure is normal; silencing slave histories of the city is normal; to stretch that silence and placard the city with nostalgia and admiration for Europe is normal. It is this normality that maintains the unequal landscapes and architectures of division of the city.

Chapter five

Intervention through art – Performing is making visible

Introduction

In this chapter, I will use the performative archive as a source of study and analysis. Before I start to elaborate the concept of political intervention through art, I will explain, how I see the role of social movements related to housing in this book and why I choose to study performative art, rather than the related movements.

South Africa is unthinkable without the many manifestations, strikes, and road blockades the different social movements, workers, farmers, shack dwellers, students, etc. organise on an everyday basis. Within the immediate struggle of the people affected against forced eviction, different campaigns and movements against evictions and urban development policies have been initiated. The most famous example is the shack dwellers movement Abahlali baseMjondolo that is predominantly active in Durban and other parts of KwaZulu Natal province. Since its initiation, its members are being punished, murdered, and criminalised for the political challenge they present as an effective and organised social movement. They continuously face being killed in demonstrations or being assassinated, as was/is the case particularly during the first months of the year 2013 and the first half of 2017.[1] In order to repress their political gatherings, the national, provincial, and city

---

[1] Cf. Pithouse, Richard: *Outcry Over Oppression in Cato Crest*. in: Rhodes University publications. October 5, 2013; Gibson, Nigel: *Fanonian Practices in South Africa – From Steve Biko to Abahlali*. Scottsville 2011; pp.192-193; Abahlali baseMjondolo article: *The Criminalisation of the Poor*. February 25, 2011. Source: http://abahlali.org/node/7820/; Langford, Malcom and Kahanovitz, Steve: *South Africa: Rethinking Enforcement Narratives*. in: Langford, Malcom; Rodriguez-Graviato, César and Rossi, Julieta (eds.): *Social Rights Judgments and the Politics of Compliance: Making it Stick*. Cambridge 2017.

governments use a law that was passed by the apartheid regime in 1993. *The Regulation of Public Gatherings Act* secures the prevention, banning, and brutal disruption of demonstrations that the governments values as intolerable. After having visited members of the shack dwellers movement, Depelchin describes: "Here were people who, living among the poorest of the poor, were standing up and insisting on being treated with respect and dignity, as called for by the South African constitution, but who, strangely, were being charged, beaten up and arrested by the police as though they were criminals. How could a police force, under the political leadership of the ANC, behave in a way that is reminiscent of the apartheid police?"[2]

In the Housing Assembly, residents of different parts of the Cape Flats have come together to protest for dignified housing and against exclusion and marginalisation. They criticise the concept, implementation, and distribution of RDP houses (Reconstruction and Development Programme Houses) and try to illuminate why the working class has been neglected systematically.[3] Another younger example is the Reclaim the City campaign that was launched in February 2016 in Cape Town. Domestic workers and other low-income residents have come together to struggle against forced evictions, forced relocations to Temporary Relocation Areas, and for social housing in Cape Town's suburbs that have remained racialised sites of exclusion and segregation.

Several scholars have tried to make sense of the movements and their demands. Anna Selmeczi's work for example, is a very meaningful engagement with Abahlali that tells a lot about how the movement organises itself, about its struggles and oppression.[4] In addition, the social movements themselves describe and analyse their work on their websites. One only has to browse for a few minutes and will find many articles on the movements' goals, strategies, methods, and contents.

This adequate representation of the social movements that struggle for dignified housing, against forced eviction and relocation and for an inclusive city, made me think of the analysis of social expressions and interventions that engage the city through a different tool. What I would like to engage with in this last chapter of the study of forced evictions and criminalisation is

---

2   Depelchin, Jacques: *Reclaiming African History*. Cape Town 2011: p.44.
3   Cf. Matlawe, Kenneth: *Housing Assembly and the Decent Housing for All Campaign*. Housing Assembly article. April 11, 2017.
4   Cf. for example Selmeczi, Anna: *Abahlali's Vocal Politics of Proximity: Speaking, Suffering and Political Subjectivization*. in: Journal of Asian and African Studies. October 2012. Volume 47: pp.465-481.

something very unique to Cape Town and maybe some other cities in the postcolony. As in the previous chapter, I will change my perspective and method of analysis. In this chapter, I turn my attention to performative art interventions, which challenge forced eviction and practices of urban development that perpetuate inequality and segregation. I treat performance art and other artistic production in two ways. Firstly, as a direct social and political response to long-term unequal politico-economic conditions and secondly as a method of processing and digesting the pain, trauma and anger that humiliation and inequality generate. How does art attempt to inhabit the spaces of inequality? As suggested by V.Y. Mudimbe, I read the attempt of finding expression through creative forms as literary and visual text[5], or, as an archive, and its outputs as statements inside the archive, because I treat its operations as performative or other artistic formations of meaning-making that can be thought through and read as any other oral or written statement and thus as a valid source of study. As Diana Taylor puts it, it is to "take seriously the repertoire of embodied practices as an important system of knowing and transmitting knowledge" and "to expand what we understand as 'knowledge'".[6]

One of the aims of this chapter is further to elaborate on the power of arts to undo and disrupt the seamlessness of biopolitics. How this takes place, I will elaborate on later. In this introduction, I would like to prepare the reader to engage with the analysis of the artworks and the elaboration of this idea. The notion is that performance can be both, self-reflexive as a means to deal with the artist's own location inside the constellation of domination and subjugation, as well as a reflection of the relations of power within the social outside. As elaborated in chapter three, self-location and social outside have a reciprocal relationship through which they decisively affect the physical body. Art as a method of intervention bears the ability to shift visibility and audibility. There are many examples of artists and arts collectives in the greater Cape Town area who use their work to intervene in processes of silencing, one-sided media coverage, and dominant city, provincial, state and business sector discourses. Interventionist art has the potential to trigger the senses of its interlocutor in a different way than written text or oral speeches. Jacques

---

5   Cf. Mudimbe, V.Y.: Reprende: *Enunciations and Strategies in Contemporary African Arts.* in: Oguibe, Olu and Enwezor, Okwui (eds): *Reading the Contemporary: African Art from Theory to the Marketplace.* London 1999: p.32.
6   Taylor, Diana: *The Archive and the Repertoire – Performing Cultural Memory in the Americas.* Durham 2003: p.26,16.

Rancière speaks about this relationship of art and its interlocutors, when he argues about the social regulation of the senses, essentially the partitioning and distribution of the senses. Rancière states:

> "Politics revolves around what is seen and what can be said about it, around who has the ability to see and the talent to speak, around the properties of spaces and the possibilities of time. It is on the basis of this primary aesthetics that it is possible to raise the question of 'aesthetic practices' as I understand them, that is forms of visibility that disclose artistic practices, the place they occupy, what they 'do' or 'make' from the standpoint of what is common to the community. Artistic practices are 'ways of doing and making' that intervene in the general distribution of ways of doing and making as well as in the relationships they maintain to modes of being and forms of visibility.... The arts only ever lend to projects of domination or emancipation what they are able to lend to them, that is to say, quite simply, what they have in common with them: bodily positions and movements, functions of speech, the parcelling out of the visible and the invisible. Furthermore, the autonomy they can enjoy or the subversion they can claim credit for rest on the same foundation."[7]

The notions of art as "literary and visual text" and thus as an archive as Mudimbe puts it; or as a "repertoire of embodied practices" that forms a system of knowledge as Taylor phrases it; or as a political "aesthetic practice" as Rancière conceptualises it, complement one another. All three concepts helped me to conceptualise what I was perceiving when looking at the artworks.

The intention here is not to deliver a critique of the works analysed, but to use them as evidence for the existence of a specific politico-economic violence and to work with their contents as data that speaks of that violence.

Out of the many examples one finds on Cape Town's streets, on house walls, and in galleries, four art projects have shaped my own understanding of the cities, their laws and by-laws, their security units, the role of business sector, and decisions taken on provincial and municipal level. In the analysis of art projects in South Africa, I had to temporarily shift my focus from the greater Cape Town area and include one art project performed in Johannesburg. The reason for this is firstly that South African interventionist art

---

7   Rancière, Jacques: *The Politics of Aesthetics – The Distribution of the Sensible*. London 2013: pp. 8, 14.

is unthinkable without taking into account the many manifestations of art within the greater Johannesburg area, including Soweto. The second reason is that although forced eviction and criminalisation as a politico-economic practice becomes executed in all over South Africa and especially in South Africa's urban landscape, something relatively particular in terms of visibility and discursive setting of forced eviction is happening in Johannesburg: One of the security companies frequently deployed by the city of Johannesburg and by different branches of the business sector, the *Red Ant Security Relocation & Eviction Services (PTY) Ltd*, represents a quite specific approach towards forced eviction of residents from their homes. What that means, we will encounter in the analysis of the first art project in this chapter.

To give a short explanation of what the reader can expect, I included four different art projects - a work of a long-term arts collective located in the Western Cape; a video installation; a work that is composed of three art pieces; and a performance artwork by an artist in Johannesburg. Starting with the latter, I have chosen Steven Cohen's invasive performance in the middle of the forced eviction of *illegal* squatters in Newtown/Johannesburg, as my first example.

Steven Cohen – The Chandelier

Images of The Chandelier performance in Newtown/Johannesburg 2002 by John Hogg[8]

---

8   Images by Hogg, John: Chandelier by Steven Cohen. Squatter camp behind the Market Theatre in Johannesburg, South Africa. First published by Canadianstage.

Newtown/Johannesburg's city centre, close to Mandela Bridge, 2002: Security officers of the *Red Ant Security Relocation & Eviction Services (PTY) Ltd*,[9] engaged by the City of Johannesburg government, are busy evicting the residents of an informal settlement and confiscating their goods.

The artist uses his own body as the centre of the performance. His costume and make-up are highly aestheticised, exaggerated and shrill. With oscillating and vibrant movements and without the use of a continuous choreography composed beforehand, he paces between the shacks that are awaiting to be bulldozed, between the anxious residents and the uniformed security guards who are dressed in red, processing the violence that is registered in the manner the bodies of the residents and the guards relate to each other. The scene is composed of three different worlds, overlapping in this moment of confrontation.

As discussed in chapter three, most security guards hired by city governments, provincial governments, the free market, or public-private cooperations, live in townships themselves, without any perspective of improving their economic conditions. This makes the eviction a paradoxical situation, as the lives of guards and residents are profoundly intertwined. Consistent with this chaos of different lives and different roles that collide in this scene, Cohen's trajectories are not predetermined, nor is any structured framework discernible. At the same time, this does not imply formlessness. The spontaneity and uncertainty of what happens next inherent in the performance creates a form of its own. Whereas each of his movements fold into the next, the guards seem shocked and unsettled at the same time. While continuing their work of removing the residents' belongings from the shacks, they try to ignore this uncomfortable situation and pretend to not see the artist. This act of trying not to see, becomes part of the performance. The turning a blind eye of the guards represents a highly symbolic metaphor. This, the removing of belongings, and the pure presence of the guards itself, stage a performance of power that is omnipresent in the space.

At the other end of the performance, Cohen's semi-nude body represents both vulnerability that is offensively put out there, without it creating fear or insecurity, and the sacrificing of the body as the last possible instance of

---

9   The Red Ant Security Relocation & Eviction Company is a private security company that the City of Johannesburg government continuously engages for the execution of forced evictions of people from their homes. The grade of violence the security company exercises increased over the years. (see Epilogue).

opposition and accordingly, as the most radical method of taking a subject position and raising one's voice. Offense, here, means active disruption, towards the political and economic structures that favour the eviction and the space of class privilege Cohen comes from. The body is also central to the language the performance uses. The language of the body as the most possible intimate language penetrates every corner and the whole interior body of the space. Cohen is not performing to touch on the surface; he is concerned with the core of unequal power relations.

Although *illegal* squatters are in permanent pursuit of being able to rent in formal housing, forced eviction from the structures they created as home is what residents of informal settlements fear the most. It is this feared and at the same time familiar situation that Cohen has come to face and to defy. Even though it seems as he identifies deeply with the residents and their social position, it is true that in relation to the space and the residents, he appears detached or unanchored. To intervene means he has to surmount the insecurity this brings with it. As illustrated in chapter two, forced evictions have become routine in the everyday of urban life in South Africa and are no departure from the metropolitan norm. Cohen's performance is set to disrupt this normality that has created an aesthetics of its own – an aesthetics of normalised violence and fear. At the intersection of state force, the experience of loss and an artist's body contesting the whole situation and the discourse behind it with an intentionally stylised mode of articulation, collision is inevitable.

The chandelier that also lends the art piece its name is wrapped around the artist's body. I suggest that it symbolises the privileged bourgeoisie that the artist identifies as complicit in the present-day forced evictions and its victims being silenced, passively watching and affirming the neoliberal project of the city. Cohen pushes for encountering the city from this view above the informal settlement with its residents being evicted, which turns the site into a space of ruins, physically, but also of ruined identity and self-determination. This is not to argue that people lose their identity through the loss of their homes. But since one's ability to self-determination becomes so substantially shattered, one's identity and socialisation become target of insecurity and fear and thus have to be built almost anew.

The Christmas-tree ornaments decorating the chandelier evoke associations with "northern suburb privilege"[10] and the identity-enclaves based on numbness, consumption, ownership, perpetual beautification of the home, guarding belongings, and, as Frantz Fanon puts it, "aesthetic forms of respect for the status quo"[11], that come with uncritical privileged life. At the same time, the chandelier is also about illuminating and "bringing to light", as the subtitle of the performance tells us. The artist's intended hypervisibility stands in great contrast to the policies of invisibilising sites as the informal settlement and its residents that are inscribed as superfluous, degraded to the status of ghosts in the city. Highly alien to the atmosphere of the squatter camp, Cohen's body interferes with and disturbs the routine of the security guards in charge of the eviction.

The scene seals off the world outside and it seems as if only Cohen, the residents of the Newtown informal settlement and the security guards exist on the surface of the earth. But time does not halt. The guards continue to remove the residents' belongings from the shacks, preparing them for demolition. For Cohen, the performance is a political act and the position from which he speaks is accordingly politicised. In one of his interviews he explains: "In South Africa, everything is political. Even shit is political, because you have a toilet and there are many people who don't have a toilet. Everything is politicised, even space... And performance for me is about attacking the street and leaving the stage."[12] Through attacking the street and raising his body, he connects his own humanity to the humanity of the residents, becoming not *the* voice, but *a* voice inside the location of those who were denied speech and who are living a life under erasure.

Cohen's performance forces the audience to have an engagement with the effects of forced evictions through illuminating and visibilising the actual scene of eviction. In other words, Cohen's performance presses weight upon the ground of the happening that now has to be recognised, that now has to be spoken of. What makes it a radical approach is also its unilateral choice of its audience, who through the volume added to the event, are forced to recognise its message. In so doing, the performance disrupts the routine of

---

10   Bunn, David: *Art Johannesburg and Its Objects*. in: Nuttal, Sarah and Mbembe, Achille (eds.): *Johannesburg – The Elusive Metropolis*. Johannesburg 2008: p.165.
11   Fanon, Frantz: *The Wretched of the Earth*. New York 2004: p.3.
12   Cohen, Steve: Interview with arte. Source: https://vimeo.com/113489663.

evicting and destabilises the power relations between the security force and their targets of eviction.

The performer does not speak on behalf of the subjects located on the bottom of this relation of domination, rather he speaks for himself. Knowing that the residents possess other means to generate social power, he stresses the need to investigate how through our stepping back and emphasising powerlessness, according to the motto of, "there is nothing I can do", policies of displacement and their executers are handed obstacle-free pathways. Hinting at the ability of every individual to react, even while witnessing a defeat, his performance sets a statement inside discourses of nihilism.

In his performance, Cohen reflects on access to basic facilities like electricity and water and how informal settlements and townships are created as sites of non-access. In another interview on the Chandelier, he expresses how it is unbearable that millions of people are living without electricity, toilets, and water and that the chandelier itself also alludes to that.[13] That he chose a crystal chandelier and not a simple lamp refers to the stark contrast of non-access and luxury or highly comfortable life. The fact of the artist himself being read as *white*, distances the art piece from unavailingly seeking to arrange itself in an imposed empathy with the situation of those being evicted. The real materiality of empathy emanates from the background of the artist acting out of a reaction to the inactivity of the middle classes, the very social position he himself comes from. At this, the performer does not appear helpless or desperate. Inherent to his movements is the will to take agency and to demonstrate/perform self-determination. The use and active exhibition of his own body and its offering as a tool of resistance contributes to this. Stuck in a combination of unpreparedness and anger, the security guards hesitate to react to the performance. The artist's body positions itself as an evidence of the witnessed injustice, as it transports the urgency with which the decision was taken to run the risk of being arrested by the security force. Having chosen semi-nudity as performative material, the artist underlines this urgency. It also demonstrates the force behind the performance, meaning that the artist saw himself as obliged to respond and the response as an urgent one. During his moving inside the settlement, no comfort or eases can be interpreted in his bodily gestures. The spontaneous, flexible and uneven movements suggest aesthetics of fight and struggle, not of composed harmony. For the *black* body

---

13   Cohen, Steve: Interview with Festival Extra. Source: https://www.youtube.com/watch?v=nkwJ29fUQyk.

that was constructed and brutally objectified as exotic spectacle with the beginning of colonialism[14], Cohen subtends his own body, placing it at the centre of attention, relieving the *black* body from the heavy burden of being inspected and exhibited. In so doing, he establishes a counter-narrative to *white* superiority and the biological discourses of scientific racism that have been used to justify the exploitation of the *black* subject and lists questions about imposed identity and the inscription of colour on the body. The domains of power related to the order to evict had not foreseen an unusual attack like that. His performance leaves traces of an imagination, an imagination of what seems unreachable, especially in the face of this scene of forced eviction, an imagination of a more equal city. The performance, then, is not only making visible but also a form of imagining. After the eviction is executed and the shacks bulldozed, what stretches out over the city are not only the physical ruins and the misery, but also this imagination.

The Xcollektiv – *Non-Poor Only*

American District Telegraph private security company Central City Improvement District (see chapter three)

---

14 Cf. Gqola, Pumla Dineo: *What is slavery to me? Postcolonial/Slave Memory in Post-Apartheid South Africa.* Johannesburg 2010: p.193; and Enwezor, Okwui: *Reframing the Black Subject: Ideology and Fantasy in Contemporary South African Representation.* in: Oguibe, Olu and Enwezor, Okwui (eds): *Reading the Contemporary: African Art from Theory to the Marketplace.* London 1999: p.381.

Intervention through art – Performing is making visible   221

The Parade in central Cape Town, where Rosheda Muller and MyCiti Bus company routes (see chapter three) other informal traders have their stalls (see chapter three)

The Old Biscuit Mill Neighbourgoods Market (see chapter three); University of Cape Town Administration Building during the Rhodes Must Fall Movement (see chapter four)[15]

Cape Town. Xcollektiv. Ongoing project since 2013: In this section of the chapter, I would like to turn to an art project of the Cape Town-based Xcollektiv. The Xcollektiv is a long-term political collective. It includes artists, academics, writers, filmmakers and activists, who started to work together in February 2013, thematising present day forced evictions, the criminalisation of individuals, and the takeover of public and private space through construction companies and the broader business sector. The collective offers a socio-

---

15   All images taken from Xcollektiv's website. Source: https://xcollektiv.wordpress.com/stickers/.

political response to what is called "city development" or "spatial and economic development"[16] that perpetuates poverty and ignores the majority of people in South Africa.[17] The streets of Cape Town are their main sphere of activity. Their projects are always about disrupting and intervening in normalised structures of exclusion and marginalisation. The only time they accepted to be part of a conventional exhibition inside a gallery was when they brought a bucket toilet from one of Cape Town's townships that still contained excrement and placed it in the middle of the gallery space. The stench stretched out over the entire gallery space, confronting the visitors promptly with everyday township troubles.

The specific art project I would like to focus on in this book is the *Non-poor Only* project. Stickers that feature the statement "Non-poor only" build the project's material. Members of the collective place them all over Cape Town, including on benches in the Company Gardens, backpacker lodges, private security signs, first class train carriages, and on walls in Cape Town's main train station. They also place the stickers at bus stops of the *My City Bus* company that is highly criticised for operating mainly between middle-class and wealthy districts[18]. Other destinations of the sticker are benches in an area called "the Fringe", a part of District Six that, as explained in chapter three, is being renamed and redeveloped under a new urban planning project of the city. Remarkable to notice here is that the company in charge of the "redesigning" and redevelopment, the *Cape Town Partnership*, is also the one who instructs the Central City Improvement District, which has been discussed as well in chapter three. In a public discussion in the *District Six Homecoming Centre* on "the Fringe", Andrew Putter of the *Cape Town Partnership* made clear how he evaluates the project's ambitions: "Our aim is to turn shit into gold."[19]

The Xcollektiv's art project *Non-Poor-Only* speaks directly to the dispraise and degradation of *poor* life to "shit", to the criminalisation and marginalisa-

---

16   Cf. the Integrated Development Plan (IDP) of the City of Cape Town; or the national Economic Development Department Annual Report 2011-2012.
17   Terreblanch, Sampie: *Lost in Transformation*. Sandton 2012: p.101.
18   The My Citi Bus company started to operate between the city and Khayelitsha and Mitchell's Plain in July 2014. Until today, many townships, other working-class areas, and informal settlements have been excluded from the cities infrastructural development plans that centre in the My Citi Bus project.
19   Putter, Andrew: talk at the public discussion. Title of the event: *The absence of memory in design-led urban regeneration*. Organisers: District Six Home Coming Centre and African Centre for Cities of the University of Cape Town. May 29, 2013.

tion of low-income residents, to forced evictions and to the silencing and erasure of the reasons of poverty. It does not play with any conceptual metaphors or use figurative language and its implied complexities, but written text as its material. While evoking associations with apartheid segregationist policies as the declaration of *"whites* only" and "non-*whites* only" areas, the project invites to an engagement with present-day neoliberal urban planning and its effects on the lower classes. Drawing from the *"whites* only"/"non-*whites* only" signs implemented during apartheid, the text traces a line between the inability to invade *white*-declared areas in the past and the inability to end exclusion and forced evictions today. Through emphasising the connections between the past and the present, the text secures its historical aspect to be recognised.

The repetition of its appearance in different places throughout the city aims to reach as many interlocutors as possible. This approach secures a markedly heterogeneous audience, preventing only an already politicised one that visits art galleries and engages with critical art on a regular basis to be confronted. The interlocutor's reaction, sitting on the bench or standing in front of the sticker after having read the statement, can be seen as part of the installation. The confrontation that happens on that site cannot be reversed. As such, the artwork already preoccupies the interlocutor. Its message has to be thought of. The messages the art intervention wants to put across, will take on a special urgency and destabilise the ways in which one has thought of public space before.

At the same time, the sticker itself becomes part of an archival "system of transfer"[20], because it speaks about the oppression of the past and its conti-

---

20   For the expression "archival system of transfer", I have been inspired by Diana Taylor's concept "acts of transfer": "Performances function as vital acts of transfer, transmitting social knowledge, memory, and a sense of identity through reiterated, or what Richard Schechner has called "twice-behaved behaviour". "Performance," on one level, constitutes the object/process of analysis in performance studies, that is, the many practices and events - dance, theatre, ritual, political rallies, funerals - that involve theatrical, rehearsed, or conventional/event-appropriate behaviors. These practices are usually bracketed off from those around them to constitute discrete foci of analysis. Sometimes, that framing is part of the event itself-a particular dance or a rally has a beginning and an end; it does not run continuously or seamlessly into other forms of cultural expression. To say something is a performance amounts to an ontological affirmation, though a thoroughly localised one. What one society considers a performance might be a nonevent elsewhere. On another level, performance also constitutes the methodological lens that enables scholars to analyze events as performance. Civic obedience, resistance, citizenship, gender, ethnicity, and sexual identity, for example,

nuities in the present, suggesting a new understanding of public spaces and their pasts. As such, aiming at the interlocutor's imagination and their ability to contextualise, the sticker departs from the present and lands in the past, not allowing any neutral space in which the interlocutor can hide. The presence of the interlocutor and the supposable absence of a person labelled as undesirable and superfluous, becomes the embodiment of and functions as the ultimate symbol for what the artwork is pointing at. Displacement is represented through this constellation in an unpredictable non-artistic manner, without the need of any inventiveness of the audience. Without the interlocutor aiming for it, he or she is placed in a field of direct interaction. Although the interlocutor's reaction is unpredictable, he or she is still caught in an unescapable situation. And this situation is embedded in a larger social condition that shapes all particulates of the fragmented urban.

The places of this interaction are chosen meaningfully, each either inhabiting a historical relation to the forced removals, or constituting public spaces where the "undesirables" are being constantly evicted from. Including the histories of the removed during apartheid, the artwork gestures towards the continuation of removals, opposing the collective amnesia mentioned in chapter three that Murray stresses.[21] By focussing on this continuation, the stickers try to process the experiences of humiliation in both, past and present, so as to be able to generate the possibility to react and accordingly to resist. Through its inherently provocative feature, catching the audience by surprise and therefore, navigating the ways of being looked at, the sticker addresses the ignorance and political opportunism of society's elite that does not question its own privilege inside the signified spaces. Presented to the public as an urgent project, the sticker's simple but aggressive characteristics are composed to it on purpose.

The Urban Development Discourse with "safety", "cleanliness", "liveability" and "profit" as its rationalising parameters against which the artwork can be read, becomes challenged, essentially finding itself opened for a new kind

---

are rehearsed and performed daily in the public sphere. To understand these as performance suggests that performance also functions as an epistemology. Embodied practice, along with and bound up with other cultural practices, offers a way of knowing. The bracketing for these performances comes from outside, from the methodological lens that organizes them into an analyzable "whole." Taylor, Diana: *The Archive and the Repertoire – Performing Cultural Memory in the Americas*. Durham 2003: pp.2-3.

21 Murray: Martin J.: *Taming the Disorderly City: The Spatial Landscape of Johannesburg After Apartheid*. New York 2008: p.224.

of questioning. Disempowered and suspended, the discourse makes way for new meanings, emerging to reveal the paradoxes one finds in the relation between the position of the self and the breeding grounds for the discourse, for it being read against the backdrop of the past, re-thought and replaced. The interlocutor is put back into a situation, where the utilising of the ability to link and position the different information about processes of criminalisation and marginalisation and to establish the connections in between, is restored. The artwork also stimulates the imagination of suppressed stories of the excluded that were, along with them, consigned to the margins of official narrative, or, at worst, completely erased. These are the stories behind the homelessness or *poor* living conditions of a person, not only in terms of individual loss, but also in terms of the political and economic dynamics behind it. Entering the consciousness, the stickers render the reasons of poverty a pervasive question. The stickers' public appearance resists the concept of the positioning of art into restricted installation spaces.

Through the stickers' ability to penetrate the places of interrogation and eviction, the artwork does not remain a symbolic act, but becomes a physically intervening one. As in the case of Cohen's performance in Johannesburg, it takes place in everyday social spaces rather than in more isolated artistic spaces of a gallery or a museum. Here, it does not necessarily point to something that is new to the interlocutors. Much more likely, it underlines a process that is well known between most Capetonians. The silence and lack of sensitivity about lower-class subjects being criminalised and marginalised does not mean that it is not part of common knowledge. Because of its illuminating a process that is being recognised but pushed aside, it disrupts the interlocutor's perception of public space as an equal zone of interaction, movement, and bringing people together. Through its deliberate provocation, the sticker echoes the violence inflicted on the body that is labelled undesirable in all over the space that surrounds the sticker. The sticker locates the site of exclusion and functions as a non-ambiguous medium that does not offer different possibilities of interpretation for the interlocutor. To repress feelings about the specific city spaces or to push them aside is almost impossible. One either has to react with incomprehension and/or disgust, or, empathy, and the will to put oneself in the position of a marginalised *poor* person. Pointing fingers in a very direct manner, it renders the violence central to the atmosphere and performs as the material manifestation of exclusion and humiliation. In this way, the flatness that might be inherent to some artworks that use text as their main material, becomes repealed.

In addition, the text endows stability to the message. Although the work does not carry any title, there is a subtitle attached to it that is the calling to act, or at least introducing the possibility to act. The technology behind apartheid segregationist policies, from which the *whites* only/ non-*whites* only signs stem, was, at least on the institutional level, defeated. But the artwork invites to rethink this defeat and think of collective organisation and opposition through establishing narratives of resistance. Demonstratively taking sides with the criminalised and marginalised, it suspends all rationalising arguments that allow the violence, as the above-mentioned argument of "more safety" and so forth. Instead, it turns the technologies used for exclusion into a persistent question that can only be answered through increased sensitisation and concentrated mindfulness to the structures of the marginalisation of "the *poor*".

Ayesha Price – Save the Princess

Images of the video installation

The Lovell Gallery, Woodstock/ Cape Town. November 2013: Within the scope of one of its projects, the construction company *Insight Property Developers* was planning to build a 9000 square meters shopping mall on the very ground of Princess Vlei, a wetland to whose surrounding area, people classified as *coloured* under the apartheid regime, were forcibly removed. Holding a diverse ecosystem that purifies the water before it runs into the ocean, the wetland is of the few protected natural landscapes that is accessible for leisure for the communities of the Cape Flats. Situated right in between Grassy Park, Southfield, Heathfield, and Retreat, it also connects communities from different parts of the Cape Flats and builds a central meeting point. The schools of the area take their learners to walk-arounds to the Vlei to teach them about indigenous birds and plants. The imposed exclusionary feature of nature that I have analysed in the first part of the previous chapter, letting natural landscape emerge as sites of non-access for many low-income families[22], invests a special importance on the wetland's sustainment. Different values are attached to it, touching various spheres of the communities' lives. Constituting particularly a place of historical value, social identification, and refuge, it enabled the excluded communities to engage and personalise *The Princess*, inscribing new meanings on their histories of being exposed to alienation, allowing multiple narratives and a variety of identity building processes that entail the continuous attempt of creating home/homeland to co-exist. When discussing this co-existence, it is important to underline that one of the central uses of the Vlei is leisure. In the Urban Development Discourse, leisure of working-class and other low-income people is set as such a faraway imagination that it becomes practically denied as a category or activity to working-class communities. Bearing this discursive imaginary in mind, leisure as a central aspect of the social value and use of the Vlei becomes important for any analysis of the Princess Vlei demolition threat.

Princess Vlei has been created as a site of belonging by the people living in its surrounding areas. As such, it is not only used for recreation but also for ceremonies. These can range from Rastafari rituals, to Christian baptising ceremonies, to commemoration of Khoi ancestors. To explain the latter, the history of the Vlei of before the forced removals of people to that area is an analogy to the development plans of the company. The Khoi inhabitants of this very same land that they used as a main water source and to grow their food and graze their animals, were deprived of the land and banished from the area. At the same time as it is a site of ceremony, it is also used by local fisherman for fishing, as the lake holds a variety of fish. Following the logical consequences of these dynamics, the formation of community movements against the development plans speaks for itself.[23] How else should have the residents form a political response against the destruction of the site if not

---

22 See chapter four.
23 Cf. for example: The Princess Vlei Forum. Source: http://www.princessvlei.org/.

united? If the City of Cape Town and the Western Cape Government Environmental Affairs and Development Planning section would have decided in the company's favour and sell the land, not only the eviction of communities that live in immediate proximity and hence on the sold land would have been guaranteed, but also a dehistoricising of the area and yet another denial of the possibility to connect with nature for communities that structurally have less access to nature reserves, mountain sites etc.

It is this project of destruction and displacement against which Ayesha Price's video installation was composed. The naming of the artwork *Save the Princess* speaks to the identification of surrounding communities with the area who gave the wetland its short name "the Princess". Holding the images in the colours black and white, the installation plays with shadows and light, with illumination, fading and flashing, and thereby features highly flexible capabilities. Eight different projections and three sound tapes play at the same time and are woven into a single narrative. Artist, musician and arts educator Garth Erasmus provided the music that is used, indigenous tones that go in loops, alluding to the cyclical nature of life, as Price described it in our conversation. The soundscape harmonises with the landscapes portrayed, each sound meshing with one of the nature elements. The images projected on the wall are tall, narrow, and huge, dominating the room from the floor to the ceiling, sucking the visitor directly into the atmosphere they aim to create. One has to walk around the room as all walls are covered by images. "You couldn't stand still, you had to move around and make choices about the way you want to go", Price explained. While incorporating nature elements as trees, stones, creeks, lakes, and grassland, the bodily gestures of human shadows are set in dialogue and interaction with the nature space. The ways in which the bodies interact with nature display codes of belonging that are not imitable. All grass and stones and trees have stories to tell, as it is the land and the lake that preserves history. It seems as if everything that has ever been said at the lakeshore, is inscribed on the landscape. Highly intimate and familiar with their surrounding, the bodies epitomise their inhabiting and embracing of the space. The nakedness of the bodies underlines this intimacy and rootedness, containing the desire for its preservation. This embodiment of harmony, not as sterile decorative aesthetics but as a circuit of contextualised political expression, performs as an antagonism towards the disharmony and defamiliarity inherent to the development plans. The manner in which the bodies' engagement with the nature elements is composed, is set as an allegory for the actual relationship Princess Vlei has with its communities. Taking full possession of the wetland means marking it inextricable from the definition of home and belonging. The relationship between the two imports complexity into the interwoven formations of the communities' lebensraum and the natural space. Besides, it is this complexity that determines the bodies' vocabulary as the only adequate source of representation. The movement of the bodies is the literal transfer of what the installation wants to say. "You can use the movement as literature", Price said. Nature and bodies share a common denominator that is dance. It means that aesthetical movement is as much inherent to the nature elements as it is to the displayed bodies, releasing nature from its objectness and investing it with subjecthood within the meaning-making processes of the installation. It also reveals a very personal relationship of the artist herself with the Princess itself but also with natural spaces in general, weaving her own essential realities into the work.

In order to be able to capture and fully absorb the audience, the images entirely cover the walls of the installation room. That way, it secures the interlocutors to become emotionalised towards what the wetland embodies, on the one hand, and the potential loss and destruction, on the other hand. Teasing out their empathy and providing the full emotional knowledge about the contemporary condition of the wetland, the interlocutors find themselves placed in the centre of the distress. The bilaterally influenced processing of the impulses becomes translated into a contemplative, corporeal experience. The atmosphere created is neither melancholic nor does it indicate victimhood. The gestures in the images rather suggest worried, unsettled and questioning bodies invested with a historical consciousness that, while trying to re-personalise the space, are engaged with the threats that shadow them. Historical consciousness here means that their bodily expressions transmit the traumatic memory of displacement that has been reproduced throughout history. In principle, the concept of worry/anxiety that can readily turn into sorrow, is central to the installation. The image in which the lake is pictured reveals layers that build upon one another, forming the understory of the lake, comprising indistinctly held faces, frontally catching and confronting the interlocutor's eyes. Read against Princess Vlei's historical background, they stand for the many layers that constitute its past, gesturing towards the different histories of forced removals and re-identification that are connected to the place, their rediscovery and restoration. The interlocutor's confrontation with these layers might represent the most emotive moment in the story of the Princess told in the installation. The land and the lake recall that trauma and the water is symbol of everything that is subconscious or everything that has been forgotten, as Price explained. The indicated reciprocal relationship between identity formation and "the Princess" stabilises the position of the wetland as characterised by the preservation of memory and its function as a real public space.

Through playing with fragments that hint at a meaningful past, the artwork challenges the politico-economic processes that resurrect and perpetuate apartheid policies, using the ability of art to record images of history even after the occurrence of the historical event. The bodies that represent community members of the past and the present, who bear the readiness to take agency and aspire towards self-determination and thus hold maturity, are positioned as the antipode of the fluidity that is inherent to political decisions that are navigated by market rule. This demonstration of resoluteness towards the business plans destabilises arguments in favour of neoliberal urban planning and thus its rationalisation and justification. The setting of the bodies conflicts narratives of modernisation and development as necessary progress that is invested with a positional superiority, turning the politico-economic discourse behind it upside down. Price also explained, that although the City cancelled the plans of the construction company for now[24], the people engaged against the development plans did not celebrate any victory. The City cancelled the plans during election time and the people do not forget that the land is prime land that could make any investor very rich, she further remarked. Hence, trust in the city government is impossible. Too many times were investment companies the winners when it came to a decision between residents' concerns and market-driven development projects. But what I could also understand from Price's explanations is that the only positive aspect of the development plans was that the communities grew together as a unit, discovering that they were able to make themselves heard and build fronts whose struggle, in addition, was able to accumulate the power to reach success collectively, without any financial backing, without any material interests, and for the only sake of maintaining the space they have created as a space of belonging.

Just as the installation is set to overwhelm the visitor, it is not surprising that Price had originally planned to set it up on the site of Princess Vlei itself.

---

24   The plans were cancelled after this section was written. Nevertheless, the process until it was cancelled, the community's struggle, and the artwork itself, remain highly meaningful in relation to the understanding of the Urban Development Discourse and community work that is positioned against it.

The lack of resources prevented it to become an open-air installation right on the site of the struggle. But in our conversation, she explained how for her, the artwork is as much an intervention as her activism against the construction plans and her involvement in the Princess Vlei Forum, of which she was part from the beginning of its formation. She wanted to radically disrupt accepted forms of art and let the images of the installation create conversations and debates. The installation's concept was developed in consultation with her fellow activists. Price wanted it to form part of the community struggle, and not an isolated art exhibition somewhere in town, to which only certain audience circles interested in art would go. The artwork thus represents a political engagement and is used as a tool to be able to express the different meanings Princess Vlei occupies. Different than written or spoken words, it is able to transmit what direct text cannot articulate. How else would it have been possible to let the underworld of the lake speak? Or to materialise what it means to create nature as a space of belonging and that it is the body that does not surrender to sadness and loss but that reclaims that space even though it does not possess the equal means to compete with the economic power of investment companies? Or to locate those who have come to engage, in a corporeal experience in which dialogue is established from body to body? Hence, Price facilitated an engagement with the struggle for Princess Vlei that personalised the Vlei even for those who have never visited the site. The interlocutors become almost intrigued by the sense of familiarity with the Vlei that the installation produces. This sense Price could evoke because of her reaching out from an insider position, from the position of a deeply affected person that has stories to tell that narrate against the City's plan, using a language that is creative and at the same time deeply radical.

Donovan Ward – Living on the Edge

Cape Town, at Donovan Ward's house in Woodstock. The artwork's material: Cement, Collage, acrylic, and soot on masonite: This last artwork that I include in my approach of reading art as an archive against criminalisation and marginalisation are selected works of a series of three art pieces by the artist Donovan Ward, who is particularly well-known in South Africa for his co-creation of the Gugulethu Seven memorial that commemorates the seven Umkhonto we Sizwe cadres murdered by the apartheid security force's Civil

First piece. Untitled

Co-operation Bureau who were all shot dead in a false flag operation on 3rd of March 1986.

Between 2013 and 2017, Ward and I hold several personal conversations on his artworks and the way he views forced eviction and criminalisation. In one of our conversations, he characterised the concept of *Living on the Edge*:

> "These works attempt to link the earliest signs of habitation in Southern Africa and claims to place with present day dislocations. The earliest records of habitation are the rock art paintings and engravings of the indigenous tribes. Today the remnants of these people are often found living on the margins, often landless and homeless. In these works, I was referencing the places where homeless people seek shelter. As you know, many seek shelter in shop front doorways and under bridges and elsewhere.
>
> Often the signs of 'home' are the soot marks on bridge sidings caused by cooking or heating fires. These blackened surfaces also serve as 'canvases'

Second piece. Untitled; Third piece. Under the Bridge

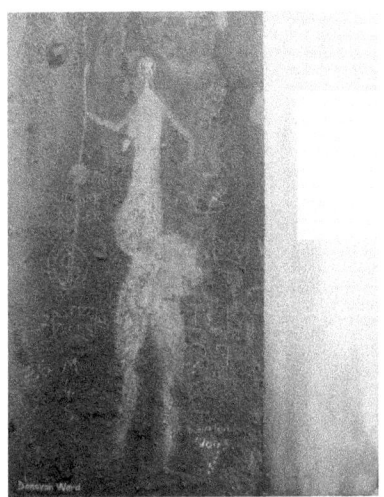

with names, and graffiti etc. scrawled or scratched into it. I symbolically represented the territorial contestation between the homeless and state, and/or corporate power by accretions of fresh cement and paint."[25]

In the first two pieces, the white colour, tending to grey, of the deformed bodies sets the bodies apart from the dark and heavy background. Although distinguished from the heaviness and darkness, the bodies are not set as their opposites, legerity and lightness, but as highly affected by the absorbing and all-embracing power of the ground they are positioned on. The contours of the bodies converge with the heaviness and darkness of the ground. The simplicity in which the bodies are held alludes to a practice of erasure through which people are rendered indiscernible and ghosts to the city. Bordering on both representations, the silhouette of a body as well as the body itself, they are suggesting the seesaw between visibility and invisibility to which poor people/homeless people are exposed. The bodies also speak about how in certain situations, people living on the streets need to regulate their visibility for not being called upon to leave or not being displaced from the space they occupy. Often, they need to cover as anonymous shadows, informal beings that assure

---

25 Email conversation with Donovan Ward. December 2, 2013.

to not touch upon formal life. The decision of where to reside becomes a practical one. The bodies' movements need to be navigated toward spaces where they attract less attention, and still, all movements are unsecured, bare and vulnerable, exposed to any kind of intervention by security forces, the police, or ordinary residents. To be able to sit or sleep somewhere depends on the constant activation of their alertness. There is no moment of ease. As we have seen homeless people re-inhabit the semi-demolished District Six houses in chapter two, the only temporary safe place to occupy is a ruin, an abandoned, decayed place in which nobody enters until the bulldozers arrive. So ruins are the only legitimate part of their trajectories. At the same time, the painted bodies are not demonstrating any theatricality, nor are they performing as spectacle. The bodies' shapes are taken from ancient rock art figures, creating a link between the present and the past. This time, they are not placed in mystical caves or mountain passes, hinting at an ancient history. In fact, there is nothing mystical about these figures. This time, the bodies speak about the present and about naked realities of a repressive social order. The only thing handed down from the past is the continuation of a violent condition.

Although the bodies are not stylised at all, they are still claiming a certain aesthetics – an aesthetics of deformation and disharmony. The weight of deformation conglomerates in every piece differently. In the first piece, it centres at the bodies' spine, suggesting the formation of a blastoma, raising associations with an inextricable burden that the body has to carry. Embodied memories of a social condition, or the condition itself has weighed down the body. In the second piece, the lower extremities, more precisely, the underside, backside and legs are deformed, pictured through swellings that weigh down and occupy a more feminine body. The underside of a female's body as the part where new life is created and protected is here exposed to disease, presumably caused in consequence of social mistreatment. Although moving, that can be indicator of both, moving as moving on or as being existent/surviving, the bodies suggest states of isolation and being left to their own resources. The texts and symbols painted and carved into the background allude to wall paintings suggestive of bare and remorseless streets with their coldness and coarseness. In one of our conversations, Ward explained how the graffiti and wall paintings are actual copies from the streets. He took photos of them, projected them onto the wall and copied them into the artworks. Only the scales become adjusted. "So I really just take what is out there", he says.[26] The graffiti-like text at the bottom of the first piece stating "toxic pills" activates our imagination about the dangers of street life and the hardship that it implies, converting the expectation of life into an expectation of death that is possible at any time, anywhere, whether the cold brings it, or through physical violence, malnutrition or disease. It hints at the biopolitical power over bodies that is in the Foucauldian sense the power to "make live and let die".[27]

In principle, the texts are harsh and bitter, not aesthetically striking or romantic. The dollar sign carved into the background of the second piece, I suggest, stands for the mercilessness of the market rule, as well as for the influence of foreign interests and dictations of economic policies, as the dollar is a foreign currency – "images of power that are seeping through", as Ward puts it, absorbing the body into their inner. The indicated British flag beneath the dollar sign evokes the same. Both, dollar sign and British flag are reminiscent of apartheid legacies that flow from the politico-economic power the apartheid regime established by means of British and US-American allocation of apparatus and the mutual profit this presupposed. They are also symbols of the birth, realisation and export of neoliberal urban planning, if one remembers for instance where the implementation of CCTV had its debut and where the security sector gained its significance. At the same time, the British flag is the emblem of a Cape Flats gang based in Mannenberg that is coincidentally named The Hard Livings. The carved crown that faces the dollar sign on the other side of the deformed body proposes associations with the wealthy elite of society that lives royally, constituting the extreme antipode of poor life towards what the artwork gestures.

The third piece that is named *Under the bridge*, shares the same heaviness and darkness, although not as dominant as in the first two pieces. Holding a collage as the background it is positioned on, the painted body is held in a comic-like mode. The protruding semicircle on the back of the body can be both, a swelling as well as exaggerated buttocks. The collage integrates text and pictures, one of a young woman and one of a young man, both seeming to hold a *white* middle or upper-class background. The manner in which the woman and the man stare frontal and straight ahead, comprises ambiguity, but can be read as exhibiting viewership while standing on the side-lines.

---

26   Conversation with Donovan Ward. June 2, 2013.
27   Foucault, Michel: *Society must be defended. Lectures at the College de France, 1975-76*. New York 2003: p.241.

Their posture involves a kind of artificiality, something plastic and stiff attached to it. What appears as the remnants of the anti-apartheid slogan "Freedom now" is drowned out and paled, as it would slowly fade away. The large-scale painted letters "YGB" stand for the Cape Town based gang "Young Gifted Boys". Its integration in the piece incorporates Cape Town's wall scenery that displays the immortalisation of different gangs and their marking out of territory. Against the backdrop of poverty that causes weak family structures, gangs constitute social establishments that provide a specific kind of social security and spaces for the formation of identity and socialisation.[28] Interwoven with the life of the lower classes, they are inherent part of South African cities' social landscape.

All three pieces speak out on the silencing of homelessness and the policy of "let die" in terms of placing homeless life at the very bottom of the hierarchy of values, letting them die social deaths. The painted bodies themselves are hold as line drawings, pointing to their dehumanisation and erasure and at what people have been reduced to, as Ward explains. They aim to make visible what assumingly, a considerable number of the upper classes clandestinely wish outside their range of vision and in case of encounter turn a blind eye to it and in so doing, erase what is existent but undesirable. The artwork challenges this contradictory positioning of homeless life in simultaneous spheres of being and non-being, of life and ghost life. It also points to the processes through which discourses of homelessness equating diseased life are constructed, turning them around through interchanging the misplaced positions of cause and effect. Through the bodily gestures of the painted bodies that imply movement, the pieces lay emphasis on survival even under the condition of abject poverty rather than on collapse. Survival as a theme runs as a thread throughout all three art pieces. Thereby, the pieces pose as much an archive of rehumanisation as they pose an archive of suffering. To end with the artist's own words, it is about "lives that have been degraded... I am trying to show how people are being cleaned up".

---

28 Cf. conversation with Edith Kriel, psychologist of the Child Trauma Centre in Cape Town: Februray 2, 2012.

Conclusion

The artworks analysed above must be read as political responses, as "The political arises when the given order of things is questioned; when those whose voice is only recognised as noise by the policy order, claim their right to speak, acquire speech, and produce the spatiality that permits and sustains this right. As such, it disrupts the order of being, exposes the constituent antagonisms, voids and excesses that constitute the police order, and tests the principle of equality."[29] But they are also attempts of putting across the histories of the excluded and the physical lives of crisis, making them understandable and tangible, opposing their narratives being flushed away, creating and amplifying social memory in this regard, and thereby, writing history and producing knowledge from below. Just as the people immediately affected by forced eviction who stored their narratives in counter-archives, the artworks I looked at are too, creating counter-archives against what they are created that is the dominant discourse. They must therefore also be seen as attempts of memorialising all that is aimed to become forgotten and silenced, controverting the memorialising needs of the dominant discourse and the political power behind it. In this relation, memory itself becomes a site of struggle in which its permanent reclaiming and reprocessing has become a permanent task.

Without claiming that they release as much power as social movements, the artworks, through the many layers of meaning they are transmitting, provide the same abundance of archives of suffering, impacts of violence and dehumanisation, as well as of rehumanisation and freedom. Here, the concept of rehumanisation stands for redistributing the refused humanity of the subjects whose stories are told and in so doing, restoring the ability to possess the body. As they are responding to, broadly speaking, relations of domination, they are evidence of processes of politico-economic violence, functioning as the mirrors of these processes and therefore, disrupt discourses that inscribe regimes of shame and dispensability on specific bodies and that attempt to justify the inflicted violence and trivialise its impacts. In this vein, although they remain nonverbal practice, they take a discursive place, holding up against which they are composed and invite to a critical re-thinking of the normalising effects of biopolitical power that emanate from this justification and trivialisation and from the repetition of that violence in everyday

---

29   Swyngedouw, Erik: *Where is the political?* Manchester 2008: p.24.

urban sceneries. As such, they also contest the liberal idea of art as an entity standing for itself, art for art, depoliticised and decontextualised from social questions, packageable, saleable, and consumable. As Rancière describes: "Political activity is whatever shifts a body from the place assigned to it or changes a place's destination. It makes visible what had no business being seen, and makes heard a discourse where once there was only place for noise; it makes understood as discourse what was once only heard as noise."[30]

Gaining access to their audience through a creative language that stimulates the interlocutors' senses, the artworks increase the sustainability of the messages transported. What I mean is that in comparison with messages propagated through mass media, such as newspaper articles, television reports or radio podcasts, interventionist art creates an alternative medium whose contents are no longer dependent on the mercy of mass media and its structures of desire. This is especially the case with those intervening artworks that are located outside more isolated spaces such as conventional museums and galleries and that are therefore able to choose their audience themselves. While revealing forced evictions, criminalisation, exclusion, and marginalisation as violence, they register the locations of its appearance and thereby render visible what is aimed to be erased. It is this locating of violence that can trigger the public imagination to revise the relationship between the city and its inhabitants and distribute the ability to identify unjust exclusion on the very site it is happening. Through this, the artworks take a political position and transgress the boundaries that are set to enable a distinction between desirable and undesirable, between conducive and superfluous. Although they differ stylistically, all artworks analysed above choose the body as their focal point. This feature bears witness of a lineal engagement with and defiance of biopolitics which is directly targeted on the body and its control or so to say on the flesh. Perhaps this feature of the body as the point of origin, the point from which everything begins, derives from a subconscious knowledge that one has to set off from the body itself in order to be able to create an archive that positions itself against dominant discourses. Moreover, the artworks are also about reclaiming the body. Although they remain intangible acts of meaning-making, they challenge a very material and concrete social condition. Occupying, or at least intervening in spaces that are designated to the implementation of those politics targeted on the body, the artists take an additional step beyond pure responding and mature to the stage of creating

---

30   Rancière, Jaques: *Disagreement*. Minneapolis 1998: p.30.

art as a political revolt against the normalising effects of the Urban Development Discourse. Revolt here primarily means to re-politicise and re-historicise space, to locate the violence and unveil the sites of exclusion and displacement. For this purpose, the artists incorporate their own subjectivities and redefine them in relation to the inequalities they are alluding to.

Conclusions

This book has examined the technologies of capitalism applied to urban development, and the ways they are informed by colonial and apartheid discourses. It has shown that it is the mergence of past and present discourses that makes the urban condition of the postcolony so special. Through disentangling the role of business sector, security sector, government, as well as media, in how displacement and criminalisation of low-income residents is being framed, this work has revealed that these practices are not accidental side-effects of urban development, but that they are a necessary part of the realisation and regulation of urban development projects that strive for a competitive, marketable, profitable and investor-attracting city. I defined and analysed the Urban Development Discourse as the corporate institution for regulating city spaces and the public that resides in the space, practices of inclusion and exclusion, and displacement of low-income residents.

The book identified the ways in which the discourse has created a body of practice in which the *People's Post* produces a specific notion of the local and criminalises or at least depicts the rest as an homogenous entity that is the Outsider; in which the security sector is established to maintain gated neighbourhoods and produce fear towards the disorderly, low-income city; in which informal traders are set as the polar opposite of the desirable milieu and become criminalised and marginalised; in which the business sector delivers discursive material through identifying their specific target groups and excluding the rest from the narration of their development and design projects; in which city officials present low-income people as lacking the right attitude for improving their lives; in which institutions as the South African Heritage Agency are forced by provincial government units to alter their reports in favour of construction companies; in which development projects of City, Province, and the private sector are almost always favoured over residents; in which no institution speaks about the enslaved peoples and forced labour who built the city; and in which the Urban Development Discourse governs the imagination of how the city should look and imposes limits upon thought about possible inclusion and more equal urban spaces.

I argued that this body of practice continuously gives birth to and reproduces a web of classed, raced, and gendered concepts of belonging.

Each eviction case I delved into was caused by a different reason. The District Six evictions of the pensioners were profit-driven in a very immediate manner; the Joe Slovo evictions were set to make space for a development project that would bring Cape Town closer to the status of a world-class city; the Symphony Way evictions ended a two years-long occupation and with it a community struggle that taught people how to organise themselves and fight for a collective cause; and the Tafelsig evictions were to set a sign that no empty space would be allocated to the working class for free and to demonstrate the determination with which city government would address the attempt of takeover of land by people. This difference in cause and effect also meant that the motivations to struggle against the evictions differed in each community. Whereas the one community fought to maintain the houses that were home to them for decades and with them the social relations and networks they had built with each other, the other was determined to break out of the instability and humiliation of backyard dwellers' life, even if that meant taking on huge risks for their families and starting from scratch on an empty field.

The common feature at stake is that all four cases derive from a discursive condition in which the lower-class *black* subject has no negotiating power. To not be fully absorbed by this powerlessness, the people affected decide to treasure their own memory, to be able to access it even if years pass, and to present it and make it accessible for others. The concern of access to their own memory and of the possibility of presentation to others, makes them narrate their own history, create visual evidences, and store them in what I called with reference to Combé and Derrida, forbidden archives. The fact that political powers always seek to control the archive does not mean that contradicting narratives do not exist. They do exist in people's homes. I assume that the risks involved in raising one's voice depends on the way the violence inflicted on them has shattered them, as well as the realities of the ongoing afterlives of those violences and shatterings. In the cases I looked at, all people affected had organised themselves as a community and had decided to struggle against the evictions together. The collective power this releases and the dynamics it brings, assists to formulate one's own narrative to make it understandable for others. It also reduces the fear of vocalising what has happened and thus helps to create one's own archive against the dominant narrative of forced eviction and urban development. Most notably, it sets examples for other communities that face the same threat of being forcibly evicted and removed. With the experiences of Symphony Way, Joe Slovo, District Six, and Tafelsig in mind, other communities have the opportunity to better the formulation of their political contents, forms of organisation and legal strategies. I hope that this work can help to form this bridge between these experiences, more current ones, and those that have yet to come.

One of the most surprising features of the residents' struggle against forgetting and the systematic and discursive production of silence, distortion and falsification of their stories, was an almost absent process of mourning. Caught in the duality of discourse and anti-discourse, the people affected by eviction had no time and space to mourn their losses, or at least I could not gather from our encounters that loss and grief had turned into mourning and nostalgia. This absence of mourning, if my perception did not intrigue me, might be related to their continuous hope of finding home at the end. The loss is not an accepted loss. To create home and build a new community has remained an essential aim around which everything else becomes negotiated. This shows that the archives they compiled are as much about the recording and narration of the past, as about the creation of the future. Every document archived and the process of archiving itself stands in a direct relationship to the evicted resident's future, how they envision it and how they approach it. And again, Derrida's words ring in my ear when he says that "...the question of the archive is not, we repeat, a question of the past. It is not the question of a concept dealing with the past that might *already* be at our disposal or not at our disposal, an archivable concept of the archive. It is a question of the future, the question of the future itself, the question of a response, of a promise and of a responsibility for tomorrow."[1]

The same intention can be identified for the prevailing power that is constructed by both the political and the business sector. Controlled by political power and the rule of the market, the Urban Development Discourse ordains the archive of the postapartheid. The fact that the question of who built the city finds no public response and is entirely absent from the narrative of the city and its past, shows the degree in which the discourse aims at collective memory. Memorialising South Africa's histories of enslavement and forced

---

1   Derrida, Jacques: *Archive Fever*. Chicago 1996: p.39.

labour in a publicly organised way could lead many of the excluded majority to not only link this past to their present-day socio-economic condition, but also to address and articulate the manners in which inequality has been produced historically. The erasure of the history of a people helps to maintain the politico-economic status quo.

But the above-mentioned powerlessness translates not only in situations of very direct and bare exclusion like forced evictions, but also in the cityscapes both architecturally and spatially. Walking the streets of the Western Cape, social inequality is a highly visible condition one cannot shut the eyes to. The difficulty is to phrase it, to make it tangible and allegeable. This book has shown that we can speak of an institutionalised regime of inequality to which highly securitised city spaces, law and criminalisation practices are central. Urban Development and City Improvement have become dogmatic projects that facilitate the enlargement of that inequality, excluding the majority of society from the design-focused, creative, fashionable, liveable, in short, normative narrative of cities. This regime includes institutions such as the Mayoral Committee, Provincial Government, the Anti-Land Invasion Unit, the High Court, the South African Heritage Agency, the Metro Police, Law Enforcement, City Improvement Districts, other public-private security companies, as well as private security companies, the Cape Town Partnership, construction companies, developers and specific media services.

This book has illuminated their role in framing and implementing the Urban Development Discourse that uses articulations of power and a specific rhetoric of criminalisation, informed by colonial doctrines, theses, and framings of the *black* subject. The ways in which the *black* subject was produced ideologically and politically, continues to nurture present-day depictions of the lower-class *black* subject. Just as the colonial and apartheid regime and the settler society gained strength and identity through creating the imagination of the inferior other, the Urban Development Discourse gains a dispositive rationalisation model through creating the working-class *black* subject as demotivated, irresponsible, lazy, and incapable of taking life in his or her own hands. These labels I identified as direct descendants of colonial and apartheid discourse. Colonial and apartheid understandings of the human are not discursive material of the past, boxed into dusty archival places. They have been evaporated onto dominant discourses of the present, in this case, onto the Urban Development Discourse. This also speaks of the strength with which the colonial discourse of superiority and inferiority has reproduced itself from one century to the other. Linked to this discourse was the political practice of forced removal under colonialism and especially under apartheid. But to be able to create them as an isolated social condition, forced evictions of the present become dehistoricised. On the one hand, the Urban Development Discourse maintains the political and economic conditions that enable the reproduction of apartheid technologies of power, and on the other hand, disguises the links between forced removals of the past and forced evictions of the present.

Collective memory is being driven away from establishing these links. As I have emphasised repeatedly in this work, this dehistoricisation leads to the depoliticisation of the practice of forced eviction. From the nourishment of the Urban Development Discourse by colonial and apartheid discourse and the control of archive and memory in this regard, I derived that we are facing a colonial condition of postapartheid archive and memory, a state that I marked as coloniality.

The Urban Development Discourse creates imaginaries of the city in which the social realities of the majority of people in South Africa become totally erased. One of these imaginaries is a prestigious imagery embellishing the route from the Cape Town International Airport to the city, disqualifying the Joe Slovo part of Langa township from the scenery. Within this frame, the first thing tourists, business entities, foreign investors and heads of states witness on the way from airport to city, cannot be shacks. And as a continuation of the logic these imaginaries emanate from that is the rule of the market, the new housing units in Joe Slovo cannot be accessible for the very residents of Joe Slovo, as the aim of the development project was not an improvement of the residents' living conditions, but beautification and the replacement of the residents by higher income families. City improvement is not allocated to the townships but reserved for the affluent, profitable parts of the city.

The city as an object of the capitalist desire for profit sets Temporary Relocation Areas as inhuman misconducts of the right to housing. TRAs are the only response city and provincial governments have to forced eviction. Spatially, TRAs are not located on the city margins, but are created as totally separate and insular spaces fully suspended from the city. The manner and scale at which urban development becomes imagined prevents any radical engagement with social inequality and spatial division. The modernities articulated and conceptualised, of which the TRA is but one example, are set by the capitalist elite and derive from fixed visions of how a profitable city must look like and from the modes of production that enable these visions. The promised prosperity this brings with is inaccessible for the ones suspended and marginalised. It materialises in that parallel world that is set to be the beneficiary, the wheel that keeps this condition intact. This world is formed by the capitalist elite and the middle classes that impose themselves in this social position and its practices. At the other side of this world, the humanity of all those criminalised and excluded has been stripped down to their production value and to the degree they contribute to the profitable city – a condition that translates into perpetual displacement and segregated city spaces.

The artists, the members of the Housing Assembly, Reclaim the City activists and the shack dweller's movement have another vision for the city. It is not only the Urban Development Discourse that is interested in liveability and joy. Individuals and movements opposed to the discourse envision vibrant neighbourhood lives as well, but not within the frame the dominant discourse dictates.

We need to create our own narrative and to articulate our own imaginaries of the urban. The artists whose work I analysed, the people affected by forced evictions I encountered and Abahlali, Housing Assembly and Reclaim the City activists show that this is possible. One of the main tasks a long-term intervention into the Urban Development Discourse requires is to address people's imagination through understanding that it is a responsibility to rethink our social, political, and economic worlds. All people that have been excluded and marginalised wait for a tomorrow in which they can perform their own urban practices and create belonging to the city. If this tomorrow is what the majority of the population is waiting for, what must be done to reach it and how does it look like?

Epilogue

The conclusion of this work was edited during the days after the killing of the people in the Lenasia-South land occupation. The *Red Ants Security Relocation & Eviction Services* had attacked the occupiers on Friday 22nd of September 2017. The City of Johannesburg has spoken of two people killed, whereas the number residents have announced is nine dead: eight residents and one security officer.[1]

The video of 14-years old Ona Dubula from Imizamo Yethu, who could have lost his ability to speak forever, after a police officer shot repeatedly into his mouth with rubber bullets, shocked all those who were not aware of the bareness with which police brutality is being applied in housing protests. Dubula's mother, Pinckie Dubula, had lost her home in the last fire that broke out in Imizamo Yethu in February 2017. She explained that she does not even have the means to get back to Imizamo Yethu from hospital. Hangberg residents, who have been threatened for years to be forcibly evicted and in whose protest action Dubula was shot, collected the boy from hospital four days later. They also raised R900 for the boy and his mother. The good news: Dubula did not lose his ability to speak.[2]

The ongoing protests in Imizamo Yethu against Cape Town city government plans to "temporarily relocate" the residents in order to upgrade the area and make it fire-resistant as the City claims, have left several persons killed. Nineteen-years old Siyamthanda Betana, our fellow University of the Western Cape student and Imizamo Yethu resident, was shot in a protest on the 23rd of July 2017. Two days after his death, his father, Thabiso Betana, collapsed and died in hospital[3].

---

1   Conversation with Shaheed Mahomed. September 27, 2017; Holder, Thomas: *City of Johannesburg Defends Removal of Illegal Land Grabbers in Univille*. September 22, 2017.
2   GroundUp article. De Greef, Kimon: *Ona Dubula Returns Home*. September 19, 2017.
3   SA Breaking News article: *Father dies after hearing of son's death*. July 25, 2017.

Earlier, in January 2017, Songezo Ndude was wounded by stun grenades and rubber bullets during related protests in Imizamo Yethu. He died a couple of hours later in hospital.

> "In a meeting in Parliament in June, IPID [Independent Police Investigative Directorate] reported that in the first half of 2016/17, there were 3,313 cases reported to it and that 1,857 of these were assault cases. There were 207 deaths as a result of police action and another 154 deaths in police custody. The Western Cape had the highest number of assault cases at 425."[4]

Perceiving these deaths as ceaseless shocks that shatter our everyday might at least mean that we have not become used to catastrophe. But there is a question that me and my friend Mohammad Shabangu have asked each other in our last conversation: Have we not all become Fukuyamists, if we do not interrogate the idea of the social, political, and economic? Are we not complicit in the reproduction of this idea of "the End of History", if we do not debate and work for these new imaginations? And at the same time, has this thirst of wanting to "change the world" and the hopelessness such a will brings with, not made us narrow our own imagination about what is possible, what is impossible, and how can these two be put into an effective relationship?

The shack dwellers movement, the metal workers' movement, the farm-workers movement, the students' movement, - why does what they envision for the future of the people of South Africa, not materialise? Is it systematic oppression of the movements, or weaknesses in organisation and political analysis, or a mixture of both? These are questions that should not be answered intuitively. Future studies conducted by members of the movements that deal with the intricacies of social movements in South Africa and their oppression, could possibly help to understand why these movements do not succeed in reaching their demands. From the specific internationalist perspective from which I thought, perceived, and analysed the gathered data, another, very central question developed as well: The worker's movement in Iran is not nearly as strong as the one in South Africa. The political radicalisation of about 300 000 metal workers in South Africa, their split from the reformist Congress of South African Trade Unions (COSATU), and their reorganisation within the National Union of Metal Workers of South Africa (NUMSA), is a bottom-up political formation that seems unthinkable in present-day Iran.

---

4   Times Live article. Furlong, Ashleigh; De Greef, Kimon; Gontsana, Mary-Anne and Hendricks, Ashraf: *A History of Violence: Police Action in Hout Bay*. September 13, 2017.

When NUMSA was expelled, seven other worker's unions left COSATU as well: The Food and Allied Workers Union (FAWU), The South African State and Allied Workers Union (SASAWU), the Public Allied Workers Union (PAWUSA), the South African Commercial, Catering, and Allied Workers Union (SACCAWU), the Democratic Nursing Organization of South Africa (DENOSA) and the Communication Workers Union (CWU).

What if in Iran, despite the systematic oppression of sugarcane workers, bus drivers, metal and machine workers and workers from other sectors, will be able to unite to a stronger and bigger movement than they form at the moment and reorganise themselves in official democratically organised unions? How devastating will it be, if the experiences of systematic oppression of workers' movements in countries like South Africa are not taken into account to become an integral part of the political and economic analysis of oppression on the one hand, and self-organisation on the other hand? The same concerns apply for the shack dwellers; farm workers; and student movements.

If shack dwellers and other spatially marginalised in other geographies would like to learn from Abahlali baseMjondolo, how exactly must they evaluate the murdered, assassinated, people shot in protests and the disappeared? At the same time, how can they learn from Abahlali's past and present strategies, discussions and political contents?

It is one thing to exchange about the forms of politico-economic violences applied in different geographies. The other is to thoroughly learn from the strengths of social movements and from the socio-political energy they release. The analysis of the role of city and provincial governments, the business sector and media as a mediator of governmental/business sector discourse, in forced evictions and criminalisation of "the people" that this work was devoted to, can help in the formulation of these new questions and the gathering of their responses.

The main aim of this book was to make an argument for de-segregating and de-partitioning city space and natural landscape and challenge fixed ideas of class and *race* that reproduce politico-economic inequality. It remains indebted to "the people" of South Africa, from whom I learned that suffering and struggling are not the same thing, that an individual who only suffers without imagining to actually change his or her own condition, will never endeavour to disrupt political and economic violence or to gather for a collective cause. The many conversations held during the process of this work will travel with me, to put it in Mrs. George's words, "wherever I go". In the face of the politico-economic oppression analysed in this work on the one side, and the thousands of protests, strikes, and political events organised every year in the Western Cape and in other parts of South Africa on the other side, I remain in hope.

Bibliography

Books, journal articles, reports and court judgments

Achebe, Chinua: *Hopes and Impediments*. New York 1988
Agamben, Giorgio: *Homo Sacer: Souvereign Power and Bare Life*. 1998
Alexander, Peter; Lekgowa, Thapelo; Mmope, Botsang; Sinwell, Luke and Xezwi, Bongani: *Marikana – A View from the Mountain and a Case to Answer*. Johannesburg 2012
Amster: Randall: *Street People and the Contested Realms of Public Space*. New York 2004
Archival Platform: *State of the Archives: An Analysis of South Africa's National Archival System, 2014*. Cape Town 2014
Asad, Talal (ed.): *Anthropology and the Colonial Encounter*. London 1975
Auditor-General on the special audit of the N2 Gateway project at the National Department of Housing. RP 177/2008
Aylward, Bruce A. and Lutz, Ernst (eds.): *Nature Tourism, Conservation, and Development in Kwazulu-Natal, South Africa*. World Bank Publication. Washington 2003
Benjamin, Walter: *Critique of Violence / Zur Kritik der Gewalt*. In: *Walter Benjamin – Gesammelte Schriften*. Frankfurt a.M. no date. First published in 1921
Bénit-Gbaffou, Claire: *Community Policing and Disputed Norms for Local Social Control in Post-Apartheid Johannesburg*. Journal of Southern African Studies. Vol. 34, No. 1. 2008
Bickford-Smith, Vivian: *Mapping Cape Town: From Slavery to Apartheid*. in: Field, Sean (ed.): *Lost Communities, Living Memories – Remembering Forced Removals in Cape Town*. Cape Town 2001
Blair Howe, Lindsay: *City-making from the Fringe: Control and Insurgency in the South African Housing Landscape*. Zurich 2016

Bogues, Anthony: *Empire of Liberty. Power, Desire & Freedom*. New Hampshire 2010

Bolaane, Maitseo: *The Impact of Game Reserve Policy on the River BaSarwa/Bushmen of Botswana*. in: Social Policy Administration. Volume 38, No 4. 2004

Bond, Patrick: *Urban Social Movements – The Housing Question and Development Discourse in South Africa*. In: Moore, David B. and Schmitz, Gerald J.: *Debating Development Discourse – Institutional and Popular Perspectives*. Hampshire 1995

Borcherds, P.B.: An Auto-Biographical Memoir. Cape Town 1861

Brown, Joel Nathan: *Kant, Derivative Influence, and the Metaphysics of Causality*. Dissertation. Syracuse 2012

Bunn, David: *Art Johannesburg and Its Objects*. in: Nuttal, Sarah and Mbembe, Achille (eds.): *Johannesburg – The Elusive Metropolis*. Johannesburg 2008

Centeno, Miguel Angel and Newman, Katherine S. (eds.): *Discrimination in an Unequal World*. New York 2010

Center on Housing Rights and Evictions (COHRE): *Any Room for the Poor? Forced Evictions in Johannesburg, South Africa*. Johannesburg 2005

Center on Housing Rights and Evictions (COHRE): *N2 Gateway Project: Housing Rights Violations As Development in South Africa*. COHRE 2009

Césaire, Aimé: *Discourse on Colonialism*. Originally published in Présence Africaine. Paris 1955 -Chukwudi Eze, Emmanuel: *Hume, Race, and Human Nature*. in: Journal of the History of Ideas. Volume 61: 4. 2004

Churchill, Winston to Palestine Royal Commission, 1937

Coetzee, J.M.: *White writing: On the Culture of letters in South Africa*. New Haven 1988

Coetzer, Nicolas: *Building Apartheid: On Architecture and Order in Imperial Cape Town*. New York 2016

Comaroff, Jean and Comaroff, John: *Ethnography and the Historical Imagination*. Colorado and Oxford 1992

Combe, Sonia: *Forbidden Archives*. Paris 1994

Community Organization Resource Centre (CORC) and Joe Slovo Community Task Team: *Joe Slovo Household Enumeration Report 2009*

Constitutional Court of South Africa: *Court Case CCT 22/08, [2009] ZACC 16. In the matter between: Residents of Joe Slovo Community, Western Cape and Thubelisha Homes, Minister for Human Settlements, and MEC for Human Settlements*. Cape Town 2011

Constitutional Court of South Africa: South African Informal Traders Forum and Others versus City of Johannesburg and Others; South African National Traders Retail Association versus City of Johannesburg. Judgement of April 4, 2014

Crais, Clifton: *White Supremacy and Black Resistance in Pre-Industrial South Africa – The Making of the Colonial Order in the Eastern Cape, 1770-1865*. Cambridge 1992

Dapper, Olfert: *Kaffraria or Land of the Kafirs*. originally published: Amsterdam 1668. in: Schapera, Isaac (ed.): *The Early Cape Hottentots - Writings of Olfert Dapper, Willem Ten Rhyne and Johannes Gulielmus de Grevenbroek*. Cape Town 1933

Dart, Raymon A.: *Racial Origins*. in: Schapera, Isaac (ed.): *The Bantu-Speaking Tribes of South Africa*. London 1937

Depelchin, Jacques: *Silences in African History*. Dar Es Salaam 2005

Depelchin, Jacques: *Reclaiming African History*. Cape Town 2011

Derrida, Jacques: *Archive Fever*. Chicago 1995

Derrida, Jacques: Transcript of the seminar on *Archive Fever* at the University of Witwatersrand, August 1998. in: Hamilton, Carolyn, amongst others (eds.): *Refiguring the Archive*. Dordrecht 2002

Desai, Ashwin: *We are the Poors – Community Struggles in Post-apartheid Soutrh Africa*. New York 2002

Desmond, Cosmas: *The Discarded People - An Account of African Resettlement in South Africa*. Harmondsworth 1971

Du Toit, André and Giliomee, Hermann: *Afrikaner Political Thought: Analysis and Documents –Volume One: 1780-1850*. Cape Town 1983

Elphick, Richard: *Kraal and Castle – Khoikhoi and the Founding of White South Africa*. New Haven and London 1977

Enwezor, Okwui: *Reframing the Black Subject: Ideology and Fantasy in Contemporary South African Representation*. in: Oguibe, Olu and Enwezor, Okwui (eds): *Reading the Contemporary: African Art from Theory to the Marketplace*. London 1999

Erasmus, Zimitri: *Coloured by History, Shaped by Space – New Perspectives on Coloured Identities in Cape Town*. Roggebaai 2001

Erasmus, Zimitri and Pieterse, Edgar: *Conceptualising Coloured Identities in the Western Cape Province of South Africa*. In: Palmerg, Mai (eds.): *National Identity and Democracy in Africa*. Uppsala 1999

Escobar, Arturo: *Worlds and Knowledges Otherwise*. in: *Cultural Studies*. Volume 21: 2-3. 2007

Fanon, Frantz: *A Dying Colonialism*. New York 1965

Fanon, Frantz: *Black Skin, White Masks*. London 1986

Fanon, Frantz: *The Wretched of the Earth*. New York 2004

Farouk, Ismail: *Conflicting rationalities: post-apartheid spatial legacies and the creative city*. Cape Town 2013

Feuchtwang, Stephan: *The Colonial Formation of British Social Anthropology*. in: Asad, Talal (ed.): *Anthropology and the Colonial Encounter*. London 1975

Field, Sean (eds.): *Lost Communities, Living Memories – Remembering Forced Removals in Cape Town*. Cape Town 2001

Foucault, Michel: *Archaeology of Knowledge*. London and New York 2002

Foucault, Michel: *Discipline and Punish*. London 1977

Foucault, Michel: *Society must be defended. Lectures at the College de France, 1975-76*. New York 2003

Foucault, Michel: *The History of Sexuality – Volume I: An Introduction*. New York 1978

Freire, Paulo: *Pedagogy of the Oppressed*. New York 2000

Garuba, Harry: *Race in Africa: Four Epigraphs and a Commentary*. New York 2008

Gibson, Nigel: *Fanonian Practices in South Africa – From Steve Biko to Abahlali*. Scottsville 2011

Gqola, Pumla Dineo: *What is slavery to me? Postcolonial/Slave Memory in Post-Apartheid South Africa*. Johannesburg 2010

Gqola, Pumla Dineo; Hoffmeyer, Murray; Shefer, T amara; Malunga, Felix; and Mashige, Mashudu (eds.): *Discourses on Difference, Discourses on Oppression*. Cape Town 2002

Godfrey James, Wilmot and Simons, Mary (eds.): *The Angry Divide: Social and Economic History of the Western Cape*. Cape Town 1989

Grosfoguel, Ramon: *The Epistemic Decolonial Turn: Beyond Political Economy Paradigms*. in: *Cultural Studies* 21: Volume 2-3. 2007

Grunebaum, Heidi: *Memorializing the Past: Everyday Life in South Africa after the Truth and Reconciliation Commission*. New Jersey 2012

Grunebaum, Heidi and Henri, Yazir: *Where the Mountain Meets Its Shadows: A Conversation on Memory, Identity, and Fragmented Belonging in Present-Day South Africa*. in: Strath, Bo and Robins, Ron: *Homelands: The Politics of Space and the Poetics of Power*. Brussels 2003

Guha, Ranajit: *Dominance without Hegemony – History and Power in Colonial India*. Chapter: *Colonialism in South-Asia: A Dominance without Hegemony and its Historiography*. London 1997

Haupt, Adam: *Statics: Race and Representation in Post-Apartheid Music, Media and Film*. Cape Town 2012

Hegel, Georg Wilhelm Friedrich: *Phenomenology of Spirit*. Delhi 1998 hooks, bell: *Black Looks – Race and Representation*. Boston 1992

Hume, David: *Of National Characters*. Original text published in 1748 and revised in 1754. in: Library of Economics and Liberty– *David Hume*

James, Wendy: *The Anthropologist as Reluctant Imperialist*. in: Asad, Talal (ed.): *Anthropology and the Colonial Encounter*. London 1975

Khan, Farieda: The Politics of Mountaineering in the Western Cape, South Africa – Race, Class and the Mountain Club of South Africa: The First Forty Years, 1891 – 193. in: researchgate.net. Bloemfontein 2017

Kant, Immanuel: *Of the Different Human Races*. Original text published in 1777. in: Bernasconi, Robert and Lott, Tommy Lee: *The Idea of Race*. Cambridge and Indianapolis 2000

Katz, Cindi: *Me and My Monkey: What's Hiding in the Security State*. in: Pain, Rachel and Smith, Susan: *Fear: Critical Geopolitics and Everyday Life*. Hampshire 2008

Kelling, George L.: *"Broken Windows" and Police Discretion*. Research Report for the US National Institute of Justice. Washington 1999

Kidd, Dudley: *Savage Childhood – A Study of Kafir Children*. London 1906

Krog, Antje: *Country of my Skull*. New York 1999

Lalu, Premesh: *A Subaltern Studies for South African History*. in: Jacklin, Heather and Vale, Peter (eds.): *Re-imagining the Social in South Africa – Critique, Theory and Post-apartheid Society*. Pietermaritzburg 2009

Lalu, Premesh: *The Deaths of Hintsa. Postapartheid South Africa and the Shape of Recurring Pasts*. Cape Town 2009

Langford, Malcom and Kahanovitz, Steve: South Africa: *Rethinking Enforcement Narratives*. in: Langford, Malcom; Rodriguez-Graviato, César and Rossi, Julieta (eds.): *Social Rights Judgments and the Politics of Compliance: Making it Stick*. Cambridge 2017

Legassick, Martin: *Western Cape Housing Crisis: Writings on Joe Slovo and Delft*. Cape Town 2008

Luxemburg, Rosa: Die Akkumulation des Kapitals. Ein Beitrag zur ökonomischen Erklärung des Imperialismus. Berlin 1923

Makki, Fouad: *Development by Dispossesion: Terra Nullius and the Social-Ecology of New Enclosures in Ethiopia*. in: Rural Sociology. Volume 79, No 1. 2014

Maldonado-Torres, Nelson: *On the Coloniality of Being*. Cultural Studies. Volume 21: 2-3. 2007 -Mandela, Nelson: *Long Walkt o Freedom*. Boston 1994

Marais, J.S.: *The Cape Coloured People 1652-1937*. Johannesburg 1962

Mare, Gerhard: *African Population Relocation in South Africa*. Johannesburg 1980

Mariita, Nicolas O.: *The impact of large-scale renewable energy development on the poor: environmental and socio-economic impact of a geothermal power plant on a poor rural community in Kenya*. in: Elsievier Science Direct. Volume 30, No 11. 2002

Marks, Rafael and Marco Bezzoli: *Palaces of Desire – Century City and the Ambiguities of Development*. Dordrecht 2001

Marx, Karl: *Das Kapital – Kritik der Politischen Ökonomie*. Paderborn (no date)

Marx, Karl: *The Eighteens Brumaire of Louis Bonaparte*. First published in 1852. Marxists.org

Marx, Karl: *Wage-Labour and Capital*. First published in 1849. Dodo Press

Massumi, Brian: *Navigating Movements*. In an Interview with Mary Zournazi. 2002

Massumi, Brian: *Parables for the Virtual. Movement, Affects, Sensation*. Durham 2002

Mbembe, Achille: *Aesthetics of Superfluity*. Journal of Public Cultures. Vol. 16, No. 3. 2004

Mbembe, Achille: *The Power of the Archive and its Limits*. in: Hamilton, Carolyn, amongst others (eds.): *Refiguring the Archive*. Dordrecht 2002

Mbembe, Achille and Nuttal Sarah: *Johannesburg – The Elusive Metropolis*. Johannesburg 2008

Mc-Call Theal, George: History of South Africa Since September 1795. First published in Cape Town 1908. Cambridge 2010

Mentzel, O.F.: *A Geographical and Topographical Description of the Cape of Good Hope*. Reprinted in 1944

Merriman, Archdeacon: *The Kafir, The Hottentot, and the Frontier Farmer – Passages of Missionary Life*. London 1853

Mignolo, Walter: Delinking: the rhetoric of modernity, the logic of coloniality, and the grammar of de-coloniality. in: Cultural Studies. Volume 21: 2-3 2007

Miraftab, Faranak: *Colonial Present: Legacies of the past in contemporary urban practices in Cape Town, South Africa*. Journal of Planning History. Vol. 11, No. 4. 2012

Mkhize, Sibongile, Dube, Godwin and Skinner, Caroline: *Street Vendors in Durban, South Africa*. Durban 2013

Mtimkulu, Abner: "*The Native Problem*". Cape Times article of May 30, 1924

Mudimbe, V.Y.: *The Invention of Africa*. Bloomington and Indianapolis 1988

Mudimbe, V.Y.: Reprende: *Enunciations and Strategies in Contemporary African Arts*. in: Oguibe, Olu and Enwezor, Okwui (eds):

Reading the Contemporary: African Art from Theory to the Marketplace. London 1999

Murray: Martin J.: *Taming the Disorderly City: The Spatial Landscape of Johannesburg After Apartheid.* New York 2008

Murray, Martin J.: *City of Extremes: The Spatial Politics of Johannesburg.* Durham and London 2011

Nasson, Bill: *Delville Wood and South African Great War Commemoration.* in: The English Historical Review. Volume 119, No 480. February 2004

National Department of Housing, Western Cape Department of Housing and the City of Cape Town: *Briefing Document for the N2 Gateway Project.* Cape Town 2004

Ndebele, Njabulo: *Fine Lines from the Box – Further Thoughts About Our Country.* Cape Town 2007

Nuttall, Sarah and Coetzee, Carli: *Negotiating the Past – The Making of Memory in South Africa.* Cape Town 1998

Nuttall, Sarah and Mbembe, Achille (eds): *Johannesburg – The Elusive Metropolis.* Johannesburg 2008

Parnell, Susan and Robinson, Jennifer: *(Re)theorizing Cities from the Global South: Looking Beyond Neoliberalism.* in: Urban Geography. Volume 33:4. 2013: pp. 593-617

Peterson, Bhekizizwe: *The Archives and the Political Imaginary.* in: Hamilton, Carolyn, amongst others (eds.): *Refiguring the Archive.* Dordrecht 2002

Philip, John: *Researches in South Africa.* Cape Town 1828

Pieterse, Edgar: *City Futures – Confronting the Crisis of Urban Development.* Cape Town 2009

Pinnock, Don: *Ideology and Urban Planning: Blueprints of a Garrison City.* in: Godfrey James, Wilmot and Simons, Mary (eds.): *The Angry Divide: Social and Economic History of the Western Cape.* Cape Town 1989

Platzky, Laurine and Walker, Cherryl: *The Surplus People: Forced removals in South Africa.* Johannesburg 1985

Prins, Jo-Anne: *Mediating Difference – Politics of Representation in Antje Krog's Chronicling of the Truth and Reconciliation Commission in Country of my Skull.* in: Duncan, Norman; Gqola, Pumla Dineo; Hoffmeyer, Murray; Shefer, Tamara; Malunga, Felix; and Mashige, Mashudu (eds.): *Discourses on Difference, Discourses on Oppression.* Cape Town 2002

Quijano, Anibal: *Coloniality and Modernity/Rationality.* in: Cultural Studies. Volume 21: 2-3. 2007

Rancière, Jaques: *Disagreement.* Minneapolis 1998

Rancière, Jacques: *The Politics of Aesthetics – The Distribution of the Sensible.* London 2013

Rasool, Ciraj: *Memory and the Politics of History in the District Six Museum.* in: Shepherd, Nick; Murray, Noeleen and Hall, Martin (eds): *Desire Lines: Space, Memory and Identity in the Post- apartheid City.* New York 2007

Rhyne, Wilhelm Ten: *A Short Account of the Cape of Good Hope.* originally published: Schaffhausen 1686. in: Schapera, Isaac (ed.): *The Early Cape Hottentots - Writings of Olfert Dapper, Willem Ten Rhyne and Johannes Gulielmus de Grevenbroek.* Cape Town 1933

Roth, Mia: *The Rhetorical Origins of Apartheid – How the Debates of the Natives Representative Council, 1937-1950, Shaped South African Racial Policy.* Jefferson 2016

Rothbard, Murray N.: *Economic Thought Before Adam Smith – An Austrian Perspective on the History of Economic Thought.* Aldershot 1995

Roy, Arundhati: *Come September.* speech: September 11, Santa Fe 2002

Said, Edward: *Orientalism.* London 1977

Said, Edward W.: *Representing the Colonised: Anthropology's Interlocutors.* in: *Critical Inquiry,* Volume 15, No. 2. 1989

Sarmiento, Nicole Oddveig: *On Burial Grounds and City Spaces – Reconfiguring the Normative.* in: Haber, Alejandro and Shepherd, Nick: *After Ethics - Ancestral Voices and Post-Disciplinary Worlds in Archaeology.* New York 2015

Schapera, Isaac (ed.): *The Bantu-Speaking Tribes of South Africa.* London 1937

Schapera, Isaac (ed.): *The Early Cape Hottentots. Writings of Olfert Dapper, Willem Ten Rhyne and Johannes Gulielmus de Grevenbroek.* Reprinted in 1933

Seekings, Jeremy: *The Broader Importance of Welfare Reform in South Africa.* in: Social Dynamics: A Journal of African Studies. Volume 28:2. 2002. pp. 1-38

Selmeczi, Anna: *Abahlali's vocal politics of proximity: speaking, suffering and political subjectivization.* In: Journal of Asian and African Studies. October 2012, Vol. 47, Issue 5

Selmeczi, Anna: *Dis/placing political illiteracy.* Unpublished paper. Cape Town 2013

Semple, Robert: *Walks and Sketches at the Cape of Good Hope- to which is subjoined- A Journey from Cape Town to Blettenberg's Bay.* London 1805

Shabangu, Mohammad: Globality: *The Double Mind of African Migrant Writing.* Stellenbosch University. September 2017

Shell, Robert; Shell, Sandra and Kamedien, Mogamat (eds.): *Bibliographies of Bondage.* Cape Town 2007

Shepherd, Nick and Ernsten, Christian: *The World Below – Post-apartheid Urban Imaginaries and the Bones of the Prestwich Street Dead*. in: Murray, Noëleen, Shepherd, Nick and Hall, Martin: *Desire Lines – Space, Memory and Identity in the Post-apartheid City*. New York 2007

Shepherd, Nick; Murray, Noeleen and Hall, Martin (eds): *Desire Lines: Space, Memory and Identity in the Post-apartheid City*. New York 2007

Sibanda, Octavia: *Social pain and social death: poor white stigma in post-apartheid South Africa, a case of West Bank in East London*. in: Anthropology Southern Africa. Volume 35: 3-4. 2012

Simons, H.J. and Simons, R.E.: *Class and Colour in South Africa 1850-1950*. Aylesbury 1969

Sitze, Adam: *History and Desire*. in: Safundi - The Journal of South African and American Studies. Volume 13, No 1-2. 2012

Smith, Adams: *The Death of David Hume*. Letter to William Strachan. November 9, 1776

Sontag, Susan: *On Photography*. New York 1977

Social Housing Regulatory Authority: *Project Review Series – N2 Gateway – Joe Slovo*. Issue 3. Houghton and Johannesburg 2006

Sparrman, Anders: *A Voyage to the Cape of Good Hope, 1772-1776*. Reprinted in 1975

Spivak, Gayatri Chakravorty: *Can the Subaltern Speak?* In: Nelson, Cary and Grossberg, Lawrence (eds.): *Marxism and the Interpretation of Culture*. Illinois 1988

Stoler, Ann Laura: *Carnal Knowledge and Imperial Power – Race and the Intimate in Colonial Rule*. Berkeley and Los Angeles 2002

Stoler, Ann Laura: *Colonial Archives and the Arts of Governance*. in: Hamilton, Carolyn, amongst others (eds.): *Refiguring the Archive*. Dordrecht 2002

Survival International report.: *The Persecution of Botswana's Bushmen 1992-2014*. November 2014

Swanson, Felicity: *District Six Forced Removals*. in: Field, Sean (eds.): *Lost Communities, Living Memories – Remembering Forced Removals in Cape Town*. Cape Town 2001

Swyngedouw, Erik: *Where is the political?* Manchester 2008

Symphony Way Pavement Dwellers: *No Land! No House! No Vote! – Voices from Symphony Way*. Cape Town 2011

Tay, Eddie: *The Mental Life of Cities*. Hong Kong 2010

Taylor, Diana: *The Archive and the Repertoire – Performing Cultural Memory in the Americas*. Durham 2003

Terreblanche, Sampie: *A History of Inequality in South Africa*. Sandton 2002

Terreblanche, Sampie: *Lost in Transformation*. Sandton 2012

Tuhiwai Smith, Linda: *Decolonizing Methodologies - Research and Indigenous Peoples*. London and New York 2008

Valentijn, Francois: *Description of the Cape of Good Hope with the Matters Concerning*. Reprinted in 1975

van Bever Donker, Maurits: *On the Limit of Community: Coming to Terms with Apartheid's Grounds*. Unpublished paper. Cape Town 2013

Voltaire, Francois-Marie: *Of the Different Races of men*. in: Voltaire, Francois-Marie: The Philosophy of History. Original text published in 1766. New York 2007

wa Thiong'o, Ngugi: *Decolonising the Mind*. Harare 1987

wa Thiong'o, Ngugi: *Writing Against Neo-Colonialism*. London 1986

Watson, Vanessa: *Change and Continuity in Spatial Planning – Metropolitan Planning in Cape Town under Political Transition*. London 2002

Webster, Dennis: *The End of the Street? Informal Traders' Experiences of Rights and Regulations in Inner City Johannesburg*. Report for the *Socio-Economic Rights Institute of South Africa*. Johannesburg 2015

Western, John: *Outcast Cape Town*. Minneapolis 1982

Worden, Nigel: *Slavery in Dutch South Africa*. Cambridge 1985

Worden, Nigel and Crais, Clifton: *Breaking the Chains: Slavery and its Legacy in the Nineteens-Century Cape Colony*. Johannesburg 1994

Worden, Nigel; van Heyningen, Elizabeth; and Bickford-Smith, Vivian: *Cape Town: The Making of a City*. Cape Town 1998

Wynter, Sylvia: *1492: A New Worldview*. In: Lawrence Hyatt, Vera and Nettleford, Rex: *Race, Discourse, and the Origin of the Americas*. Washington and London 1995

Social Sciences

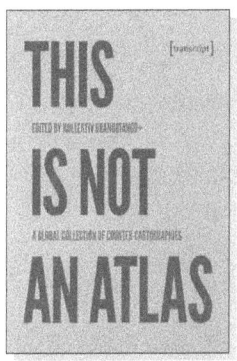

kollektiv orangotango+ (ed.)
This Is Not an Atlas
A Global Collection of Counter-Cartographies

2018, 352 p., hardcover, col. ill.
34,99 € (DE), 978-3-8376-4519-4
E-Book: free available, ISBN 978-3-8394-4519-8

Gabriele Dietze, Julia Roth (eds.)
Right-Wing Populism and Gender
European Perspectives and Beyond

April 2020, 286 p., pb., ill.
35,00 € (DE), 978-3-8376-4980-2
E-Book: 34,99 € (DE), ISBN 978-3-8394-4980-6

Mozilla Foundation
Internet Health Report 2019
2019, 118 p., pb., ill.
19,99 € (DE), 978-3-8376-4946-8
E-Book: free available, ISBN 978-3-8394-4946-2

**All print, e-book and open access versions of the titles in our list
are available in our online shop www.transcript-verlag.de/en!**

Social Sciences

James Martin
Psychopolitics of Speech
Uncivil Discourse and the Excess of Desire

2019, 186 p., hardcover
79,99 € (DE), 978-3-8376-3919-3
E-Book: 79,99 € (DE), ISBN 978-3-8394-3919-7

Michael Bray
Powers of the Mind
Mental and Manual Labor
in the Contemporary Political Crisis

2019, 208 p., hardcover
99,99 € (DE), 978-3-8376-4147-9
E-Book: 99,99 € (DE), ISBN 978-3-8394-4147-3

Iain MacKenzie
Resistance and the Politics of Truth
Foucault, Deleuze, Badiou

2018, 148 p., pb.
29,99 € (DE), 978-3-8376-3907-0
E-Book: 26,99 € (DE), ISBN 978-3-8394-3907-4
EPUB: 26,99 € (DE), ISBN 978-3-7328-3907-0

All print, e-book and open access versions of the titles in our list are available in our online shop www.transcript-verlag.de/en!

GPSR Authorized Representative: Easy Access System Europe, Mustamäe tee 50, 10621 Tallinn, Estonia, gpsr.requests@easproject.com

www.ingramcontent.com/pod-product-compliance
Lightning Source LLC
Chambersburg PA
CBHW051534020426
42333CB00016B/1920